Linux Shell Scripting

From Basics to Expert Proficiency

Contents

Introduction

The versatile and powerful world of Linux offers a robust environment for systems administration, development, and automation. One of the most compelling features of Linux is its command-line interface, where users can leverage the power of shell scripting to perform complex tasks efficiently. This book, "Linux Shell Scripting: From Basics to Expert Proficiency," aims to be a comprehensive guide, providing the foundational knowledge needed to script effectively in Linux, as well as advanced techniques for optimizing and securing scripts.

Linux, an operating system known for its stability and flexibility, offers multiple shells to interact with the system. Among these, the Bourne Again Shell (bash) is the most widely used. Shell scripting involves writing a sequence of commands for the shell to execute, enabling users to automate repetitive tasks, manage system operations, and develop complex workflows. Understanding the essentials of shell scripting can significantly enhance your productivity and capabilities within a Linux environment.

This book is structured into carefully curated chapters, each focusing on core concepts vital for mastery of shell scripting. We begin with an exploration of Linux and its ecosystem, followed by an introduction to basic commands essential for any Linux user. As we progress, we delve into the art of shell scripting, starting from the basics and gradually moving to more advanced topics.

The journey into shell scripting starts with a fundamental understanding of Linux commands. You will learn to navigate the file system, manipulate files and directories, and utilize various command-line utilities. A solid grasp of these commands is crucial, as they form the building blocks of shell scripts. You will then be introduced to shell scripting itself, where you will learn to write, execute, and test your first scripts.

Control structures, such as conditionals and loops, are essential for writing dynamic and flexible scripts. You will learn to use these structures to perform different actions based on various conditions, iterate through data, and handle complex logical operations. Working with variables and user input will further enhance your scripts, allowing them to adapt to different scenarios and user requirements.

File and directory management is another essential aspect of shell scripting. This book covers techniques for handling files and directories efficiently, including setting permissions, creating links, and finding files. Processing text using filters and regular expressions is also covered in-depth, providing you with the tools to manipulate and analyze text data effectively.

Functions and libraries can greatly improve the modularity and reusability of your code. You will learn to write functions, pass arguments, handle return values, and organize your scripts into libraries. Advanced scripting techniques are also covered, including array manipulation, background processing, and performance optimization.

Debugging and troubleshooting are critical skills for any script writer. This book provides strategies for identifying and resolving common errors, using debugging tools, and writing robust scripts that handle errors gracefully. Security and best practices are also emphasized, ensuring that your scripts are not only functional but also secure and maintainable.

Finally, a chapter dedicated to practical shell script examples will provide you with real-world scenarios where shell scripting can be applied. From automating system maintenance to managing user accounts and generating reports, these examples will demonstrate the practical applications of the concepts covered in this book.

As you immerse yourself in the chapters that follow, you will gain a comprehensive understanding of Linux shell scripting. Whether you are a beginner seeking foundational knowledge or an experienced user looking to refine your skills, this book will serve as a valuable resource on your path to shell scripting proficiency.

Chapter 1

Introduction to Linux and Shell Scripting

This chapter provides a foundational overview of Linux and the essentials of shell scripting. It begins by explaining what Linux is and introduces the different types of shells available. The historical evolution of shell scripting is discussed, followed by guidance on setting up a Linux environment and accessing the command line. The chapter distinguishes between various shells like sh, bash, and zsh, and offers a basic example to illustrate how a shell script works. It emphasizes the utility of the terminal and the advantages of using shell scripts for automating tasks, concluding with resources for obtaining help in Linux.

1.1 What is Linux?

Linux is a robust, open-source operating system that forms the backbone of countless systems worldwide, from personal computers to supercomputers. Originally created by Linus Torvalds in 1991, Linux has grown through contributions from developers around the world, emphasizing collaboration and transparency.

Open-source refers to software for which the original source code is made freely available and may be redistributed and modified. This philosophy of openness has allowed Linux to evolve rapidly and securely, as a diverse community continuously audits and improves the code.

Linux operates on a monolithic kernel architecture. The kernel acts as the core interface between a computer's hardware and its processes, managing resources and facilitating communication between software and hardware components. The **Linux kernel** is specifically designed to handle complex multitasking and multiuser functionalities inherent in modern computing environments.

The operating system itself is typically distributed in the form of **Linux distributions** (often abbreviated as **distros**). A Linux distribution packages the Linux kernel with a set of software applications, management tools, and libraries tailored to meet user needs. Notable distributions include:

- **Debian**: Renowned for its stability and vast repository of software packages, making it a preferred choice for server environments and those requiring a rock-solid system for application deployment.

- **Ubuntu**: Derived from Debian, bundles user-friendly desktop environments with rich community support, appealing to both new and experienced users.

- **Fedora**: Backed by Red Hat, known for integrating cutting-edge features and technologies, serving as a testing ground for future innovations.

- **CentOS**: Based on Red Hat Enterprise Linux (RHEL), designed for enterprise use, offering robust performance and long-term support without the associated cost of RHEL.

A fundamental feature of Linux is its **command-line interface** (CLI), providing powerful tools and scripting environments for detailed system management and automation. The CLI enables users to perform complex operations more efficiently than relying solely on graphical user interfaces (GUIs). It is through the terminal that shell scripts, covered extensively in this book, come into play.

Moreover, Linux embodies **security** and **permission models** that are integral to its architecture. Permissions in Linux govern the access levels users or processes have regarding files and directories. These are defined for the owner, the group, and others, distinctly acknowledging read, write, and execute capabilities:

```
-rwxr-xr--
```

In this example, a file exhibits permissions where the owner has read, write, and execute (rwx) access; the group can read and execute (r-x); and others can only read (r–).

Additionally, Linux supports a modular approach with the inclusion of loadable kernel modules. These allow for dynamically extending the functionality of the kernel without the need to reboot the system. Commonly used modules can be inspected via:

```
lsmod
```

This command lists all currently loaded modules.

Importantly, Linux is known for its extensive support for a wide variety of software applications and development tools, making it a preferred environment for developers. Programming languages such as C, Python, Java, and PHP are natively supported, along with sophisticated compilers, debuggers, and text editors like gcc, gdb, and vim, respectively.

Finally, Linux's ubiquity across diverse computational platforms—ranging from embedded systems to large-scale server farms—underlines its flexibility and scalability. The operating system's open-source nature encourages innovation, enabling it to adapt rapidly to technological advancements and diverse user requirements, perpetuating its relevance in an ever-evolving digital landscape.

1.2 Introduction to the Linux Shell

The Linux shell is a powerful tool that serves as the interface between the user and the kernel of the operating system. As an interpreter that executes commands typed by the user, the shell plays a critical role in the functional efficacy of the Linux environment.

When a user logs into a Linux system, they are greeted with a command-line interface (CLI) where they can input commands. This interface is the shell. Unlike graphical user interfaces (GUIs), the shell relies solely on text input and output, which makes it lightweight and flexible, particularly well-suited for scripting and task automation.

To understand the operation of the shell, it's essential to comprehend both its command interpretation process and its executable functionalities. When a user types a command, the shell breaks this command down into the command name and a set of arguments. The shell then searches for the command in its designated paths (defined in the PATH environment variable), executes it, and displays any output or errors.

```
$ echo "Hello, World!"
Hello, World!
```

In this example, the echo command is employed, followed by the argument "Hello, World!". The shell interprets this command and prints the specified text.

Different shells provide distinctive features and behaviors. However, some of the common functionalities across most shells include:

- **Command Execution:** Interpreting and running commands provided by the user.
- **Scripting:** Writing scripts to automate repetitive tasks.
- **Piping and Redirection:** Redirecting the output of one command as input to another using pipes (|) and redirection operators (>, », <, etc.).
- **Environment Variables:** Storing values that can affect the way processes run.
- **Job Control:** Managing multiple processes, including stopping, starting, and backgrounding jobs.

```
$ ls -l > file_list.txt
$ cat file_list.txt | grep ".sh" > shell_scripts.txt
```

Here, the ls -l command lists the files in the current directory, which are then redirected into a file named file_list.txt. The cat command concatenates and displays the content of file_list.txt, which is then piped to the grep command to filter out lines containing ".sh". The filtered results are redirected into shell_scripts.txt.

The shell is also capable of handling variables and control flow constructs, which enhances its scripting capabilities. Variables in shell scripts are used to store data that can be referenced and manipulated throughout the script.

```
$ name="Linux User"
$ echo "Welcome, $name."
Welcome, Linux User.
```

Control flow constructs, such as loops and conditional statements, enable the creation of more dynamic and complex scripts.

```
if [ -f /etc/passwd ]; then
    echo "File exists."
else
    echo "File does not exist."
fi
```

This script checks if the /etc/passwd file exists. If it does, the script prints "File exists."; otherwise, it prints "File does not exist."

The user can also define functions within shell scripts, facilitating modularity and readability.

```
greet_user() {
    echo "Hello, $1! Welcome to the Linux shell."
}

greet_user "Alice"
```

This function greet_user takes an argument and prints a personalized greeting. The function is then called with "Alice" as the argument.

Understanding the shell is critical for automating system tasks and effective system administration. Proficiency with the shell allows users to harness the full potential of the Linux operating system.

1.3 Types of Shells

Bash, zsh, and sh represent various types of Unix shells, each endowed with unique features and capabilities best suited to different scenarios. Understanding the differences and capabilities of each shell is crucial in choosing the most suitable one for specific tasks or scripts.

The **Bourne Shell** (sh) represents one of the earliest and most fundamental Unix shells. Designed by Stephen Bourne at Bell Labs, it served as the default shell in Unix versions and established many conventions that continue to influence other shells. Among its merits are simplicity and compatibility with a substantial body of legacy scripts. However, it lacks numerous modern amenities found in contemporary shells, such as advanced scripting features and user interactivity enhancements.

Next, **Bash** (Bourne Again Shell) stands out as an extended version of sh. Developed by the Free Software Foundation in the GNU project, Bash incorporates features from both the sh and C shells, contributing to a more versatile scripting environment. Bash is the default shell on many Linux distributions due to its robust scripting capabilities and user-friendly interactive experience. It includes enhancements such as command line editing, improved scripting keywords, and a rich set of built-in commands. The following example demonstrates a simple Bash script:

```
#!/bin/bash
echo "Hello, World!"
```

Executing this script displays the output:

```
Hello, World!
```

Zsh (Z Shell), derived from sh, incorporates features from bash, tcsh, and ksh. It distinguishes itself through extensive customization options, theme and plugin support, and features like spelling correction and automatic folder switching. These capabilities significantly enhance shell usability and developer productivity. Zsh users can also benefit from the Oh My Zsh framework, which simplifies the customization process and provides a vast repository of themes and plugins.

Korn Shell (ksh), engineered by David Korn at Bell Labs, fuses the syntax and features from both sh and csh. It introduces advanced scripting capabilities, including sophisticated string manipulation and associative arrays, thus bridging the gap between users seeking traditional sh compatibility and advanced features.

The **C Shell** (csh) and its enhanced variant, **TCSH**, offer a syntax resembling the C programming language. This shell is particularly advantageous for users familiar with C programming. Features such as history substitution, aliasing, and job control improve interactive use. Despite its popularity among earlier Unix users, csh is less frequently used today due to its non-standard scripting syntax and limited portability compared to sh and bash.

When selecting a shell type, several factors must be weighed, including:

- Scripting needs
- System compatibility
- User convenience
- Specific features of the shell

Many modern systems provide multiple shells, allowing users to switch as per the task's requirements. Proficiency in multiple shell environments can be beneficial, as distinct tasks may necessitate distinct tools. Understanding these shells' characteristics enables users to harness their unique strengths effectively and choose the most appropriate tool for their scripting and operational needs.

1.4 History and Evolution of Shell Scripting

The history of shell scripting is deeply intertwined with the development of Unix and Linux operating systems. Shell scripting emerged as a powerful tool for automating repetitive tasks and simplifying complex operations by leveraging the shell—a command-line interpreter that provides the traditional user interface for Unix-like operating systems.

Unix, developed in the late 1960s at AT&T's Bell Labs by Ken Thompson, Dennis Ritchie, and others, laid the groundwork for shell scripting. The first Unix shell, known as the Thompson shell (or "sh"), was introduced in the early 1970s. It was a simple, primitive shell that allowed users to execute commands interactively and create basic scripts using constructs like loops and conditional statements.

In 1977, the Bourne shell (also abbreviated as "sh"), written by Stephen Bourne, made significant advances over the Thompson shell. The Bourne shell incorporated more sophisticated programming constructs and comprehensive scripting capabilities. It became the standard shell for Unix operating systems and set the foundation for subsequent shell developments. Most Unix and Linux systems still recognize scripts written for the Bourne shell, ensuring its legacy endures.

The 1980s saw further advancements with the creation of the C shell ("csh"), developed by Bill Joy at the University of California, Berkeley. The C shell introduced features inspired by the C programming language, such as improved syntax for control flow and enhanced interactive capabilities. One notable enhancement was its job control mechanism, which allowed users to manage multiple tasks within a shell session more easily.

During the same period, the Korn shell ("ksh"), developed by David Korn at Bell Labs, emerged as another powerful shell. The Korn shell combined the scripting capabilities of the Bourne shell with the user-friendly features of the C shell. Its backward compatibility with the Bourne shell made it an attractive upgrade for users looking for enhanced functionality without losing existing scripts.

The Bourne Again Shell ("bash"), written by Brian Fox for the GNU Project and released in 1989, became one of the most influential and widely used shells in Unix and Linux environments. Bash extended the Bourne shell with features from the Korn and C shells while providing a rich set of new functionalities. Bash scripts are versatile and robust, making them suitable for various applications, from simple task automation to complex system administration.

Around the same time, the TC shell ("tcsh"), an enhanced version of the C shell, also gained popularity. TC shell incorporated numerous improvements, such as command-line editing, filename completion, and better scripting support.

The 1990s and early 2000s saw the introduction of other notable shells, such as the Z shell ("zsh"), which offered even more powerful features for both interactive use and scripting. Zsh's advanced capabilities include improved globbing, extended pattern matching, and customizable key bindings, making it a favorite among power users.

Parallel to the development of these shells, various scripting languages emerged, further expanding the possibilities of shell scripting. Languages such as Perl, Python, and Ruby allowed users to write more complex and modular scripts with functionalities beyond the traditional shell's scope. However, the shell remains an indispensable tool for quick, lightweight scripting and interactive command execution.

The evolution of shell scripting has been driven by the need for efficiency, flexibility, and user convenience. Each new shell built upon the strengths of its predecessors while introducing innovative features that addressed the limitations and challenges faced by users. The result is a rich and diverse ecosystem of shells and scripting languages, each with unique strengths that cater to various use cases and preferences.

As we continue to explore the capabilities of modern shell scripting, it is important to build on the foundational knowledge established by these historical developments. Understanding the evolution of shells allows users to appreciate the design choices and improvements that have led to the powerful tools available today. This historical context also underscores the importance of maintaining compatibility and embracing advancements in scripting practices, ensuring that shell scripting remains a vital instrument for automation and productivity in Unix-like environments.

1.5 Setting Up a Linux Environment

Setting up a Linux environment involves choosing the appropriate Linux distribution, installation method, and ensuring that the necessary configurations are applied for a functional and optimized system. This section will guide you through the essential steps required to establish a robust Linux environment suitable for shell scripting and general use.

Choosing a Linux Distribution

Selecting the right Linux distribution is a critical first step. Popular choices include Ubuntu, CentOS, Fedora, and Debian. Each distribution has its unique features, package management systems, and use cases:

- **Ubuntu** is beginner-friendly, has extensive community support, and uses the apt package manager.
- **CentOS** is often used in server environments and utilizes the yum package manager.
- **Fedora** offers cutting-edge features and uses the dnf package manager.
- **Debian** is known for its stability and uses the apt package manager similar to Ubuntu.

Installation Methods

There are several methods for installing a Linux distribution, including:

- **Live USB/CD/DVD**: Bootable media containing the Linux OS for installation.
- **Virtual Machines**: Using software like VirtualBox or VMware to install Linux on a virtual environment.
- **Dual-Boot**: Installing Linux alongside another operating system such as Windows.
- **Cloud-based Installations**: Provisioning Linux environments on cloud platforms like AWS, Google Cloud, or Azure.

Creating a Bootable USB

To create a bootable USB drive for installation, use tools like Rufus, UNetbootin, or dd command on an existing Linux system. For example, using dd:

```
sudo dd if=/path/to/linux.iso of=/dev/sdX bs=4M status=progress
```

Replace /path/to/linux.iso with the path to your ISO file and /dev/sdX with your USB device identifier.

Installing Linux

Upon booting from the live USB:

1. Follow the on-screen prompts to select your preferred language, keyboard layout, and time zone.
2. Partition your disk. Options typically include:
   - **Use entire disk**: Replaces any existing data.
   - **Manual partitioning**: For experienced users wishing to control partition sizes and types.
3. Set up a user account with a username and password.
4. Install the bootloader, which allows you to choose between operating systems if dual-booting.
5. Complete the installation process and reboot.

Post-Installation Configuration

Once Linux is installed, perform the following configurations to optimize your system:

- **Update the System**: Ensure you have the latest updates and security patches.

  ```
  sudo apt update && sudo apt upgrade # For Debian-based systems
  sudo dnf update # For Fedora-based systems
  ```

- **Install Essential Packages**: Tools and utilities necessary for shell scripting and daily use.

  ```
  sudo apt install build-essential git curl vim # For Debian-based systems
  sudo yum groupinstall "Development Tools" # For CentOS-based systems
  sudo dnf install @development-tools git curl vim # For Fedora-based systems
  ```

- **Configure the Firewall**: Set up firewall rules for security.

```
sudo ufw enable # For Ubuntu and Debian using UFW
sudo firewall-cmd --add-service=ssh --permanent # For CentOS and Fedora
    using Firewalld
sudo firewall-cmd --reload
```

- **Set up SSH**: To enable remote access to your system.

```
sudo apt install openssh-server # For Debian-based systems
sudo dnf install openssh-server # For Fedora-based systems
sudo systemctl enable ssh
sudo systemctl start ssh
```

Accessing the Shell

After configuring your Linux environment, access the shell by opening a terminal emulator such as gnome-terminal, konsole, or xterm. Execute the following commands to verify your shell version and user details:

```
echo $SHELL # Displays the current shell
whoami # Displays the current user
```

Setting Environment Variables

Customize your environment by setting variables in configuration files like ~/.bashrc, ~/.zshrc, or ~/.profile. For example, to add a directory to your PATH:

```
export PATH=$PATH:/path/to/directory
```

Execute the following command to apply changes immediately:

```
source ~/.bashrc # Or source ~/.zshrc for zsh
```

Installing a Code Editor

While any text editor can be used, selecting an efficient and powerful editor can streamline your scripting process. Popular choices include:

- **Vim**: A highly configurable command-line text editor.
- **Emacs**: Known for its extensibility and lightweight.
- **Visual Studio Code**: A feature-rich, multi-platform code editor.

Verifying the Installation

Confirm that your system is configured correctly by executing common commands and verifying outputs:

```
uname -a # Displays system information
df -h # Shows disk usage
top # Monitors system processes
```

In this manner, setting up a Linux environment from choosing a distribution to verifying the installation prepares the ground, making it conducive for executing and developing shell scripts effectively.

1.6 Accessing the Command Line

Accessing the command line in a Linux environment is an essential skill for leveraging the power of shell scripting and system administration. The command line interface (CLI) enables users to interact directly with the operating system by executing text-based commands. This section details the various methods available to access the command line in different Linux distributions, ensuring a thorough understanding of how to initiate and use the terminal effectively.

In most Linux distributions, the terminal emulator is the application that provides access to the command line. Common terminal emulators include gnome-terminal, konsole, xterm, and terminator. These emulators provide a text-based interface to execute shell commands, scripts, and programs.

Finding and Launching the Terminal Emulator: To access the terminal, one typically needs to launch the terminal emulator application. The specific steps to find and open the terminal emulator can vary slightly depending on the desktop environment (DE) and window manager used, but the general procedure remains similar across various setups.

- **GNOME Desktop Environment:**
  - Press Super (Windows) key to open the Activities overview.
  - Type terminal in the search bar.
  - Click on the Terminal icon from the search results.
- **KDE Plasma Desktop Environment:**
  - Press Alt + Space to open KRunner.
  - Type konsole and press Enter.

  - Alternatively, click on the menu icon, navigate to System, and select Konsole.

- **XFCE Desktop Environment:**
  - Press Alt + F2 to open the application launcher.
  - Type xfce4-terminal and press Enter.
  - You can also open the terminal through the application menu under Accessories.

- **Command Line Shortcut:** In most Linux distributions, the terminal can also be launched using a keyboard shortcut, such as Ctrl + Alt + T.

Accessing the Command Line via SSH: In addition to local access, the command line can be accessed remotely using the Secure Shell (SSH) protocol. SSH provides a secure channel over an unsecured network, allowing users to execute commands on remote machines. To access a remote Linux system, you need the SSH client installed on your local machine and the SSH server running on the remote machine.

```
ssh user@remote_host
```

```
$ ssh user@remote_host
user@remote_host's password:
Welcome to Ubuntu 20.04.1 LTS (GNU/Linux 5.4.0-52-generic x86_64)
...
user@remote_host:~$
```

Replace user with the username on the remote machine and remote_host with the IP address or domain name of the remote server.

Virtual Terminals: Linux systems also offer virtual terminals, giving users direct command line access without the graphical interface. Virtual terminals are accessed via console mode and are available on most Linux systems by default.

To switch to a virtual terminal, use the following key combinations:

- Ctrl + Alt + F1 through Ctrl + Alt + F6 to access different virtual terminals.

- Ctrl + Alt + F7 or Ctrl + Alt + F8 to return to the graphical desktop environment.

After switching to a virtual terminal, log in using your username and password. Virtual terminals provide a robust environment for performing system maintenance and troubleshooting, especially when graphical interfaces are unavailable or unresponsive.

Navigating within the Terminal: Navigating within the terminal involves using various commands to move through directories, list files, and execute programs. Essential commands include:

- pwd: Prints the current working directory.

```
pwd
```

```
$ pwd
/home/username
```

- cd: Changes the current directory.

```
cd /path/to/directory
```

```
$ cd /usr/local
$ pwd
/usr/local
```

- ls: Lists the files and directories in the current directory.

```
ls
```

```
$ ls
bin etc include lib share
```

These basic navigation commands form the foundation of interacting with the Linux filesystem and will be expanded upon in subsequent sections.

Understanding how to access and navigate the command line is vital for proficiency in Linux shell scripting and system management. This knowledge enables efficient and effective execution of commands and scripts, forming the bedrock upon which advanced skills will be built.

1.7 Differences Between Shells (sh, bash, zsh, etc.)

When navigating the landscape of Linux shells, understanding the differences between sh, bash, zsh, and other shells is critical for making informed decisions about which shell to use for specific tasks. Each shell has unique features, syntax, and performance characteristics, which can impact the efficiency and capabilities of your scripts.

sh, or the Bourne Shell, is one of the earliest and most fundamental shells. Developed by Stephen Bourne at AT&T's Bell Labs, sh set many standards for shell scripting. It provides a basic, no-frills environment, prioritizing POSIX compliance and simplicity. While it can be seen as lacking in features compared to modern shells, it is highly portable and predictable. Many scripts written in sh can run on any POSIX-compliant system without modification.

bash, the Bourne Again Shell, developed by the Free Software Foundation, extends sh's capabilities significantly. It incorporates a wealth of features such as command-line editing, improved scripting capabilities, and an extensive built-in help system. Syntax enhancements include:

```
# Example of an enhanced feature in bash
for file in *.txt; do
    echo "Processing $file"
done
```

Here, looping constructs in bash are more versatile, and variable handling is more intuitive compared to sh. bash supports arrays and can perform arithmetic natively within the shell script, increasing its utility for more complex scripts.

zsh, or the Z Shell, is renowned for its flexibility and user-centric design. It includes all features of bash and introduces many more. Notable features include spelling correction, shared history between sessions, and enhanced globbing abilities:

```
# Example of zsh globbing
print *.txt(.)
```

The zsh globbing example above showcases advanced pattern matching capabilities, such as file type qualifiers, which simplify file selection tasks. Additionally, zsh supports powerful prompt customization and theming via frameworks like oh-my-zsh, making it a favorite among developers for personal environments.

Comparing csh (C Shell) and tcsh (TENEX C Shell), they deviate more significantly from the Bourne shell syntax, aligning more closely with C programming language constructs. While csh introduced features like aliasing, command history, and job control, it is often criticized for its less predictable scripting behavior. tcsh, an enhanced version of csh, addresses some of these issues with additional features and improved scripting reliability.

```
# Example of tcsh command aliasing
alias ll 'ls -l'
```

PowerShell, predominantly a Windows shell, is integrated in this comparison due to its availability on Linux through PowerShell Core. Unlike traditional Unix shells, PowerShell treats data as objects rather than text, providing robust object-oriented scripting capabilities:

```
# Example of PowerShell in Linux
Get-ChildItem *.txt | ForEach-Object { $_.Name }
```

PowerShell introduces a paradigm shift in shell scripting with its emphasis on structured data manipulation, offering powerful tools for complex administrative scripts.

In summary, choosing the appropriate shell hinges on the specific requirements of your tasks. For portability and simplicity, sh is unmatched. For rich features, bash and zsh provide extensive capabilities. For specific use cases like object-oriented scripting, PowerShell may be advantageous. Understanding these differences ensures optimized and effective usage of the Linux shell environment.

1.8 Basic Shell Script - An Example

A practical understanding of shell scripting begins with crafting a basic script and examining its components. In this section, we will write a simple script, dissect its structure, and explore how it functions within the Linux environment.

A shell script is essentially a text file containing a sequence of commands for the shell to execute. It enables automation of repetitive tasks, efficient processing of files, and performing system administration tasks with ease. To write a shell script, we follow these steps:

- **Create the script file**: We start by creating a text file with a '.sh' extension, which is a common convention for shell scripts but not a strict requirement.
- **Add the shebang line**: The first line of the script should specify the interpreter using the shebang ('#) followed by the path to the shell.
- **Write commands**: Insert the desired sequence of shell commands.

- **Save and close**: Save the script file and close the text editor.
- **Make the script executable**: Modify the file permissions to make the script executable.
- **Execute the script**: Run the script from the command line.

Consider the following example script named 'example.sh':

```
#!/bin/bash
# This script displays a welcome message and the current date and time

# Display a welcome message
echo "Welcome to Linux Shell Scripting!"

# Display the current date and time
current_date=$(date)
echo "Current date and time: $current_date"
```

Let's break down the key elements of this script:

- **Shebang Line**: '#!/bin/bash'

- This instructs the system to use the Bash shell to interpret the following commands. The path '/bin/bash' points to the location of the Bash interpreter.

- **Comment**: '# This script displays a welcome message and the current date and time'

- Comments are preceded by '#' and are not executed. They help in documenting the script for better understanding and maintenance.

- **Command**: 'echo "Welcome to Linux Shell Scripting!"'

- The 'echo' command prints the specified string to the terminal.

- **Command with Command Substitution**: 'current_date=$(date)'

- The 'date' command retrieves the current date and time. The '$(command)' syntax performs command substitution, capturing the output of the 'date' command and storing it in the variable 'current_date'.

- **Variable Expansion**: 'echo "Current date and time: $current_date"'

- The variable '$current_date' is expanded to its stored value and printed by the 'echo' command.

Next, we make the script executable using the 'chmod' command:

```
chmod +x example.sh
```

The 'chmod +x' command adds execute permissions to the file 'example.sh'. Consequentially, the script can be run directly from the command line:

```
./example.sh
```

Upon execution, you will observe the script's output:

```
Welcome to Linux Shell Scripting!
Current date and time: Wed Mar 15 14:55:48 UTC 2023
```

This output confirms the successful execution of the script, displaying a welcome message followed by the current date and time.

Basic scripts like this serve as foundational tools, illustrating fundamental concepts such as command execution, variable usage, and script structure. As complexity increases, scripts may incorporate control structures (e.g., loops and conditionals), functions, and advanced command-line utilities to handle more sophisticated tasks.

1.9 Understanding and Using the Terminal

The terminal, also referred to as the command line interface (CLI), is an essential tool in Linux environments. Proficiency with the terminal empowers users to interact directly with the operating system, perform complex tasks efficiently, and automate repetitive tasks through scripting. In this section, we will delve into various facets of the terminal to enhance your understanding and usage of this powerful tool.

When you open a terminal window, you are greeted by a prompt, typically indicating the user name, hostname, and current directory. For example, a common shell prompt might look like this:

```
user@hostname:~$
```

This prompt signifies that the terminal is ready to accept commands. Commands entered at the prompt are parsed and executed by the shell. Each command typically consists of a command name followed by options and arguments, with spaces separating them.

- **Navigating the Filesystem**

One of the primary tasks performed in the terminal is navigating the filesystem. The following basic commands are instrumental in moving around the directory structure:

```
ls # Lists the contents of the current directory
```

```
cd # Changes the directory
pwd # Prints the current working directory
```

For instance, to list the contents of the current directory:

```
user@hostname:~$ ls
Desktop Documents Downloads Pictures
```

Changing directories involves using the 'cd' command followed by the path of the target directory:

```
cd Documents
```

To return to the home directory, you can use:

```
cd ~
```

Or to move up one directory level:

```
cd ..
```

- **Working with Files and Directories**

The terminal allows users to create, delete, copy, and move files and directories with simple commands. Here are some of the essential commands for file manipulation:

```
touch filename # Creates an empty file
mkdir dirname # Creates a new directory
rm filename # Deletes a file
rmdir dirname # Deletes an empty directory
cp source dest # Copies a file or directory
mv source dest # Moves or renames a file or directory
```

For example, to create a file:

```
touch example.txt
```

To create a directory and then navigate into it:

```
mkdir newdir
cd newdir
```

Copying a file involves specifying the source file and the destination:

```
cp example.txt copy_of_example.txt
```

- **Viewing and Editing Files**

Viewing the content of files is also straightforward using the terminal with commands such as 'cat', 'less', and 'more':

```
cat filename # Displays the entire content of the file
less filename # Allows scrolling through the file content
more filename # Displays the file content page by page
```

To view a file using 'cat':

```
cat example.txt
```

For large files, 'less' provides a more user-friendly approach:

```
less largefile.txt
```

Editing files directly from the terminal can be done using text editors like 'nano', 'vi', or 'emacs'. For instance, to edit a file using 'nano':

```
nano example.txt
```

- **System Monitoring and Management**

The terminal also provides tools for monitoring and managing system resources and processes. Key commands for this purpose include:

```
top # Displays real-time system information and process details
ps # Reports a snapshot of current processes
kill # Terminates a process by its ID
df # Reports file system disk space usage
du # Estimates file space usage
free # Displays the amount of free and used memory in the system
```

To monitor processes in real-time:

```
top
```

To list all running processes, the 'ps' command can be augmented with options for detailed information:

```
ps aux
```

- **Using Pipes and Redirection**

Pipes and redirection are powerful features of the terminal that allow users to chain commands and manage input/output more effectively. The pipe symbol ('|') takes the output of one command and uses it as the input for another command. For example, to search for a string within the list of processes:

```
ps aux | grep 'search_string'
```

Redirection is used to control where the output of a command goes or where the input comes from. Common redirection operators include ‘>‘, ‘»‘, ‘<‘, and ‘2>‘:

```
command > output.txt # Redirects standard output to a file
command >> output.txt # Appends standard output to a file
command < input.txt # Takes input from a file
command 2> error.log # Redirects standard error to a file
```

- **Basic Shell Scripting**

Shell scripting in the terminal involves writing scripts composed of a series of commands that are executed by the shell. A simple example of a shell script is as follows:

```
#!/bin/bash
# This is a comment
echo "Hello, World!"
```

Save the script to a file, for example ‘script.sh‘, and make it executable:

```
chmod +x script.sh
```

Then execute the script:

```
./script.sh
```

These examples and commands provide a foundational understanding of using the terminal in Linux. Mastery of the terminal enhances both basic and advanced interactions with the operating system, paving the way for efficient task management and automation through shell scripting.

1.10 Benefits and Uses of Shell Scripting

Shell scripting provides a myriad of benefits and practical uses that can significantly enhance productivity in the Linux environment. These advantages stem from the innate capabilities of shell scripts to automate repetitive tasks, streamline system administration, and enable complex data manipulation with ease.

One of the primary advantages of shell scripting is automation. By writing scripts, users can automate repetitive tasks that would otherwise consume significant amounts of time if performed manually. For instance, a system administrator can automate the process of backing up system files, managing user accounts, or monitoring system performance. This automation achieves consistency and reduces the likelihood of human errors.

Shell scripts also offer extensive control over the execution of command-line utilities, allowing users to chain multiple commands together, process inputs and outputs, and handle errors effectively. A typical example is the automation of system updates. Rather than manually typing each command to update software packages, a shell script can be written to update the entire system with a single execution.

```
#!/bin/bash
echo "Starting system update..."
sudo apt update && sudo apt upgrade -y
echo "System update completed successfully."
```

Security is another sector where shell scripting proves invaluable. Scripts can be employed to automate security checks, such as auditing user activities, monitoring system logs for suspicious behavior, and ensuring compliance with security policies. By leveraging cron jobs, these scripts can be scheduled to run at regular intervals, providing continuous monitoring without manual intervention.

Shell scripting facilitates the integration of various tools and software. Users can create scripts that combine the functionalities of different command-line utilities, enabling complex data processing workflows. For example, a script could be designed to extract data from log files, filter out relevant information, and send an email report. The following script illustrates this use case:

```
#!/bin/bash
log_file="/var/log/syslog"
report_file="/tmp/report.txt"
recipient="admin@example.com"

echo "Extracting error entries from log file..." > $report_file
grep "error" $log_file >> $report_file

echo "Sending email report..."
mail -s "Error Report" $recipient < $report_file
```

Additionally, shell scripts often serve as essential tools for system bootstrapping and configuration management. During the boot process, numerous scripts are executed to initialize the system's state, configure hardware settings, start services, and perform other critical setup tasks. Scripts for configuration management can deploy and configure software across multiple servers in a consistent manner, ensuring all systems are uniformly set up.

The portability of shell scripts cannot be overlooked. Since the shell environment is almost universally available on Unix-like systems, scripts written for one Linux distribution can often be run on another with minimal or no modification. This cross-platform compatibility enhances the reusability of scripts in diverse environments, fostering the sharing of tools and solutions within the open-source community.

Shell scripting is integral to task scheduling. Using the cron and at daemons, users can schedule scripts to run at specified times or in response to certain events. This capability is crucial for tasks such as regular maintenance, backups, system monitoring, and running periodic reports. A cron job example is illustrated below:

```
# Edit the crontab entry by running 'crontab -e'
0 2 * * * /path/to/backup_script.sh
```

Furthermore, shell scripting is a powerful tool for customizing the user environment. Users can write scripts to modify their shell initialization files, set environment variables, create aliases, and enhance command-line functionalities according to their preferences.

```
# Add the following to ~/.bashrc
alias ll='ls -la'
export PATH=$PATH:/opt/myprogram/bin

# Apply changes
source ~/.bashrc
```

Incorporating shell scripting into one's skill set also fosters a deeper understanding of the operating system and its underlying principles. As users write and debug scripts, they gain insights into system processes, file system structure, kernel interactions, and performance optimization techniques.

Finally, shell scripting provides a foundation for learning other scripting languages. The syntax and principles learned through shell scripting are transferable to other programming environments, such as Python, Perl, and Ruby. This foundational knowledge opens pathways to more advanced programming and system automation tasks.

Shell scripting exemplifies the principle of "do more with less." It harnesses the power of the Linux command line, enabling users to efficiently manage systems, automate complex workflows, and perform sophisticated data analyses. Mastery of shell scripting is a pivotal asset for any Linux user, affirming its indispensable role in modern computing environments.

1.11 Getting Help in Linux

One of the fundamental advantages of using Linux is the extensive array of documentation and help resources available. These resources are essential for both new users and experienced professionals to troubleshoot issues, learn new commands, and understand the system better. This section will cover various methods to obtain help in Linux, including using manual pages (man), info pages, built-in help options, online resources, and community support.

The *man* command is the standard way to access the manual pages for different commands and programs in Linux. To use this feature, simply type man followed by the name of the command you need help with. For example:

```
$ man ls
```

This command will display the manual page for the ls command, showing detailed information about its usage, options, and examples. Manual pages are divided into sections, such as Name, Synopsis, Description, Options, Examples, and See Also. Navigating through the *man* output can be done using standard commands like the arrow keys for scrolling line by line, or PgUp and PgDn for page-wise navigation. Press q to quit the manual page viewer.

For commands that offer detailed and structured documentation, the *info* command serves as an alternative to the *man* pages. The *info* command provides a hierarchical and hyperlinked format that allows users to navigate through sections and topics more intuitively. To access the info documentation of a command, use:

```
$ info ls
```

This command will launch the Info reader with the documentation for the ls command. Use the arrow keys to navigate, and press Enter to follow hyperlinks. To search within the Info documentation, press s, type the search term, and press Enter. Like the *man* command, press q to quit the Info reader.

Many Linux commands also provide built-in help that can be accessed via command-line options. Commonly, the -h or –help flags are used to display a brief summary of the command's usage and available options. For example:

```
$ ls --help
```

The output typically includes a concise description of how the command works, its options, and occasionally some examples of its usage. This method is particularly useful when you need quick information without reading through the comprehensive manual or info pages.

Beyond the built-in help facilities, there are numerous online resources available for Linux users. Websites such as www.kernel.org/doc/man-pages/, www.tldp.org (The Linux Documentation Project), and the official documentation of various Linux distributions are valuable repositories of knowledge. These sites provide detailed guides, FAQs, tutorials, and community-contributed content that can be indispensable for users seeking assistance.

Another significant aspect of obtaining help in Linux involves engaging with the community. Various forums, mailing lists, and IRC channels are dedicated to Linux support. Sites like www.stackoverflow.com and www.reddit.com/r/linux/ are excellent platforms where users can search for solutions to their problems or ask questions directly. Additionally, subscribing to mailing lists such as linux-users@vger.kernel.org can provide access to expert advice and discussions.

When participating in community forums or seeking help online, it is important to follow best practices for effective communication. Clearly describe the issue, provide relevant details such as the Linux distribution in use, steps to reproduce the problem, and any error messages encountered. This information helps responders provide accurate and timely assistance.

In addition to these resources, many Linux distributions include graphical help systems accessible from the desktop environment. These help systems offer a user-friendly way to browse documentation and find answers to common questions.

Approaching these help resources methodically ensures that users can efficiently find solutions, learn new skills, and harness the full potential of their Linux systems.

Chapter 2

Basic Linux Commands

This chapter covers fundamental Linux commands necessary for navigating and managing the file system, performing file and directory operations, and handling file permissions. It also includes guidance on viewing and editing files, basic text processing, and searching files and directories. Additionally, system monitoring, network commands, package management, and archiving and compression techniques are explained to provide a comprehensive understanding of basic Linux command-line operations.

2.1 Introduction to Linux Commands

Linux commands are the foundational building blocks for interacting with a Linux operating system. They enable users to execute a variety of tasks, from simple file manipulation to complex system maintenance. Understanding these commands is crucial for efficient system administration and effective utilization of Linux capabilities.

Commands in Linux adhere to a specific syntax structure that typically includes the command name followed by options and arguments. This structure allows users to perform operations in a precise and controlled manner. For example, the basic syntax can be represented as follows:

```
command [options] [arguments]
```

In this structure:

- *command* is the name of the command to be executed.
- *options* are optional flags that modify the behavior of the command.
- *arguments* are the inputs the command operates on, such as file names or directory paths.

To grasp the concepts clearly, examining each component in a practical context is essential. Let's consider the following example:

```
ls -l /home/user
```

Here, 'ls' is the command to list directory contents, '-l' is an option that provides a long listing format, and '/home/user' is an argument specifying the directory to be listed.

Commands are typically entered into the Linux shell, which serves as the command-line interface (CLI). There are various types of shells available, with Bash (Bourne Again Shell) being the most commonly used. Other popular shells include Zsh, Tcsh, and Ksh.

Linux commands fall into several categories based on their functions:

- File and Directory Operations: Manipulating files and directories (e.g., 'cp', 'mv', 'rm', 'mkdir', 'rmdir').
- File Viewing and Editing: Displaying and modifying file contents (e.g., 'cat', 'less', 'nano', 'vi').
- Text Processing: Processing and analyzing text data (e.g., 'grep', 'awk', 'sed').
- System Monitoring and Performance: Monitoring system resources and performance (e.g., 'top', 'htop', 'free').
- Networking: Managing network configurations and connections (e.g., 'ping', 'ifconfig', 'netstat').
- Package Management: Installing, updating, and removing software packages (e.g., 'apt-get', 'yum', 'zypper').
- Archiving and Compression: Archiving files and compressing/decompressing data (e.g., 'tar', 'gzip', 'zip', 'unzip').

Each command typically has its own set of options and flags, which can be explored through the associated manual pages. The 'man' command is used to access these manual pages, providing detailed information about command usage. For example:

```
man ls
```

This command displays the manual page for 'ls', including available options and examples.

Understanding how to string commands together and automate repetitive tasks is paramount in Linux. Commands can be executed sequentially, conditionally, or in parallel using operators such as ';', '&&', '||', and '&'. For example:

```
mkdir newdir && cd newdir
```

In this example, 'mkdir newdir' creates a new directory named 'newdir', and '&&' ensures that the next command, 'cd newdir', is executed only if the directory creation is successful.

For conditional execution, consider the following example:

```
command1 || command2
```

Here, 'command2' will be executed only if 'command1' fails. For parallel execution, the '&' operator is used:

```
command1 & command2
```

Both 'command1' and 'command2' will run simultaneously.

The use of pipes ('|') is another powerful feature in Linux, allowing the output of one command to serve as the input for another. This chaining enables complex data transformations and processing. For example:

```
cat file.txt | grep 'search_term' | wc -l
```

This command sequence reads the contents of 'file.txt', searches for lines containing 'search_term', and counts the number of matching lines.

Mastering Linux commands demands consistent practice and exploration. Understanding how each command operates individually and in conjunction with others unlocks the full potential of the Linux operating system. Effective command usage promotes efficiency, enhances productivity, and opens avenues for advanced system management and automation.

2.2 Navigating the File System (cd, ls, pwd)

Navigating the Linux file system efficiently is an essential skill for anyone working with a Linux environment. This section covers three fundamental commands: cd, ls, and pwd, which are foundational for moving through directories, listing contents, and identifying the current directory.

The command cd, short for "change directory," allows the user to switch the current working directory. The general syntax is:

```
cd [directory]
```

For example, to change to the /home/user/Documents directory, the command is:

```
cd /home/user/Documents
```

Relative paths can also be used. To move from a directory to its subdirectory named projects, you can use:

```
cd projects
```

To navigate to the parent directory, use:

```
cd ..
```

The command ls lists the contents of a directory. Its basic usage is:

```
ls [options] [directory]
```

Without any options, ls will display the names of files and directories in the current directory. For instance:

```
ls
```

Commonly used options with ls include:

- -l: List in long format, showing detailed information about each file and directory.
- -a: Include hidden files (those starting with a dot).
- -h: Display file sizes in human-readable format when used with the -l option.

```
ls -l
```

```
ls -a
ls -lh
```

To list the contents of a specific directory, provide the directory path as an argument:

```
ls /home/user/Documents
```

The command pwd stands for "print working directory." It outputs the absolute path of the current directory:

```
pwd
```

This command is particularly useful when navigating deeply nested directories to confirm the current working path.

Consider a scenario where you need to navigate to a subdirectory, list its contents, and confirm your current location. The sequence of commands might be:

```
cd /home/user/Documents/projects
ls -lh
pwd
```

The expected output could be:

```
/home/user/Documents/projects
total 4.0K
drwxr-xr-x 2 user user 4.0K Jan  1 12:34 project1
drwxr-xr-x 2 user user 4.0K Jan  1 12:34 project2
```

Using cd, ls, and pwd effectively together enables efficient and informed navigation of the Linux file system.

2.3 File and Directory Operations (cp, mv, rm, mkdir, rmdir)

File and directory operations are fundamental actions within the Linux shell environment. This section covers essential commands such as cp, mv, rm, mkdir, and rmdir, which are indispensable for file management. Understanding these commands enhances the ability to navigate and manipulate the filesystem efficiently.

The cp command is used to copy files and directories. Its basic syntax is:

```
cp [options] source destination
```

Key options include:

- -r: Copies directories recursively.
- -i: Prompts before overwriting files.
- -v: Displays verbose output, indicating files being copied.

For example, to copy a file named example.txt to /var/tmp/:

```
cp example.txt /var/tmp/
```

Copying an entire directory with the -r option:

```
cp -r /home/user/Documents /backup/
```

The mv command is utilized for moving or renaming files and directories. Its primary syntax is:

```
mv [options] source destination
```

Essential options:

- -i: Prompts before overwriting files.
- -v: Provides verbose output.

Moving example.txt to /var/tmp/:

```
mv example.txt /var/tmp/
```

Renaming a file from oldname.txt to newname.txt:

```
mv oldname.txt newname.txt
```

The rm command serves for file and directory removal. Its syntax is straightforward:

```
rm [options] file
```

Important options:

- -r: Removes directories and their contents recursively.
- -i: Prompts before deletion.
- -f: Forces removal without prompting.

To remove a file named example.txt:

```
rm example.txt
```

For removing a directory and its contents:

```
rm -r /home/user/old_directory
```

Using rm with the -f option:

```
rm -rf /var/tmp/old_files/
```

The mkdir command facilitates the creation of directories. Its syntax includes options to enhance functionality:

```
mkdir [options] directory
```

Key options:

- -p: Creates parent directories as needed.
- -v: Verbose output.

Creating a single directory:

```
mkdir /home/user/new_directory
```

Using -p to create nested directories:

```
mkdir -p /home/user/projects/2023/jan
```

The rmdir command removes empty directories only. Its basic usage is:

```
rmdir [options] directory
```

Optionally:

- -p: Removes parent directories if they are empty.

Removing a single empty directory:

```
rmdir /home/user/empty_directory
```

Recursively removing directories using -p:

```
rmdir -p /home/user/projects/2023/jan
```

These commands, cp, mv, rm, mkdir, and rmdir, provide a robust toolset for manipulating files and directories in a Linux environment.

Their options and usage variations contribute to a flexible and powerful file management system.

2.4 Viewing and Editing Files (cat, less, more, nano, vi)

Interacting with files through the command line often requires tools for viewing and editing content. This section delves into some of the most commonly used commands and editors in Linux: cat, less, more, nano, and vi. These utilities facilitate efficient file manipulation directly from the terminal, each offering unique functionalities suited for different tasks.

The cat command, short for "concatenate," is a versatile utility for displaying or concatenating file contents. To display the contents of a file:

```
cat filename.txt
```

This command prints the entire contents of filename.txt to the terminal. Multiple files can be concatenated and displayed sequentially:

```
cat file1.txt file2.txt
```

Redirection functionality with cat allows combining files into a new file:

```
cat file1.txt file2.txt > combined.txt
```

Appending additional data to a file can be achieved as follows:

```
cat additional_data.txt >> existing_file.txt
```

The less command is invaluable for viewing large files by enabling forward and backward navigation within the file. It loads content incrementally, which is efficient for performance:

```
less largefile.txt
```

Upon invocation, use the arrow keys for line-by-line navigation and the spacebar for paging. Pressing q exits less.

The more command, conceptually similar to less, displays file contents page by page. However, unlike less, more only allows forward navigation:

```
more bigfile.txt
```

The interaction commands are straightforward: spacebar for the next page, Enter for the next line, and q for quitting.

For textual editing within the terminal, nano and vi are popular choices. nano is known for its simplicity and ease of use:

```
nano filename.txt
```

In nano, the commands are intuitive and displayed at the bottom of the screen. For instance:

- Ctrl+O saves the file.
- Ctrl+X exits the editor.
- Ctrl+K cuts a line.
- Ctrl+U pastes the cut line.

The editor supports syntax highlighting and basic search-and-replace operations, making it suitable for quick edits.

On the other hand, vi (and its improved version, vim) provides a robust suite of features for more advanced editing needs:

```
vi filename.txt
```

Initial interaction with vi might seem complex due to its modal nature, which separates command and insert modes. In command mode, various keystrokes perform actions, while insert mode allows text input:

- To enter insert mode, press i.
- To return to command mode, press Esc.
- Save and exit with :wq.
- Exit without saving with :q!.

Navigational commands include:

- h, j, k, l for left, down, up, and right movements respectively.
- gg to go to the start of the file.
- G to jump to the end of the file.
- /pattern for searching forward.

- n to find the next occurrence of the pattern.

Advanced features of vi enable practical macro recording, complex search-and-replace via regular expressions, and integration with scripting languages, making it highly efficient for power users.

These utilities — cat, less, more, nano, and vi — provide a comprehensive toolkit for viewing and modifying text files within a Linux environment. Mastery of these commands is fundamental for effective file manipulation and text editing directly from the command line.

2.5 File Permissions and Ownership (chmod, chown)

In a multiuser environment, file permissions and ownership are fundamental for maintaining security and ensuring proper access control. Linux employs a robust permission mechanism that specifies who can read, write, or execute a file. The chmod and chown commands are quintessential tools for managing these permissions and ownerships.

Each file and directory in Linux is associated with three types of owners: the user (u), the group (g), and others (o). Permissions are defined for each of these owners and are represented by three types of access: read (r), write (w), and execute (x).

To view the current permissions of files and directories, one can use the ls -l command. The output displays the permissions in a 10-character string format: the first character indicates the type of file (e.g., - for regular files, d for directories), followed by three groups of three characters. Each group represents the permissions for the owner, group, and others, respectively.

```
$ ls -l
total 16
-rw-r--r-- 1 user user 0 Jan 1 12:34 example.txt
drwxr-xr-x 2 user user 4096 Jan 1 12:34 example_dir
```

Here, -rw-r–r– indicates that the file example.txt is a regular file where the user has read and write permissions, while the group and others have only read permissions. The directory example_dir (drwxr-xr-x) has read, write, and execute permissions for the user, and read and execute permissions for the group and others.

- **Using chmod to Modify Permissions**

The chmod (change mode) command modifies file permissions. Permissions can be set using symbolic or numeric (octal) modes.

- **Symbolic Mode**

In symbolic mode, permissions are specified using letters and symbols to add (+), remove (-), or set (=) specific permissions:

```
# Add execute permission for the user
$ chmod u+x example.txt
# Remove write permission for the group
$ chmod g-w example.txt
# Set read and write permissions for others
$ chmod o=rw example.txt
```

- **Numeric (Octal) Mode**

In numeric mode, permissions are represented as a three-digit octal number where each digit ranges from 0 to 7. Each digit is the sum of its component bits: read (4), write (2), and execute (1).

```
# Set permissions to rwxr-xr-x (755)
$ chmod 755 example_dir
# Set permissions to rw-rw-r-- (664)
$ chmod 664 example.txt
```

- **Understanding chown for Ownership Modification**

The chown (change owner) command changes the ownership of files and directories. Ownership is specified by the user and the group. Only the root user or a user with sudo privileges can change the ownership.

To change the user owner of a file, the syntax is:

```
# Change the owner to another_user
$ sudo chown another_user example.txt
```

To change both the user and group owner:

```
# Change the owner to another_user and group to another_group
$ sudo chown another_user:another_group example.txt
```

To recursively change ownership of a directory and its contents:

```
# Recursively change owner and group for example_dir and its contents
$ sudo chown -R another_user:another_group example_dir
```

Correctly setting file permissions and ownership is vital to system security and user collaboration, preventing unauthorized access and modifications.

By understanding and utilizing chmod and chown, users and administrators can maintain precise control over access rights, ensuring system integrity and security.

2.6 Basic Text Processing (head, tail, wc)

Text processing is an essential part of shell scripting and Linux command-line operations. It involves reading, analyzing, manipulating, and modifying text files. This section will focus on three fundamental utilities for basic text processing: head, tail, and wc. These tools are invaluable for inspecting file contents, especially when dealing with large log or data files, as they allow us to view selective lines and count various file attributes efficiently.

head and tail are used to display the beginning and end of files respectively. The wc command, on the other hand, provides word, line, character, and byte counts for specified files, aiding in file analysis and reporting.

1. The head Command

The head command outputs the first part of files. By default, it displays the first 10 lines of each file specified. The syntax is as follows:

```
head [options] [file...]
```

Common options include:

- -n N: Display the first *N* lines.
- -c bytes: Display the first *bytes* bytes.

Example usage:

```
$ head -n 5 /var/log/syslog
```

This command displays the first 5 lines of the /var/log/syslog file.

2. The tail Command

The tail command outputs the last part of files. By default, it shows the last 10 lines. The syntax is similar to head:

```
tail [options] [file...]
```

Common options include:

- -n N: Display the last *N* lines.
- -c bytes: Display the last *bytes* bytes.
- -f: Follow the output as the file grows (useful for monitoring log files in real-time).

Example usage:

```
$ tail -f /var/log/syslog
```

This command will continuously display the last 10 lines of the /var/log/syslog file and update the output as new lines are added.

3. The wc Command

The wc (word count) command provides a count of lines, words, and characters in files. The syntax is:

```
wc [options] [file...]
```

Common options include:

- -l: Print the number of lines.
- -w: Print the number of words.
- -c: Print the number of bytes.
- -m: Print the number of characters.

Example usage:

```
$ wc -l /var/log/syslog
```

This command outputs the number of lines in the /var/log/syslog file.

Combining wc with other commands enables more advanced text processing. Using pipe (|) and head, one can count the number of lines in the first *N* lines of a file:

```
$ head -n 20 /var/log/syslog | wc -l
```

This counts the lines in the first 20 lines of the /var/log/syslog file.

Using tail, one can count the number of words in the last *N* lines:

```
$ tail -n 10 /var/log/syslog | wc -w
```

This counts the words in the last 10 lines of the /var/log/syslog file.

Understanding and effectively using head, tail, and wc facilitates efficient data inspection and manipulation, enabling more complex and powerful text processing tasks in Linux shell scripting.

2.7 Searching Files and Directories (find, grep, locate)

Efficiently searching for files and directories is a crucial skill in Linux. The command-line tools 'find', 'grep', and 'locate' provide powerful functionalities to help users locate files based on various criteria. Here, we will explore the detailed usage and options for each of these tools.

The 'find' Command

The 'find' command traverses a directory hierarchy to locate files and directories based on specified criteria. It requires a starting point and allows for numerous options.

The basic syntax of the 'find' command is:

```
find [starting-point] [options] [expression]
```

Examples: 1. To find all files with the name example.txt starting from the root directory:

```
find / -name example.txt
```

2. To search for files that are of type directory and named sample:

```
find /path/to/search -type d -name sample
```

3. To find files larger than 10MB:

```
find /path/to/search -type f -size +10M
```

4. To find files modified within the last seven days:

```
find /path/to/search -type f -mtime -7
```

Common Options: - '-name' or '-iname': Searches for files using a specific name or case-insensitive name match. - '-type': Specifies the type of file (e.g., 'f' for file, 'd' for directory). - '-size': Finds files based on their size. - '-mtime': Finds files based on their modification time. - '-user': Searches for files owned by a specific user.

The 'grep' Command

The 'grep' command is used for searching text using pattern matching. Unlike 'find', 'grep' can search contents within files.

The basic syntax of the 'grep' command is:

```
grep [options] pattern [file...]
```

Examples: 1. To search for the pattern example in a file named file.txt:

```
grep 'example' file.txt
```

2. To search recursively for the pattern example within a directory:

```
grep -r 'example' /path/to/directory
```

3. To perform a case-insensitive search:

```
grep -i 'example' file.txt
```

4. To display lines that do not match the pattern:

```
grep -v 'example' file.txt
```

Common Options: - '-r' or '–recursive': Recursively searches directories. - '-i': Ignores case distinctions in patterns. - '-v': Inverts the match to display lines not containing the pattern. - '-l': Lists files with matching lines. - '-n': Shows the line numbers of matching lines.

The 'locate' Command

The 'locate' command finds files by querying a database pre-built by the 'updatedb' utility. It is significantly faster than 'find' because it doesn't search the filesystem at runtime.

The basic syntax of the 'locate' command is:

```
locate [options] pattern
```

Examples: 1. To locate files named example.txt:

```
locate example.txt
```

2. To find files containing the pattern config in their path:

```
locate config
```

3. To limit the number of results to 10:

```
locate -n 10 example.txt
```

Common Options: - '-n': Limits the number of results. - '-r': Accepts a regular expression for more complex pattern matching. - '-i': Ignores case distinctions in both the database and the user query.

These commands, each with its own set of powerful options and use cases, allow users to find files and directories with precision and efficiency. By understanding and combining these tools, users can navigate and manage their Linux file systems more effectively.

2.8 System Monitoring and Performance (top, htop, free, df, du)

Effective system monitoring is essential for maintaining optimal performance and ensuring that resources are not overburdened. This section details several critical commands for monitoring system performance and resource usage in a Linux environment. We will discuss the commands top, htop, free, df, and du. These commands provide comprehensive insights into various aspects of the system, including CPU usage, memory utilization, disk space, and more.

The top command is one of the most widely used tools for real-time system monitoring. It provides a dynamic and interactive view of the running system, displaying system summary information and a list of tasks currently being managed by the Linux kernel. The output from top includes valuable information such as CPU usage, memory consumption, and process-specific data.

```
top
```

Upon executing top, a frequently updating display appears, showing detailed information. Typically, the display is divided into different sections:

```
top - 15:27:41 up 3 days,  1:44,  2 users,  load average: 0.28, 0.31, 0.29
Tasks: 185 total,   1 running, 184 sleeping,   0 stopped,   0 zombie
%Cpu(s):  7.3 us,  2.2 sy,  0.0 ni, 90.1 id,  0.2 wa,  0.0 hi,  0.3 si,  0.0 st
KiB Mem :  8159276 total,  1593428 free,  3307760 used,  3258088 buff/cache
KiB Swap:  2097148 total,  2095740 free,     1408 used.  4492412 avail Mem

  PID USER      PR  NI    VIRT    RES    SHR S  %CPU %MEM     TIME+ COMMAND
 1367 root      20   0  434100  52056  34852 S   1.3  0.6   9:24.03 Xorg
 1503 user      20   0 1280216 168544  60288 S   0.7  2.1   6:51.24 gnome-shell
 2697 user      20   0   42044   3768   3168 R   0.3  0.0   0:00.19 top
```

The first line provides system uptime, user sessions, and load average, which reflects the system's load over the past one, five, and fifteen minutes. Following this, the tasks currently being managed are displayed, indicating running, sleeping, stopped, and zombie processes. CPU usage metrics denote user space, system space, nice tasks, idle CPU, I/O wait, hardware interrupts, software interrupts, and steal time. Memory and swap usage are also listed.

To complement top, htop offers an improved and more user-friendly interface, making it easier to monitor real-time system information. htop is not included by default in all distributions, but can typically be installed via package managers such as apt-get or yum.

```
sudo apt-get install htop
htop
```

htop provides a color-coded and interactive display, making it simple to identify resource consumption. It supports mouse interactions and includes features such as vertical and horizontal scrolling to view the full list of processes and complete command lines.

Memory usage is crucial for understanding how your system allocates and utilizes RAM. The free command provides a snapshot of memory and swap usage.

```
free -h
```

The -h option presents the output in a human-readable format, as shown below:

```
              total        used        free      shared  buff/cache   available
Mem:           7.8G        3.2G        1.5G        200M        3.1G        4.0G
Swap:          2.0G          0B        2.0G
```

The free command output details total, used, and available memory. These metrics are useful for determining if the system is utilizing memory efficiently or if adjustments are needed.

To inspect disk usage, the df (disk filesystem) command is highly useful. It reports the amount of disk space used and available on all mounted filesystems.

```
df -h
```

Including the -h flag makes the output human-readable:

```
Filesystem      Size  Used Avail Use% Mounted on
/dev/sda1        50G   30G   18G  63% /
udev            7.9G     0  7.9G   0% /dev
tmpfs           1.6G  2.0M  1.6G   1% /run
tmpfs           7.9G   70M  7.8G   1% /dev/shm
tmpfs           5.0M  4.0K  5.0M   1% /run/lock
tmpfs           7.9G     0  7.9G   0% /sys/fs/cgroup
```

Each line includes the filesystem name, size, used space, available space, usage percentage, and its mount point. This inspection is vital for ensuring that there is adequate disk space for applications and system tasks.

Lastly, the du (disk usage) command offers detailed reports on disk space usage for files and directories. It is especially useful for identifying large files or directories consuming excessive storage.

```
du -h /path/to/directory
```

Here, the -h option again renders the output readable by humans, as in the example:

```
4.0K    /path/to/directory/file.txt
20K     /path/to/directory/subdir
25M     /path/to/directory
```

The command recursively summarizes the disk usage, enabling users to locate large directories or files quickly.

Combining these tools provides a comprehensive overview of system performance, allowing administrators to make informed decisions about resource utilization and system management. These commands are indispensable for maintaining optimal performance in a Linux environment.

2.9 Networking Commands (ping, ifconfig, netstat, ssh)

Networking commands are essential tools used for diagnosing, managing, and configuring network-related tasks on a Linux system. This section will delve into four critical networking commands: ping, ifconfig, netstat, and ssh, providing detailed explanations and practical usage examples.

1. Ping

The ping command is used to test the reachability of a host on a network and measure the round-trip time for messages sent from the origin to the destination and back. It uses the Internet Control Message Protocol (ICMP) Echo Request to send packets and waits for Echo Reply messages.

```
ping <hostname_or_IP_address>
```

Example:

```
ping google.com
```

Output:

```
PING google.com (142.250.72.238) 56(84) bytes of data.
64 bytes from yyz12s08-in-f14.1e100.net (142.250.72.238): icmp_seq=1 ttl=116 time=21.7 ms
64 bytes from yyz12s08-in-f14.1e100.net (142.250.72.238): icmp_seq=2 ttl=116 time=22.1 ms
64 bytes from yyz12s08-in-f14.1e100.net (142.250.72.238): icmp_seq=3 ttl=116 time=22.2 ms
--- google.com ping statistics ---
3 packets transmitted, 3 received, 0\% packet loss, time 4004ms
rtt min/avg/max/mdev = 21.694/22.052/22.187/0.212 ms
```

The output shows the packets sent, packets received, packet loss, and the round-trip time statistics.

2. ifconfig

The ifconfig (interface configuration) command is used to configure network interfaces in Unix-like operating systems. It is primarily used to set up IP addresses, enable or disable interfaces, and view network interface configurations.

Displaying network interfaces:

```
ifconfig
```

Example Output:

```
eth0: flags=4163<UP,BROADCAST,RUNNING,MULTICAST>  mtu 1500
    inet 192.168.1.105  netmask 255.255.255.0  broadcast 192.168.1.255
    inet6 fe80::f816:3eff:fe29:c6e4  prefixlen 64  scopeid 0x20<link>
    ether fa:16:3e:29:c6:e4  txqueuelen 1000  (Ethernet)
    RX packets 2083153  bytes 1723848400 (1.7 GB)
    RX errors 0  dropped 0  overruns 0  frame 0
    TX packets 192247  bytes 24852155 (24.8 MB)
    TX errors 0  dropped 0 overruns 0  carrier 0  collisions 0
```

To assign an IP address to an interface:

```
ifconfig eth0 192.168.1.10 netmask 255.255.255.0
```

3. netstat

The netstat (network statistics) command displays various network-related information such as network connections, routing tables, interface statistics, masquerade connections, and multicast memberships.

Checking active connections and their ports:

```
netstat -tuln
```

Example Output:

```
Active Internet connections (only servers)
Proto Recv-Q Send-Q Local Address          Foreign Address        State
tcp        0      0 0.0.0.0:22              0.0.0.0:*               LISTEN
tcp6       0      0 :::80                   :::*                    LISTEN
udp        0      0 0.0.0.0:68              0.0.0.0:*
udp6       0      0 :::546                  :::*
```

To view network interface statistics:

```
netstat -i
```

Example Output:

```
Kernel Interface table
Iface     MTU    RX-OK RX-ERR RX-DRP RX-OVR TX-OK TX-ERR TX-DRP TX-OVR Flg
eth0      1500  2079679 0      0      0      192003 0      0      0      BMRU
lo        65536 582     0      0      0      582    0      0      0      LRU
```

4. ssh

The ssh (Secure Shell) command is used for securely logging into a remote machine and executing commands over an encrypted connection. It utilizes public-key cryptography to authenticate the remote computer and allow it to authenticate the user if necessary.

Connecting to a remote machine:

```
ssh <username>@<hostname_or_IP_address>
```

Example:

```
ssh user@192.168.1.100
```

Generating SSH keys for password-less login:

```
ssh-keygen -t rsa
```

This generates a public/private RSA key pair:

```
Generating public/private rsa key pair.
Enter file in which to save the key (/home/user/.ssh/id_rsa):
Enter passphrase (empty for no passphrase):
Enter same passphrase again:
Your identification has been saved in /home/user/.ssh/id_rsa.
Your public key has been saved in /home/user/.ssh/id_rsa.pub.
The key fingerprint is:
SHA256:AAAAB3NzaC1yc2EAAAABJQAAAQEAgNVeirOe5yRXYuVrL6MmfKn5wCWwDAhE+kG5 user@hostname
The key's randomart image is:
+---[RSA 2048]----+
|   . o           |
|  . + .          |
|   = .           |
|  o = . .        |
|   + S * .       |
|    = + E        |
|   . E = .       |
|     o +         |
|      o          |
+----[SHA256]-----+
```

Copying the public key to the remote machine:

```
ssh-copy-id <username>@<hostname_or_IP_address>
```

Example:

```
ssh-copy-id user@192.168.1.100
```

The networking commands ping, ifconfig, netstat, and ssh provide powerful utilities for network diagnostics, configuration, and secure communication. Proficiency in these commands is an essential skill for effective network administration and troubleshooting.

2.10 Package Management (apt-get, yum, zypper)

Package management is a critical aspect of maintaining and configuring Linux systems. It encompasses tools and practices for installing, updating, and removing software applications. Different Linux distributions often employ different package management systems. In this section, we will delve into three primary package management tools: apt-get, yum, and zypper, which are used respectively in Debian-based, RedHat-based, and openSUSE-based distributions.

apt-get is a command-line tool used to handle packages in Debian and its derivatives, such as Ubuntu. yum is used in RedHat and CentOS environments, while zypper is employed in managing packages for openSUSE and SLE (SUSE Linux Enterprise). Each tool offers a variety of commands for package operations, allowing for efficient maintenance of software applications.

To begin with, let's explore some common apt-get commands used in

Debian-based systems. The following command updates the package list from all configured repositories:

```
sudo apt-get update
```

Updating the package list is often a preliminary step before installing or upgrading packages to ensure that the system has the latest information on available packages. Once the package list is updated, you can upgrade all installed packages to their latest versions using:

```
sudo apt-get upgrade
```

When you wish to install a new package, the syntax is straightforward. For example, to install the curl utility, you would use:

```
sudo apt-get install curl
```

If you need to remove a package, the remove command is used. For instance, to remove curl, the following command will suffice:

```
sudo apt-get remove curl
```

For a complete removal of a package, including its configuration files, it is advisable to use the purge command:

```
sudo apt-get purge curl
```

Switching focus to yum, a package manager used primarily in RedHat-based distributions, it follows a similar structure to apt-get. To check for updates in the repositories, you should execute:

```
sudo yum check-update
```

To install a package, for example, the tree command, you would use:

```
sudo yum install tree
```

Removing installed packages in yum is straightforward. The following command will remove the installed tree package:

```
sudo yum remove tree
```

An essential task in package management is upgrading existing packages. To upgrade all installed packages to their latest versions, the following command is utilized:

```
sudo yum update
```

Another powerful feature of yum is the ability to list installed packages or available packages in the repositories:

```
sudo yum list installed
sudo yum list available
```

zypper is the package manager for SUSE-based systems and is quite versatile. To refresh the repository data, which is similar to updating the package list in apt-get, use:

```
sudo zypper refresh
```

To install a package, such as wget, the command would be:

```
sudo zypper install wget
```

For removing a package, zypper uses the following syntax:

```
sudo zypper remove wget
```

To update all installed packages on the system, you would perform:

```
sudo zypper update
```

In addition to these basic commands, zypper also offers the capability to search for packages using:

```
zypper search <pattern>
```

Each of these package managers provides extensive options and capabilities beyond the fundamental commands covered here. They also include functionalities for handling repositories, such as adding, removing, and managing repository priorities. Furthermore, package managers can handle dependencies automatically, ensuring that all required libraries and tools are installed alongside the primary package to maintain system stability and consistency.

These command-line package management tools are critical for both system administrators and users, enabling efficient and reliable management of software on Linux systems. Understanding and utilizing these tools effectively ensures that systems remain up-to-date, secure, and functional.

2.11 Archiving and Compression (tar, gzip, zip, unzip)

Archiving and compression are essential techniques for managing files and conserving disk space in a Linux environment. These techniques facilitate easier data transfer, reduce storage requirements, and simplify file organization. Four primary tools commonly employed in Linux for these purposes are tar, gzip, zip, and unzip.

The tar (tape archive) utility is designed to consolidate multiple files into a single archive file, known as a tarball. The syntax for creating a tarball using tar is:

```
tar -cvf archive_name.tar /path/to/directory_or_file
```

In this command, c stands for 'create', v for 'verbose', and f for 'file'. The archive_name.tar specifies the name of the resulting tarball file, and /path/to/directory_or_file indicates the files or directories to be included in the tarball.

To extract the contents of a tarball, the following command is used:

```
tar -xvf archive_name.tar
```

Here, x stands for 'extract'. This command decompresses the tarball and restores the original files and directories.

Compression tools such as gzip can further reduce the size of the tarball. To compress a tarball using gzip, execute:

```
gzip archive_name.tar
```

The resulting file will be named archive_name.tar.gz. To decompress this file, use:

```
gunzip archive_name.tar.gz
```

Alternatively, you can combine both archiving and compressing into one step. The tar command allows specifying gzip compression directly using:

```
tar -czvf archive_name.tar.gz /path/to/directory_or_file
```

To extract a tar.gz file, the command is:

```
tar -xzvf archive_name.tar.gz
```

Another common tool for compression is zip. Unlike tar, zip does both archiving and compression in a single step by default. The syntax for creating a zip file is:

```
zip -r archive_name.zip /path/to/directory_or_file
```

In this command, -r stands for 'recursive', which allows the inclusion of directories and subdirectories. The resulting file is archive_name.zip.

To extract files from a zip archive, the unzip command is used:

```
unzip archive_name.zip
```

For large files or directories, it is often beneficial to split the archive into smaller parts. Using zip, this can be achieved with the split option:

```
zip -r -s 50m archive_name.zip /path/to/directory_or_file
```

This command splits the archive into chunks of 50MB each.

Linux natively supports a diverse range of archive and compression tools. While tar combined with gzip or bzip2 is the standard for many use cases, zip and unzip provide additional flexibility, especially for cross-platform compatibility.

Users can employ tar and gzip for efficient storage and transfer of data across Linux systems. Conversely, zip and unzip are advantageous when the archives need to be accessed from non-Linux operating systems, such as Windows and macOS.

Chapter 3

Introduction to Shell Scripting

This chapter introduces the fundamentals of shell scripting, starting with the definition and purpose of a shell script. Readers will learn to write and execute basic scripts, understand the syntax and structure, and incorporate comments. Key concepts such as script execution, using variables, handling basic input and output, and managing script arguments and parameters are covered. The chapter concludes with an introduction to debugging shell scripts, ensuring readers can troubleshoot and refine their scripts effectively.

3.1 What is a Shell Script?

A shell script is a text file containing a series of commands intended to be executed by the Unix/Linux shell, which is an interpreter that executes commands read from input devices or files. Shell scripts serve a multitude of purposes, ranging from task automation to complex programming solutions involving loops, conditionals, and functions.

A shell script combines the powerful command-line interface of Unix/Linux with the flexibility of scripting. Unlike compiled languages, shell scripts are interpreted by the shell, which means they are executed line-by-line. This allows for rapid testing and iteration but often results in slower execution compared to compiled binaries.

A typical shell script begins with a "shebang" (#!/bin/sh or #!/bin/bash) that identifies the script's intended shell. This line is critical as it defines the environment in which the script will run. For example:

```
#!/bin/bash
echo "Hello, World!"
```

The above script starts with the shebang pointing to the Bash shell, followed by an echo command which outputs "Hello, World!". Saving this script to a file and ensuring it has execution permissions will result in producing the expected output upon execution.

One distinguishing aspect of shell scripts is their use of shell built-ins and external programs. Built-ins are commands intrinsic to the shell, like cd for changing directories or echo for printing text. Conversely, external programs such as grep, awk, and sed expand a shell script's capabilities by offering advanced text processing utilities.

Shell scripts also facilitate the use of variables, which store data values and can be reused throughout the script. This capability allows for the dynamic handling of data, enhancing scripts' flexibility and efficiency.

```
#!/bin/bash
GREETING="Hello"
TARGET="World"
echo "$GREETING, $TARGET!"
```

In the snippet above, two variables, GREETING and TARGET, are defined and later referenced within the echo command. The shell replaces the variables with their values before execution, resulting in "Hello, World!".

Comments are another vital feature of shell scripting, denoted by the # character. Comments provide documentation within the script, explaining the purpose of commands or sections without affecting execution.

```
#!/bin/bash
# Assign a greeting to a variable
GREETING="Hello"
# Assign the target audience to a variable
TARGET="World"
# Print the greeting to the terminal
echo "$GREETING, $TARGET!"
```

Complex logic is enabled by various control flow constructs, such as conditionals (if, else, elif) and loops (for, while). These constructs allow for decision-making and repetitive task execution within scripts.

```
#!/bin/bash
# Check if a file exists and print a message
if [ -e "$1" ]; then
    echo "File $1 exists."
else
    echo "File $1 does not exist."
fi
```

Here, the script checks for the existence of a file whose name is passed as a command-line argument (accessible through the parameter $1). The if statement determines the flow based on whether the file exists, showcasing conditional logic.

Automation is a significant advantage provided by shell scripts. By combining multiple commands into a single file, repetitive tasks can be streamlined:

```
#!/bin/bash
# Backup script
# Create a backup directory
mkdir -p /backup

# Copy important files to the backup directory
cp /important/files/* /backup/

# Print completion message
echo "Backup completed."
```

In this example, the script automates the process of backing up files. It creates a backup directory (if not already existing), copies files from a specified location to the backup directory, and prints completion feedback.

Shell scripts are versatile and invaluable tools for both beginners and advanced users. Their ability to orchestrate complex operations through simple text files makes them fundamental in Unix/Linux environments. Understanding the core concepts of writing and executing shell scripts is an essential skill for efficient system administration, automation, and beyond.

3.2 Writing Your First Shell Script

When embarking on the journey to write your first shell script, it is crucial to understand the foundational concept and structure. A shell script is a series of commands written in a file and intended to be executed by the shell. These scripts can automate repetitive tasks, manage system operations, and facilitate complex workflows with minimal human intervention.

Begin by creating a new file using your preferred text editor. Common editors include nano, vim, emacs, and gedit. For simplicity, let's use nano to create our first script. Open a terminal and type:

```
nano first_script.sh
```

The file extension .sh denotes that this is a shell script, although it is not strictly necessary. Adding the extension can help to quickly identify the type of file. Once the file is open, the first line of your script should specify the interpreter that will execute the script. This is done using the shebang (#) followed by the path to the interpreter. In most cases, the interpreter for shell scripts is located at /bin/bash. Therefore, the first line of your script should be:

```
#!/bin/bash
```

The shebang ensures that the script is executed using the Bash shell, regardless of the default shell of the user running the script. Following the shebang, you can start adding commands that comprise your script. For a simple demonstration, let's add a few basic commands to our script:

```
#!/bin/bash
# This is a simple shell script

echo "Hello, World!"
date
```

In this script:

- **Comment**: The line starting with # is a comment and is ignored by the shell. Comments are useful for annotating your code and explaining the purpose of different parts of the script.
- **echo Command**: The echo command outputs the text "Hello, World!" to the terminal.
- **date Command**: The date command displays the current date and time.

After saving and closing the file (Ctrl + X in nano, then Y to confirm saving), you need to make the script executable. This is done by modifying the file permissions using the chmod command:

```
chmod +x first_script.sh
```

The +x option adds execute permissions to the file for the user. To execute the script, use the following command:

```
./first_script.sh
```

The ./ indicates that the script is located in the current directory. When you run this command, the output should be:

```
Hello, World!
Wed Oct 4 10:00:00 UTC 2023
```

This output confirms that your shell script was executed successfully, printing "Hello, World!" followed by the current date and time.

It is important to understand the syntax rules when writing a shell script. Commands in the script are executed sequentially, starting from the first command after the shebang. Each command can be placed on a new line or separated by a semicolon (;). When incorporating variables, always ensure proper syntax to avoid common errors. For example:

```
#!/bin/bash

name="John"
echo "Hello, $name!"
```

Here, the variable name is assigned the value "John" and is later referenced in the echo command using $name. This will output:

```
Hello, John!
```

To enhance script readability, maintain proper indentation and spacing. This helps in easily identifying different sections and their respective purposes within the script.

By following these steps, you can confidently write, save, and execute basic shell scripts. They form the basis for more complex scripts that you will encounter and develop as you delve deeper into shell scripting.

3.3 Making a Shell Script Executable

After writing your first shell script, the next crucial step is to make the script executable. A shell script is an ordinary text file until it is given the proper permissions to execute. This distinction allows the operating system to treat it as a program. To make a script executable, you must modify its permissions using the chmod command.

chmod stands for "change mode," and it is used to adjust the permission settings of files and directories. In Linux, file permissions determine the actions that users can perform on a file. There are three types of permissions: read (r), write (w), and execute (x). These permissions can be granted to the owner of the file, the group owner, and others.

Consider a sample shell script named myscript.sh. Initially, when you create this script, it may have the following default permissions:

```
% ls -l myscript.sh
-rw-r--r-- 1 user group  0 Apr 1 10:00 myscript.sh
```

In this example, the script has read and write permissions for the owner and read-only permissions for the group and others. However, it lacks execute permissions, which are necessary for it to be run as a program.

To make the shell script executable, you need to modify its permissions by adding the execute permission. This can be done using the following command:

```
chmod +x myscript.sh
```

The +x option tells chmod to add execute permissions for the owner, group, and others. After running this command, you can verify the new permissions using the ls -l command:

```
% ls -l myscript.sh
-rwxr-xr-x 1 user group  0 Apr 1 10:00 myscript.sh
```

Now, the script has execute permissions, as indicated by the x in the permission string (-rwxr-xr-x). This means the owner, group, and others can all execute the script.

For more granular control over permissions, you can specify explicitly which users (owner, group, others) should have execute permissions. The chmod command allows these modifications through symbolic and octal modes.

With symbolic mode, you can add specific permissions. To grant execute permissions only to the owner, use:

```
chmod u+x myscript.sh
```

In this command, u+x indicates that execute permission should be added (+) for the user (owner) only (u). After this, the script permissions are:

```
% ls -l myscript.sh
-rwxr--r--  1 user group  0 Apr 1 10:00 myscript.sh
```

Here, only the owner can execute the script, while the group and others retain read-only access.

Alternatively, permissions can be set using the octal (numeric) mode.

In octal mode, every permission set is represented by a number: 4 for read, 2 for write, and 1 for execute. These values can be combined; for example, 7 (read+write+execute = $4+2+1$) gives full permissions.

To set the shell script permissions to 755 (rwxr-xr-x), use:

```
chmod 755 myscript.sh
```

This command grants the owner full permissions (7), while the group and others receive read and execute permissions (5).

Finally, the script can be run directly from the command line, assuming the current directory is included in your PATH. If not, execute the script by specifying its relative or absolute path:

```
./myscript.sh
```

When executed, ensure the script operates as intended. If any issues arise, verify the script content, permissions, and execution environment to diagnose and resolve the problem effectively.

3.4 Basic Syntax and Structure of Shell Scripts

When crafting a shell script, understanding its fundamental syntax and structure is crucial. A shell script, essentially a text file containing a sequence of commands executed by the shell, must adhere to specific syntactical guidelines to ensure proper execution.

Shebang Line: The very first line in a shell script should be the shebang line. This line designates the script's interpreter.

```
#!/bin/bash
```

This line tells the system to use the 'bash' shell to execute the script. The path '/bin/bash' may vary depending on the environment, but it is typically the location of the Bash shell.

Comments: Comments are essential for documenting the script and explaining code functionality. They begin with the # character and extend to the end of the line.

```
# This is a comment
# Script to display current date and time
```

Command Execution: Commands are executed line by line from top to bottom. Each command is typically on a new line and may include internal or external commands.

```
echo "Hello, World!"
date
```

Variables: Variables store data that can be referenced and manipulated throughout the script. Assignment is straightforward, using the syntax 'variable_name=value' without spaces around the '=' sign.

```
greeting="Hello"
date_command=$(date) # Command substitution using $(...)
```

To access the value of a variable, prefix the variable name with $.

```
echo $greeting
echo $date_command
```

Quoting: Quoting is an essential aspect impacting how strings and variables are parsed. Double quotes ("""") preserve the literal value of all characters except for $, ${, and \. Single quotes ("") preserve the literal value of all characters within them.

```
echo "Greeting: $greeting"
echo 'Literal Greeting: $greeting'
```

Control Structures: Shell scripts support various control structures for conditional execution and loops.

If-Else:

```
if [ condition ]; then
  # commands to execute if condition is true
else
  # commands to execute if condition is false
fi
```

For Loop:

```
for var in list
do
  # commands to execute for each item in list
done
```

While Loop:

```
while [ condition ]
do
  # commands to execute while condition is true
done
```

Functions: Functions are defined blocks of code that perform specific tasks and can be reused throughout the script. Functions are declared using the following syntax:

```
function_name() {
  # code block
}
```

```
greet() {
  echo "Hello, $1"
}

greet "Alice"
```

In this example, 'greet' is a function that takes one argument.

Exit Status: Each executed command returns an exit status. A status of '0' indicates success, while any non-zero value indicates an error. The special variable $? holds the exit status of the last executed command.

```
echo "This is a test"
echo $? # displays the status of the previous command
```

Attention to these facets of syntax and structure empowers the user to write effective and efficient shell scripts.

3.5 Using Comments in Scripts

Comments are an indispensable tool in the development of shell scripts. They provide clarity, documentation, and aid in the maintenance of code over time. In shell scripting, comments are implemented with the # symbol. Any text following this symbol on the same line is treated as a comment and is ignored by the shell during script execution.

Single-Line Comments

A single-line comment begins with the # symbol and extends to the end of the line. It is useful for explaining individual lines or blocks of code.

```
#!/bin/bash
# This is a single-line comment
echo "Hello, World!" # This comment explains the echo command
```

In this example, # This is a single-line comment explains the purpose of the script or a specific line, and # This comment explains the echo command provides further insight into the echo command.

Commenting Out Code

Commenting out blocks of code is a common practice for debugging or temporarily disabling code. This can be achieved by placing the # symbol before each line of the code block you wish to comment out.

```
#!/bin/bash
# The following lines of code are commented out
# echo "This line is commented out and won't execute"
# echo "This is another commented line"
echo "Only this line will be executed"
```

Here, two echo statements are commented out and will not be executed. The third echo statement will be executed normally.

Multi-Line Comments

While there is no direct syntax for multi-line comments in shell scripts (unlike some other programming languages), consecutive single-line comments are often used to achieve the same effect.

```
#!/bin/bash
# This is a multi-line comment
# Each line starts with the \# symbol
# This can span multiple lines
echo "Multi-line comments example"
```

Every line of the multi-line comment starts with #, thus covering multiple lines.

Inline Comments

Inline comments are placed at the end of a code line. This type of comment is helpful for adding brief notes or explanations directly adjacent to the code they refer to.

```
#!/bin/bash
echo "Starting process..." # Initiates the process
process_id=$$ # Stores the process ID of the script
echo "The process ID is: \$process_id" # Outputs the process ID
```

Each comment follows a statement or command, providing a concise description of its function.

Best Practices for Using Comments

To maximize the utility of comments in scripts, consider the following best practices:

- **Clarity:** Ensure comments are clear and concise. They should add value and understanding to the code.

- **Relevance:** Keep comments relevant to the code they describe. Outdated or incorrect comments can confuse more than help.
- **Avoid Over-Commenting:** While comments are useful, over-commenting can clutter the script. Aim for the right balance.
- **Descriptive:** Use comments to describe the "why" behind a decision or action rather than the "what," which is often evident from the code itself.

Example of a well-commented shell script:

```
#!/bin/bash

# This script demonstrates the use of comments
echo "Welcome to the script demo" # Outputs a welcome message

# Define a variable to store the user input
read -p "Enter your name: " username # Prompts user to enter their name

# Greet the user
echo "Hello, \$username!" # Displays a personalized greeting

# Check if a specific file exists
if [ -f "example.txt" ]; then
    # File exists
    echo "The file 'example.txt' exists." # Informs the user
else
    # File does not exist
    echo "The file 'example.txt' does not exist." # Informs the user
fi

# End of script
echo "Script execution completed." # Indicates completion
```

The above script includes comments for initialization, user input, conditional checks, and terminal outputs, making it easy to understand each part of the script.

Effective use of comments improves code readability and maintainability, making it easier for others (and your future self) to understand and work with your scripts.

3.6 Running and Testing Shell Scripts

To effectively utilize shell scripts, it is crucial to understand the processes involved in running and testing them. This ensures that scripts perform as expected and potential issues are identified and resolved systematically. This section covers methods for executing shell scripts and strategies for rigorous testing, incorporating essential commands and scenarios.

Running Shell Scripts

Executing a shell script involves informing the shell to interpret and execute the commands written within the script file. There are multiple ways to run a shell script in a Unix-like operating system:

- Using the sh or bash Command:
  The most direct method to run a script is to invoke the shell executable with the script as an argument. This method does not require the script to have execute permissions.

  ```
  sh script_name.sh
  ```

  or

  ```
  bash script_name.sh
  ```

- Setting Execute Permissions and Running Directly:
  By changing the file permissions of a script to make it executable, the script can be run directly from the command line.

  ```
  chmod +x script_name.sh
  ./script_name.sh
  ```

  The chmod command modifies file permissions, allowing the script to be executed. Using ./script_name.sh ensures the shell looks in the current directory for the script.

- Specifying the Interpreter Line:
  At the beginning of a shell script, a shebang line (#!) specifies the path to the interpreter that should execute the script. This is typically /bin/bash or /bin/sh.

  ```
  #!/bin/bash
  echo "Hello, World!"
  ```

  Including this line allows the script to be run directly, assuming it has execute permissions.

Testing Shell Scripts

Testing is a vital phase in the development of shell scripts. It involves checking the script for correctness, efficiency, and robustness against different input scenarios. Below are practices and commands to test shell scripts:

- Debug Mode:
  Shells like bash provide a debug mode that outputs each command to the terminal before executing it, offering insight into the script's operation.

  ```
  bash -x script_name.sh
  ```

  Each command and its arguments are preceded by a plus sign, making it easier to trace and identify issues.

- Syntax Checking:
  Perform a syntax check on the script using the -n option, which parses the script without executing it, revealing any syntax errors.

  ```
  bash -n script_name.sh
  ```

  No output indicates no syntax errors, whereas errors are reported directly.

- Error Handling:
  Implement robust error handling within the script to manage unexpected scenarios. Use constructs like if-else, case statements, and the trap command to handle errors gracefully.

  ```
  #!/bin/bash

  trap 'echo "An error occurred. Exiting..."; exit 1;' ERR

  if [ -z "$1" ]; then
    echo "No argument supplied"
    exit 1
  fi

  echo "Script running with argument: $1"
  ```

- Unit Testing with Functions:
  Modularize scripts using functions to isolate and test specific components independently. Define and test each function comprehensively.

  ```
  #!/bin/bash

  greet() {
    echo "Hello, $1"
  }

  test_greet() {
    local expected="Hello, John"
  ```

```
    local result=$(greet "John")
    if [ "$result" == "$expected" ]; then
      echo "Test passed"
    else
      echo "Test failed"
    fi
}

test_greet
```

- Test with Varied Inputs:
  Execute the script with various valid and invalid arguments to ensure it handles all cases appropriately, preventing unexpected failures during actual use.

```
./script_name.sh
./script_name.sh "argument"
bash script_name.sh "unexpected argument"
```

- Logging:
  Supplement the script with logging to capture outputs and errors for further analysis. Redirect outputs to a log file for post-execution review.

```
#!/bin/bash

exec >script.log 2>&1

echo "Script started"
# other commands
```

By integrating these practices, running and testing shell scripts becomes a structured, consistent process, leading to robust and error-free scripts.

3.7 Understanding Shell Script Execution

The execution of a shell script involves several stages that transform the written code into actions executed by the shell. It is vital to comprehend these stages to effectively develop and debug scripts.

1. Reading the Script File: When a shell script is executed, the shell reads the script file line by line. It interprets each line as a command or a sequence of commands to be executed.

```
#!/bin/bash
echo "Hello, World!"
```

In the example above, the shell reads the script file starting from the first line, which is the shebang (#bin/bash), indicating the script should be executed in the Bash shell.

2. Tokenizing: After reading a line, the shell splits it into tokens. Tokens are syntactic units such as keywords, commands, arguments, and operators.

```
echo "Hello, World!"
```

Here, 'echo' is recognized as a command token, and '"Hello, World!"' is identified as a single argument token.

3. Parsing: The shell parses the tokens to understand their structure and relationship. This stage involves syntax analysis where the shell checks for syntactic correctness.

4. Execution: The parsed commands are then executed. Execution involves running built-in commands directly within the shell or invoking external programs.

Command Execution Flow:

- **Internal Commands**: Commands that are built into the shell, such as 'cd', 'echo', and 'set'.
- **External Commands**: Commands that are standalone executable programs, such as 'ls', 'grep'.

```
ls -l /home/user
```

In this command, 'ls' is an external command that lists directory contents. The shell locates 'ls' through the PATH environment variable, then executes it with the provided arguments.

5. Command Substitution: Before executing commands, the shell performs command substitution. It replaces command substitution expressions with their output.

```
echo "Today is $(date)"
```

Here, '$(date)' is executed, and its output is substituted into the 'echo' command.

6. Variable Expansion: The shell expands variables by replacing variable names with their values.

```
MY_VAR="Hello"
echo "$MY_VAR, World!"
```

'$MY_VAR' is expanded to '"Hello"', producing the output 'Hello, World¡.

7. Quoting Mechanisms: The shell processes quoting mechanisms to determine how special characters and whitespaces are interpreted.

- **Double Quotes (")**: Preserve the literal value of all characters within the quotes except '$', " ' ", and '
'.
- **Single Quotes ("'")**: Preserve the literal value of all characters within the quotes.

```
echo "The price is \$5"
```

Produces 'The price is $5'.

8. Redirection and Pipelines: The shell moves the output of commands using redirection and connects multiple commands with pipelines.

```
ls -l > output.txt
grep "search_term" < input.txt
ls -l | grep "myfile"
```

- '>' redirects standard output to a file.
- '<' redirects standard input from a file.
- '|' passes the output of one command as input to another.

9. Conditional Execution and Grouping: Commands can be conditionally executed based on the success or failure of previous commands.

```
mkdir new_directory && cd new_directory
```

The 'cd' command is executed only if 'mkdir' succeeds, indicated by the '&&' operator.

Understanding the detailed stages of shell script execution is crucial for effective scripting. Each stage from reading the script file to conditional execution plays a significant role. This knowledge facilitates writing robust scripts and debugging them with precision.

3.8 Using Variables in Shell Scripts

In shell scripting, variables provide an essential means to store and manipulate data. Understanding how to declare, assign, and utilize variables is crucial for writing efficient and effective shell scripts. This section elaborates on the syntax and semantics of using variables, their scope, and best practices.

Variables in shell scripts are used to store information which can be referenced and manipulated within the script. They can store different types of data such as strings, numbers, and even the results of commands.

The basic syntax for declaring a variable and assigning it a value is straightforward. In the Bourne shell (sh) and its derivatives, including Bash (Bourne Again Shell) which is the default on many Linux systems, variables are declared without explicit data types.

```
#!/bin/bash
# Assign a value to a variable
greeting="Hello, world!"
# Print the value of the variable
echo $greeting
```

In the example above, the variable greeting is assigned the string "Hello, world!". When we want to reference the value of the variable, we prefix the variable name with a dollar sign ($), as shown in the echo command.

- **Variable Naming Conventions**

Variable names are case-sensitive and by convention, they are written in uppercase. However, lowercase variable names are also permissible. A variable name can contain letters, digits, and underscores but must not start with a digit. Special characters and spaces are not allowed in variable names.

```
# Valid variable names
VAR1="value"
variable_name="value"
_variable="value"

# Invalid variable names
1variable="value" # Starts with a digit
var name="value" # Contains a space
var-name="value" # Contains a hyphen
```

- **Quoting Variables**

When assigning values that contain spaces or special characters, it is important to quote the value. Either single (') or double (") quotes can be used, but they behave differently. Single quotes preserve the literal value of each character, while double quotes allow for variable interpolation.

```
#!/bin/bash
# Using double quotes
greeting="Hello, $USER!"
echo $greeting # Output: Hello, current_username! (current_username is the user's
    login name)

# Using single quotes
greeting='Hello, $USER!'
echo $greeting # Output: Hello, $USER!
```

- **Variable Scope and Exporting Variables**

Variables declared within a script are local to that script and any functions within it. To make a variable available to any subsequently executed scripts or commands, it must be exported to the environment.

```
#!/bin/bash
# Local variable
local_var="I am local"
# Exported variable
export global_var="I am global"

# Another script or command can access 'global_var'
bash -c 'echo $global_var' # Output: I am global
bash -c 'echo $local_var' # Output: (nothing, as it's not exported)
```

- **Arithmetic Operations**

Shell scripting allows for basic arithmetic operations using variables. This can be done using the let command, double parentheses (()), or the expr command.

```
#!/bin/bash
num1=5
num2=10

# Using let command
let sum=num1+num2

# Using double parentheses
sum=$((num1 + num2))

# Using expr command
sum=$(expr $num1 + $num2)

echo "The sum is: $sum" # Output: The sum is: 15
```

- **Command Substitution**

Command substitution allows the output of a command to be assigned to a variable. This can be achieved using backticks (‘command‘) or the more modern and preferred syntax with $(command).

```
#!/bin/bash
# Using backticks
current_date=‘date‘

# Using $(...)
current_date=$(date)

echo "Today's date is: $current_date"
```

- **Best Practices**

- Use meaningful variable names to enhance readability.
- Initialize variables before use to avoid uninitialized variable errors.
- Quote variables appropriately to handle cases with spaces or special characters.
- Use uppercase variables for exported environment variables.
- Clean up exported variables when they are no longer needed to prevent unintended usage in subsequent commands or scripts.

Familiarity with variable manipulation in shell scripting will significantly improve your ability to write flexible and powerful scripts. Variables are the building blocks for storing data that can be processed within your scripts, enabling dynamic and robust functionality.

3.9 Basic Input and Output in Shell Scripts

Shell scripts require interaction with users and the system, making input and output mechanisms vital. Input allows scripts to receive data from users or files, while output directs script results to various destinations like the console, files, or other programs. Fundamental commands for handling basic input and output include echo, read, and redirection operators.

The echo command is an essential tool for outputting text to the console. It prints the provided string to standard output. Here is an example of echoing a simple message:

```
echo "Hello, World!"
```

Executing this script will produce the following output:

```
Hello, World!
```

To include variables within the output text, the variable name is prefixed with a dollar sign ($). For example:

```
#!/bin/bash
name="Alice"
echo "Hello, $name!"
```

If executed, the script yields:

```
Hello, Alice!
```

It's important to note that the `echo` command can interpret escape sequences if used with the `-e` option. For instance:

```
#!/bin/bash
echo -e "First line\nSecond line\tIndented text"
```

The above script would output:

```
First line
Second line     Indented text
```

For input, the `read` command collects user input during script execution. This command reads a line from standard input and assigns it to a variable. Here is an example:

```
#!/bin/bash
echo "Enter your name:"
read name
echo "Welcome, $name!"
```

When the script runs, it prompts for a name and then displays a welcome message:

```
Enter your name:
Alice
Welcome, Alice!
```

Redirection operators are crucial for managing input and output in shell scripts. The `>` operator redirects standard output to a file, creating the file if it does not exist or overwriting it if it does. For example:

```
echo "This will be written to a file" > output.txt
```

Executing this script will write "This will be written to a file" into `output.txt`. To append to the file instead of overwriting, use the `>>` operator:

```
echo "This text will be appended" >> output.txt
```

Input can also be redirected from a file using the < operator. This is useful when a script needs to process data from an existing file. For instance:

```
#!/bin/bash
while read line
do
  echo "Read line: $line"
done < inputfile.txt
```

This script reads each line from inputfile.txt and echoes it to the console:

```
Read line: Line 1 of the file
Read line: Line 2 of the file
...
```

Combining these mechanisms with pipes (|) allows the output of one command to be used as the input for another, facilitating more complex data processing. Here is an example of using a pipe with shell scripting commands:

```
#!/bin/bash
echo "This is an example" | tr 'a-z' 'A-Z'
```

The tr command translates characters from lowercase to uppercase, and the output will be:

```
THIS IS AN EXAMPLE
```

Understanding and using these basic input and output techniques effectively enhances the interaction capabilities of shell scripts by providing robust mechanisms for data flow and manipulation.

3.10 Script Arguments and Parameters

In many scenarios, shell scripts need to be flexible and reusable. This is achieved by passing arguments and parameters to the script at runtime. Arguments enable the script to handle various inputs without altering the script's codebase. In this section, we will delve into the mechanisms for passing and accessing script arguments, examine special parameters available within the shell, and understand how to deal with an arbitrary number of arguments.

When a shell script is executed, the arguments are passed to the script as a list. These arguments can be accessed using positional parameters. Positional parameters are variables that are assigned values based on the order of the arguments provided when the script is called.

For instance, consider the following shell script saved as args.sh:

```
#!/bin/bash

echo "Argument 1: \$1"
echo "Argument 2: \$2"
echo "All arguments: \$@"
echo "Total number of arguments: \$#"
```

In this script, $1 and $2 refer to the first and second arguments, respectively. The $@ variable expands to all the arguments passed to the script, and $# provides the count of arguments.

Executing the script with arguments would produce the following output:

```
$ ./args.sh Hello World
Argument 1: Hello
Argument 2: World
All arguments: Hello World
Total number of arguments: 2
```

It is important to note that arguments are separated by spaces and the order of arguments corresponds to their respective positional parameters. Let us explore more intricate details about each special parameter used with arguments:

- $0: This variable holds the name of the script itself.
- $1, $2, ...: These are positional parameters corresponding to the first, second, and subsequent arguments.
- $@: This variable expands to all positional parameters as a single word.
- $#: This variable holds the total number of arguments passed to the script.
- $*: Similar to $@, but with slightly different behavior when quoted (all parameters as a single word rather than separate words).
- $?: This variable represents the exit status of the last command executed.
- $$: This variable expands to the process ID of the script itself.
- $!: This variable contains the process ID of the last background command.

A practical example to understand these parameters better involves creating a script named param_info.sh:

```
#!/bin/bash

echo "Script Name: \$0"
echo "Argument 1: \$1"
echo "Argument 2: \$2"
echo "Total Arguments: \$#"
echo "All Arguments (quoted): \$@"
echo "All Arguments (single word): \$*"
echo "Last command exit status: \$?"
echo "Script Process ID: \$$"
```

Executing this script with arguments provides an insightful output:

```
$ ./param_info.sh arg1 arg2
Script Name: ./param_info.sh
Argument 1: arg1
Argument 2: arg2
Total Arguments: 2
All Arguments (quoted): arg1 arg2
All Arguments (single word): arg1 arg2
Last command exit status: 0
Script Process ID: 12345
```

Quotes around $@ and $* reveal their subtle differences. While $@ maintains individual arguments as separate quoted strings, $* concatenates them into a single string. These distinctions are crucial when handling arguments that contain spaces or other special characters.

Handling an unknown number of arguments can be achieved via looping constructs within the script. A for loop is particularly efficient for iterating over all arguments provided to the script. Consider the following script iterate_args.sh:

```
#!/bin/bash

echo "Iterating over all arguments:"

for arg in "\$@"
do
    echo "\$arg"
done
```

If this script is executed with multiple arguments:

```
$ ./iterate_args.sh one two three four
Iterating over all arguments:
one
two
three
four
```

This script demonstrates how to iterate over and process each argument individually. The quoted "$@" ensures that each argument is considered as a separate entity, which is critical when arguments contain spaces.

There are additional considerations for arguments and parameters in more advanced scripting scenarios, such as using getopts for parsing options and arguments systematically. However, foundational knowledge about positional parameters and special variables lays the groundwork for creating flexible and robust shell scripts.

3.11 Introduction to Shell Script Debugging

Debugging is an essential skill in shell scripting, allowing programmers to identify and fix errors in their scripts. Errors can occur for a variety of reasons, including syntax mistakes, logic errors, or incorrect usage of commands. Effective debugging ensures that scripts run correctly and efficiently. This section aims to provide a comprehensive understanding of the debugging techniques available for shell scripts, with an emphasis on practical approaches and tools.

Shell scripting languages such as Bash provide several built-in options and commands to aid in debugging. These options can be enabled when running a script or can be incorporated into the script itself. The primary methods for debugging shell scripts include enabling debugging modes, using diagnostic commands, setting breakpoints, and examining variable values.

Debugging Modes

The three most commonly used debugging modes in Bash are:

- -n: Read commands but do not execute them.
- -v: Print each command to the terminal before executing it.
- -x: Print each command and its arguments to the terminal as they are executed.

To enable these modes, either pass them as options to the Bash interpreter when running the script, or include them in the script's shebang line or within the script using the set command.

```
#!/bin/bash -x

# Alternatively, set debugging options within the script
set -x
```

```
# Sample script with a syntax error
echo "Start of Script"
for i in {1..5
do
  echo "Value: $i"
done

# Revert debugging options
set +x
```

In the example above, the -x option is used to enable debugging, causing each command and its expanded arguments to be printed as they are executed. This helps identify the specific line where an error occurs.

To execute a script with debugging options from the command line, utilize:

```
$ bash -x script.sh
```

For comprehensive debugging, combining multiple options can be advantageous:

```
$ bash -nv script.sh
```

Diagnostic Commands

Several diagnostic commands are extremely useful for debugging shell scripts. The echo command, for example, can be used to print variable values and messages to track script execution.

```
#!/bin/bash

echo "Debug Start"
myVar="Hello, World!"
echo "myVar: $myVar"

# Example block
if [ "$myVar" == "Hello, World!" ]; then
  echo "Condition met"
else
  echo "Condition not met"
fi

echo "Debug End"
```

Using echo statements at crucial points in the script can help understand the flow of execution and the state of variables. Another powerful diagnostic command is trap. The trap command intercepts signals and executes specified commands, aiding in the identification of points where a script might fail or exit unexpectedly.

```
#!/bin/bash
```

```
trap 'echo "An error occurred on line $LINENO"' ERR

# Example command that will fail
ls non_existent_file

echo "This will not be printed if the error trap is executed"
```

In this example, the trap command is set to print an error message including the line number where the error occurred whenever any command returns a non-zero exit status.

Breakpoints

Setting breakpoints within a script can temporarily halt execution, allowing for the inspection of the current state. This technique is particularly useful in longer scripts or when diagnosing complex issues.

```
#!/bin/bash

# Setting breakpoints
echo "Start of script"
read -p "Paused at first breakpoint. Press enter to continue..."

# Sample commands
echo "Executing first command"
read -p "Paused at second breakpoint. Press enter to continue..."

# Further commands
echo "Executing second command"
```

The read -p command is used to pause the script and wait for user input, effectively creating manual breakpoints.

Inspecting Variable Values

Understanding the values held by variables at various points in a script is crucial for debugging. The declare command provides insights into variable attributes and contents.

```
#!/bin/bash

myNumber=42
myString="Hello"

# Inspect variable attributes and values
declare -p myNumber
declare -p myString
```

This command prints the attributes and values of the specified variables, assisting in verifying their expected states.

Effective debugging combines these techniques to methodically isolate and resolve issues in shell scripts. By adopting these practices, developers can significantly enhance the reliability and performance of their scripts.

Chapter 4

Control Structures in Shell Scripts

This chapter delves into the control structures available in shell scripts, essential for writing dynamic and flexible code. It covers conditional statements (if, else, elif), case statements, and various looping structures (for, while, until). Additionally, it discusses the use of break and continue statements, nested loops, and conditional statements. Logical operators and the 'select' loop for creating menus are also explained. Practical examples are provided to illustrate the application of these control structures in real-world scenarios.

4.1 Introduction to Control Structures

Control structures are fundamental constructs in programming that enable the direction of program flow based on specific conditions and repetitions. In shell scripting, control structures provide the capability to create complex and dynamic scripts that can perform varied operations under different circumstances. The basic control structures include conditional statements and loops, each serving a crucial role in the logical segmentation and operational decision-making within a script.

Conditional statements such as if, else, and elif allow the execution of certain blocks of code only when specific conditions are met. These conditional checks are essential for making decisions within your script. For example, consider a scenario where you need to perform a backup only if a particular file exists or execute different commands based on the user's input. Conditional statements provide the necessary syntax to handle these situations.

A simple example of an if statement in a shell script is given below:

```
if [ -f /etc/passwd ]; then
    echo "The file exists."
fi
```

In this example, the test command [-f /etc/passwd] checks if the file /etc/passwd exists. If the condition evaluates to true, the script outputs "The file exists."

Else and elif statements extend the basic if statement, enabling more finely-tuned control over program flow by handling multiple conditions. The else clause allows the script to execute alternative commands if the initial if condition is not met, while elif provides additional conditional checks after an if statement.

An extended example using else and elif:

```
if [ -f /etc/passwd ]; then
    echo "The file exists."
elif [ -d /etc ]; then
    echo "The directory exists."
else
    echo "Neither the file nor the directory exists."
fi
```

In this snippet, the script first checks for the file's existence. If the file is not present, it then checks if the directory exists using the elif clause. If neither condition holds true, the else clause executes, confirming the absence of both the file and the directory.

Looping structures are another critical set of control structures utilized in shell scripts. They allow the repetition of a series of commands based on predefined conditions or a set of items. These loops include for, while, and until loops, each serving different use cases.

A for loop iterates over a list of items, executing the enclosed commands for each item. Here is a basic example of a for loop in a shell script:

```
for i in 1 2 3 4 5; do
    echo "Number: $i"
done
```

This script will output:

```
Number: 1
Number: 2
Number: 3
Number: 4
Number: 5
```

For more complex cases, where the loop needs to repeat based on a condition rather than a list, while and until loops come into play. A while loop continues to execute as long as the given condition remains true. For example:

```
count=1
while [ $count -le 5 ]; do
    echo "Count: $count"
    ((count++))
done
```

This script starts with count set to 1 and will continue looping and printing the value of count until count exceeds 5.

Similarly, an until loop continues to execute the commands until the specified condition becomes true. It is practically the inverse of the while loop. Here is an example:

```
count=1
until [ $count -gt 5 ]; do
    echo "Count: $count"
    ((count++))
done
```

This script produces the same output as the previous while loop example, demonstrating the interchangeability based on the logical requirement of the script.

Break and continue statements enable more intricate control over loop execution. The break statement terminates the loop completely, while continue skips the remaining commands in the current iteration and proceeds to the next iteration of the loop.

An example using break:

```
for i in 1 2 3 4 5; do
    if [ $i -eq 3 ]; then
        break
    fi
    echo "Number: $i"
done
```

This loop outputs:

```
Number: 1
Number: 2
```

The loop stops when i equals 3.

Conversely, an example using continue:

```
for i in 1 2 3 4 5; do
    if [ $i -eq 3 ]; then
        continue
    fi
    echo "Number: $i"
done
```

This loop outputs:

```
Number: 1
Number: 2
Number: 4
Number: 5
```

The value 3 is skipped due to the continue statement.

Control structures are instrumental in crafting robust and flexible shell scripts. Mastery of these constructs enables the creation of scripts that are not only efficient and concise but also capable of handling complex logic and varied operational scenarios. Understanding and utilizing these constructs effectively is a crucial skill for any proficient shell script programmer.

4.2 Conditional Statements (if, else, elif)

Conditional statements in shell scripting are fundamental constructs that enable the execution of code based on specific conditions. These conditions facilitate decision-making processes within scripts, allowing for dynamic and responsive execution paths. The primary conditional statements in shell scripting are if, else, and elif.

Basic if Statement

The if statement allows for the execution of a block of code only if a specified condition is true. The general syntax is as follows:

```
if [ condition ]
then
    # code to execute if condition is true
fi
```

The condition typically involves comparison operators and can include command execution status. The square brackets [] are a synonym for the test command.

Example of a Basic if Statement

```
#!/bin/bash

number=10

if [ $number -gt 5 ]
then
    echo "The number is greater than 5."
fi
```

In this example, the script checks if the variable $number is greater than 5. If the condition is true, it outputs a message.

Adding an else Clause

To execute a different block of code when the condition is false, an else clause can be added to the structure. The syntax is:

```
if [ condition ]
then
    # code to execute if condition is true
else
    # code to execute if condition is false
fi
```

Example with else Clause

```
#!/bin/bash

number=3

if [ $number -gt 5 ]
then
    echo "The number is greater than 5."
else
    echo "The number is 5 or less."
fi
```

Here, the script evaluates $number. If it is greater than 5, one message is printed; otherwise, another message is displayed.

Using elif for Multiple Conditions

The elif (short for "else if") construct allows for the checking of multiple conditions. This enables more complex decision-making. The syntax is:

```
if [ condition1 ]
then
    # code to execute if condition1 is true
elif [ condition2 ]
then
    # code to execute if condition2 is true
else
    # code to execute if none of the above conditions are true
fi
```

Example with elif

```
#!/bin/bash

number=7

if [ $number -gt 10 ]
then
    echo "The number is greater than 10."
elif [ $number -gt 5 ]
then
    echo "The number is greater than 5 but less than or equal to 10."
else
    echo "The number is 5 or less."
fi
```

In this script, the variable $number is evaluated against multiple conditions. Depending on its value, different messages will be printed.

Logical Operators in Conditions

Conditions can be combined using logical operators such as -a (AND) and -o (OR). This enables more nuanced controlling of flow.

```
#!/bin/bash

number=8

if [ $number -gt 5 -a $number -lt 10 ]
then
    echo "The number is between 5 and 10."
else
    echo "The number is not between 5 and 10."
fi
```

In this example, the script checks if the number is both greater than 5 and less than 10. If both conditions are true, it prints a corresponding message.

Testing File Attributes

if statements are also frequently used to test file attributes such as existence, readability, writability, and executability. Commonly used file test operators include -e (file exists), -r (readable), -w (writable), and -x (executable).

```
#!/bin/bash

file="example.txt"

if [ -e $file ]
then
    echo "The file exists."
else
    echo "The file does not exist."
fi
```

This script checks if a file named example.txt exists and outputs the appropriate message.

Command Execution Status in Conditions

The exit status of commands (0 for success, non-zero for failure) can also be used in if statements. The syntax to check command success is simplified by omitting square brackets.

```
#!/bin/bash

if ls /etc/passwd
then
    echo "The file exists."
else
    echo "The file does not exist."
fi
```

Here, the ls command is executed to check if the file /etc/passwd exists. The if statement evaluates the command's exit status.

These constructs provide the foundational tools needed to direct the flow of execution based on evaluated conditions, enhancing script versatility and functionality.

4.3 Case Statements

The case statement in shell scripting is an efficient way to execute different blocks of code based on the value of a particular variable or expression. This structure is particularly useful for handling multiple possible conditions without the need for numerous if-elif-else statements, thereby improving the clarity and maintainability of the script.

The syntax of the case statement is as follows:

```
case expression in
    pattern1)
        statements1
        ;;
    pattern2)
        statements2
        ;;
    ...
    patternN)
        statementsN
        ;;
    *)
        default_statements
        ;;
esac
```

In this structure, expression is evaluated once, and its value is compared sequentially against the given patterns. When a match is found, the corresponding block of statements is executed. Each block must end with ;; to signify the end of that particular case. The * pattern acts as the default case, similar to the default clause in many programming languages' switch statements.

- **Example of a Basic case Statement**

Consider a script that categorizes a day of the week into a weekday or a weekend:

```
#!/bin/bash

day="Monday"

case $day in
    "Monday" | "Tuesday" | "Wednesday" | "Thursday" | "Friday")
        echo "$day is a Weekday."
        ;;
    "Saturday" | "Sunday")
        echo "$day is a Weekend."
        ;;
    *)
        echo "Not a valid day."
        ;;
esac
```

In this example, the variable day is checked against a series of patterns. The | operator is used to specify multiple matches for a single block of statements. The echo command outputs whether the specified day is a weekday or a weekend.

- **Pattern Matching with case**

Patterns in a case statement can include wildcards and ranges, providing powerful matching capabilities. For example:

```
read -p "Enter a single character: " char

case $char in
    [a-z])
        echo "You entered a lowercase letter."
        ;;
    [A-Z])
        echo "You entered an uppercase letter."
        ;;
    [0-9])
        echo "You entered a digit."
        ;;
    *)
        echo "You entered a special character."
```

```
        ;;
esac
```

Here, the script reads a single character and uses character ranges to determine its type—whether it is a lowercase letter, an uppercase letter, a digit, or a special character.

- **Nested** case **Statements**

Just like other control structures, case statements can be nested within each other to handle more complex logic. For instance:

```
vehicle="car"
color="red"

case $vehicle in
    "car")
        case $color in
            "red")
                echo "You have a red car."
                ;;
            "blue")
                echo "You have a blue car."
                ;;
            *)
                echo "Car color not recognized."
                ;;
        esac
        ;;
    "motorcycle")
        echo "You have a motorcycle."
        ;;
    *)
        echo "Vehicle type not recognized."
        ;;
esac
```

In this example, a case statement is used within another case statement to first evaluate the type of vehicle and then further categorize based on its color if it is a car.

- **Handling Exit Status in** case **Statements**

The exit status of a case statement is the exit status of the last executed command within the matched pattern. This allows for easy integration into larger scripts where the success or failure of the case statement impacts subsequent logic.

```
fruit="apple"

case $fruit in
    "apple")
```

```
        echo "Processing apple."
        # Any commands related to apple
        ;;
    "banana")
        echo "Processing banana."
        # Any commands related to banana
        ;;
    *)
        echo "Unknown fruit."
        exit 1
        ;;
esac

if [ $? -ne 0 ]; then
    echo "An error occurred while processing the fruit."
    exit 1
else
    echo "Fruit processed successfully."
fi
```

In this scenario, if the fruit is unknown, the script exits with an error code, and this is subsequently checked to provide a meaningful error message.

- **Practical Application: Menu Selection**

The case statement is particularly useful for creating interactive menus in shell scripts. Below is an example that uses a case statement to provide a user with different options and executes the selected option:

```
while true; do
    echo "Select an option:"
    echo "1. Show Date"
    echo "2. List Files"
    echo "3. Show Uptime"
    echo "4. Exit"
    read -p "Enter your choice: " choice

    case $choice in
        1)
            date
            ;;
        2)
            ls -l
            ;;
        3)
            uptime
            ;;
        4)
            echo "Exiting..."
            break
            ;;
        *)
            echo "Invalid choice, please try again."
            ;;
    esac
done
```

This script continually presents a menu to the user until the user chooses to exit. Each menu option is handled by a specific case pattern, demonstrating how case statements can be utilized to handle various user inputs efficiently.

Utilizing case statements in shell scripts is a powerful way to handle multiple conditional branches succinctly. They enhance readability and maintainability, especially when dealing with numerous potential values for a variable or expression.

4.4 Looping Structures (for loops)

In shell scripting, the 'for' loop is a fundamental control structure that enables repetitive execution of commands over a list of items, files, strings, or sequences. It is essential for tasks that involve iteration, significantly reducing the need for repetitive coding.

The basic syntax of a 'for' loop in a shell script is as follows:

```
for variable in list
do
    commands
done
```

- **'variable'**: Represents a temporary variable that takes the value of each element in the list, one at a time.
- **'list'**: A sequence of items, which can be explicitly defined, generated by a command, or glob patterns.
- **'commands'**: The set of instructions that are executed for each value of the variable.

An illustrative example can clarify the concept. Consider iterating over a list of numbers:

```
for num in 1 2 3 4 5
do
    echo "The number is $num"
done
```

The output of this script will be:

```
The number is 1
The number is 2
The number is 3
The number is 4
The number is 5
```

Iteration over Files

A common use case for 'for' loops is iterating over files in a directory. Suppose you want to list all files in the current directory:

```
for file in *
do
    echo "File: $file"
done
```

'*' is a wildcard that matches all files and directories in the current directory. The output will list all items present in the current directory.

Using Command Substitution

Another powerful feature is using command substitution within 'for' loops. This allows the output of a command to be used as the list. For example, iterating over all files with a '.txt' extension and printing their names:

```
for file in $(ls *.txt)
do
    echo "Text file: $file"
done
```

Working with Sequences

Shell scripts can also iterate over sequences of numbers using brace expansion or the 'seq' command.

Using brace expansion:

```
for num in {1..5}
do
    echo "Number is: $num"
done
```

Using the 'seq' command:

```
for num in $(seq 1 5)
do
    echo "Number using seq: $num"
done
```

Nested 'for' Loops

A 'for' loop can be nested within another 'for' loop to handle more complex iterations. For instance, creating a multiplication table:

```
for i in {1..5}
do
    for j in {1..5}
    do
        result=$((i * j))
        echo "$i * $j = $result"
```

```
    done
done
```

The result is a formatted multiplication table, where the outer loop iterates over the rows and the inner loop iterates over the columns.

Utilizing Arrays

Arrays in shell scripts provide an additional layer of convenience for 'for' loops. An array can be defined and iterated over as follows:

```
arr=("apple" "banana" "cherry")
for fruit in "${arr[@]}"
do
    echo "Fruit: $fruit"
done
```

This example prints each element in the array 'arr'.

Loop Control: 'break' and 'continue'

Within a 'for' loop, the 'break' statement can be used to exit the loop prematurely, while the 'continue' statement can be used to skip the remaining commands in the current iteration and proceed to the next one.

Example using 'break':

```
for num in {1..10}
do
    if [ $num -eq 5 ]
    then
        break
    fi
    echo "Number: $num"
done
```

This loop terminates once 'num' reaches 5.

Example using 'continue':

```
for num in {1..10}
do
    if [ $num -eq 5 ]
    then
        continue
    fi
    echo "Number: $num"
done
```

This loop skips the command when 'num' equals 5 and continues with the next iteration.

Practical Application

For a practical application, consider a script that backs up files with a '.conf' extension to a backup directory:

```
backup_dir="backup"
mkdir -p $backup_dir
for file in *.conf
do
    cp "$file" "$backup_dir/$(basename "$file")"
    echo "Backed up $file to $backup_dir"
done
```

This script ensures all '.conf' files in the current directory are copied to a 'backup' directory, creating it if it does not exist.

Integrating these 'for' loop structures allows for more dynamic, efficient, and organized shell scripts, laying a strong foundation for advanced shell scripting practices.

4.5 While Loops

The while loop is a fundamental control structure in shell scripting, allowing the execution of a block of commands as long as a given condition evaluates to true. This iterative process continues until the specified condition becomes false. The syntax for a while loop in a shell script is:

```
while [ condition ]
do
    # Commands to be executed
done
```

The condition inside the square brackets is evaluated before every iteration. If the condition is true, the commands within the do block are executed. Once the condition evaluates to false, the loop terminates, and the script continues with the subsequent commands.

To illustrate the practical application of while loops, the following example demonstrates a simple counter that increments until a specified limit is reached:

```
#!/bin/bash

counter=1
while [ $counter -le 5 ]
do
    echo "Counter: $counter"
    ((counter++))
done
```

In this script:

- The counter variable is initialized to 1.
- The while loop condition checks if counter is less than or equal to 5.
- Inside the loop, the current value of counter is printed.
- The ((counter++)) command increments the value of counter by 1.

The output of executing this script would be:

```
Counter: 1
Counter: 2
Counter: 3
Counter: 4
Counter: 5
```

It is crucial to ensure that the loop condition will eventually become false, in order to avoid infinite loops. An infinite loop can occur if the condition in the while statement always evaluates to true. Consider the following example:

```
#!/bin/bash

while true
do
    echo "This is an infinite loop. Press Ctrl+C to stop."
done
```

In this case, the condition true will always evaluate to true, causing the loop to iterate indefinitely. To exit such a loop, the user must manually interrupt the script using Ctrl+C.

A practical application of while loops is in reading files line by line. This can be achieved by redirecting the file input into the while loop. Consider the following example, which reads and prints each line of a file:

```
#!/bin/bash

filename="example.txt"

while IFS= read -r line
do
    echo "$line"
done < "$filename"
```

Here, the script:

- Sets the variable filename to "example.txt".

- Uses the IFS (Internal Field Separator) to ensure that leading and trailing whitespace in each line is preserved, and the read -r option to prevent backslashes from being treated as escape characters.
- Reads each line of the file and prints it until all lines are processed.

Another common use of while loops involves waiting for a condition to be met, such as a file becoming available or a service starting. The following script checks if a specific file exists before continuing:

```
#!/bin/bash

file_path="/path/to/file"

while [ ! -f "$file_path" ]
do
    echo "Waiting for the file to be created..."
    sleep 2
done

echo "File found!"
```

In this script:

- The while loop condition uses the -f flag to check if the file at file_path exists.
- As long as the file does not exist, a message is printed, and the script sleeps for 2 seconds before checking again.
- Once the file is found, the loop exits, and the script prints "File found!".

The while loop's flexibility allows it to be integrated into various scenarios, such as monitoring system resources, handling user input, or performing repetitive tasks until a condition is met. Understanding and utilizing while loops effectively is critical for enhancing the functionality and efficiency of shell scripts.

4.6 Until Loops

until loops provide an alternative to the while loop, differing primarily in their operational conditions. In until loops, the command list within the loop executes as long as a specified condition evaluates to false. Once the condition becomes true, the loop terminates. This is particularly useful when the termination condition is more naturally expressed as the point at which the loop should cease rather than when it should continue.

The general syntax of the until loop is as follows:

```
until [CONDITION]
do
    # Command list
done
```

To understand the behavior of until loops, consider an example where you need to increment a counter variable until it reaches a certain value. Here, the loop continues execution as long as the condition evaluates to false. Once the condition is true, the loop stops.

```
#!/bin/bash
counter=0
until [ \$counter -ge 5 ]
do
    echo "Counter: \$counter"
    counter=\$((counter + 1))
done
```

Output:

```
Counter: 0
Counter: 1
Counter: 2
Counter: 3
Counter: 4
```

In this example, the until loop increments the counter variable starting from 0. The condition [$counter -ge 5] is initially false, allowing the loop to proceed. With each iteration, the counter is incremented by 1. When counter reaches 5, the condition evaluates to true, and the loop terminates.

until loops can also manage more complex operations, such as file operations or interactive user input. The following script illustrates a scenario where a user is prompted for a specific string input that matches a defined password. The loop continues to prompt until the correct password is entered.

```
#!/bin/bash
correct_password="linux_scripting"
password=""
until [ "\$password" == "\$correct_password" ]
do
    echo -n "Enter the password: "
    read password
done
echo "Access granted."
```

Output:

```
Enter the password: wrong_password
Enter the password: another_try
Enter the password: linux_scripting
Access granted.
```

In this script, the until loop repeatedly asks the user for a password until the correct password linux_scripting is entered. This ensures that the loop continues to operate under the condition where the entered password does not match the correct password.

It is advisable to use until loops when the loop's operational logic aligns better with the cessation condition. Compare this with while loops, which are more intuitive when the logic naturally expresses continuity. Here's a comparative example where the goal is to create a loop that executes until a file exists.

Consider using an until loop to monitor the existence of a file:

```
#!/bin/bash
filename="example_file.txt"
until [ -f "\$filename" ]
do
    echo "Waiting for the file: \$filename"
    sleep 2
done
echo "File \$filename found."
```

Output:

```
Waiting for the file: example_file.txt
Waiting for the file: example_file.txt
# ...repeats until the file is created...
File example_file.txt found.
```

This script checks for the existence of example_file.txt and prints a waiting message every 2 seconds until the file is created. When example_file.txt is detected, the condition becomes true, and the loop terminates.

Overall, the until loop is a potent control structure for scenarios where you need to keep executing a command list until a particular condition turns true. With careful application, until loops can improve script clarity and ensure that termination conditions are explicitly and logically handled. This complements the varying paradigms of control structures in shell scripting, allowing for greater flexibility in script design and execution flow.

4.7 Break and Continue Statements

In the context of control structures within shell scripts, the break and continue statements play a crucial role in managing the flow of iterative loops. These statements are essential for optimizing code execution by providing mechanisms to exit loops prematurely or to skip specific iterations based on certain conditions.

The break statement is used to exit the nearest enclosing loop, typically for, while, or until loops. When a break command is encountered within a loop, control is transferred immediately to the first statement following the loop. This can be particularly useful in scenarios where you need to terminate loop execution upon meeting a specific condition, thereby avoiding unnecessary iterations.

Here's a simple example demonstrating the break statement within a for loop:

```
#!/bin/bash

for i in {1..10}
do
    if [ $i -eq 5 ]; then
        break
    fi
    echo "Iteration $i"
done
echo "Loop terminated prematurely when i equals 5."
```

In this script, as soon as the variable i equals 5, the break statement is executed, and the loop terminates. The output is:

```
Iteration 1
Iteration 2
Iteration 3
Iteration 4
Loop terminated prematurely when i equals 5.
```

The continue statement, on the other hand, skips the remaining commands in the current loop iteration and proceeds directly to the next iteration of the loop. This is useful in scenarios where you want to bypass certain iterations of the loop without terminating it prematurely.

Consider the following example using the continue statement within a for loop:

```
#!/bin/bash

for i in {1..10}
do
    if [ $i -eq 5 ]; then
        continue
```

```
    fi
    echo "Iteration $i"
done
echo "Loop skipped the iteration where i equals 5."
```

In this example, when the variable i equals 5, the continue statement is executed, skipping the echo "Iteration $i" command for that iteration. The output is:

```
Iteration 1
Iteration 2
Iteration 3
Iteration 4
Iteration 6
Iteration 7
Iteration 8
Iteration 9
Iteration 10
Loop skipped the iteration where i equals 5.
```

The integration of these statements becomes even more powerful when used within nested loops and complex conditional logic. For instance, in a scenario with nested loops, break can be instructed to exit multiple levels of loops if necessary.

A more complex example involving nested loops is illustrated below:

```
#!/bin/bash

for ((i=1; i<=3; i++))
do
    echo "Outer loop iteration $i"
    for ((j=1; j<=3; j++))
    do
        if [ $j -eq 2 ]; then
            break 2 % Exits both the inner and outer loops
        fi
        echo " Inner loop iteration $j"
    done
done
echo "Exited nested loops when j equaled 2."
```

The output of this script demonstrates how the break statement with an argument can be used to exit multiple nesting levels:

```
Outer loop iteration 1
  Inner loop iteration 1
Exited nested loops when j equaled 2.
```

Analogously, the continue statement can be used within nested loops to skip to the next iteration of a specified loop level. Here is an example of how it can be employed:

```
#!/bin/bash

for ((i=1; i<=3; i++))
do
```

```
    echo "Outer loop iteration $i"
    for ((j=1; j<=3; j++))
    do
        if [ $j -eq 2 ]; then
            continue % Skips to the next iteration of the inner loop
        fi
        echo " Inner loop iteration $j"
    done
done
echo "Completed nested loops with inner loop skipping iteration when j equals 2."
```

The output indicates the selective execution facilitated by the continue statement:

```
Outer loop iteration 1
  Inner loop iteration 1
  Inner loop iteration 3
Outer loop iteration 2
  Inner loop iteration 1
  Inner loop iteration 3
Outer loop iteration 3
  Inner loop iteration 1
  Inner loop iteration 3
Completed nested loops with inner loop skipping iteration when j equals 2.
```

Understanding and effectively utilizing break and continue statements empower script developers with the capability to create more efficient and nuanced control flows within their shell scripts, thus enabling more precise and optimal script behaviors.

These principles encourage a more mindful approach to scripting, wherein loop iterations can be controlled not just sequentially but also conditionally, catering to the requirements of complex computational tasks.

4.8 Nested Loops and Conditional Statements

In shell scripting, the use of nested loops and conditional statements enhances the script's ability to handle complex tasks by allowing repeated actions within loops and conditional execution paths. This intricate control flow is particularly useful in scenarios where multiple levels of iteration or condition checking are required.

To start, let's consider nested loops. A nested loop refers to a loop inside another loop. Typically, this involves having an inner loop perform its iterations for each iteration of the outer loop. Shell scripts support nesting for loops, while loops, and until loops in various combinations. Understanding nested loops is vital for tasks that require multidimensional data handling or hierarchical processing.

Consider the following example where a for loop is nested within another for loop:

```
#!/bin/bash
# Script to demonstrate nested loops
for i in 1 2 3; do
    echo "Outer loop iteration: $i"
    for j in a b c; do
        echo " Inner loop iteration: $j"
    done
done
```

When this script is executed, the output is:

```
Outer loop iteration: 1
  Inner loop iteration: a
  Inner loop iteration: b
  Inner loop iteration: c
Outer loop iteration: 2
  Inner loop iteration: a
  Inner loop iteration: b
  Inner loop iteration: c
Outer loop iteration: 3
  Inner loop iteration: a
  Inner loop iteration: b
  Inner loop iteration: c
```

The outer loop iterates over the values 1, 2, and 3. For each iteration of the outer loop, the inner loop iterates over the values a, b, and c. This pattern of execution is essential for tasks that might involve processing items in a matrix or checking multiple conditions in different scenarios.

Next, consider a script using a while loop nested inside another while loop:

```
#!/bin/bash
# Nested while loops example
outer=1

while [ $outer -le 3 ]; do
    echo "Outer loop: $outer"
    inner=1
    while [ $inner -le 2 ]; do
        echo " Inner loop: $inner"
        ((inner++))
    done
    ((outer++))
done
```

This script produces:

```
Outer loop: 1
  Inner loop: 1
  Inner loop: 2
Outer loop: 2
  Inner loop: 1
  Inner loop: 2
Outer loop: 3
  Inner loop: 1
  Inner loop: 2
```

Here, the outer loop runs three times, and for each iteration of the outer loop, the inner loop runs twice.

In addition to nested loops, scripts often require nested conditional statements to add layers of decision-making. Nesting if-else statements allows the script to evaluate multiple conditions in a structured manner.

Consider the following example of a nested if statement within a for loop:

```
#!/bin/bash
# Nested if statements within a for loop

for number in 1 2 3 4 5; do
    if [ $number -gt 3 ]; then
        echo "$number is greater than 3"
    else
        if [ $number -eq 3 ]; then
            echo "$number is equal to 3"
        else
            echo "$number is less than 3"
        fi
    fi
done
```

The output of this script will be:

```
1 is less than 3
2 is less than 3
3 is equal to 3
4 is greater than 3
5 is greater than 3
```

In this script, for each value in the list, an outer if statement checks if the value is greater than 3. If not, an inner if statement checks if the value is equal to 3; otherwise, the number is less than 3.

Consider another use of nested if statements with a while loop. This is particularly useful when the conditions to be checked are more complex and require multiple logical tests.

```
#!/bin/bash
# Example with nested if statements inside a while loop
counter=0

while [ $counter -lt 5 ]; do
    if [ $((counter % 2)) -eq 0 ]; then
```

```
        if [ $counter -ne 0 ]; then
            echo "$counter is even and not zero"
        else
            echo "$counter is zero"
        fi
    else
        echo "$counter is odd"
    fi
    ((counter++))
done
```

The execution of this script results in:

```
0 is zero
1 is odd
2 is even and not zero
3 is odd
4 is even and not zero
```

In this example, the while loop runs five times, incrementing the counter each time. The nested if statements determine if the counter is even or odd and provide a specific message if the counter is zero.

The integration of nested loops and nested conditional statements can further be combined to build highly complex and powerful scripts. The flexibility provided by these constructs enables developers to design scripts for a wide range of sophisticated tasks.

Consider a comprehensive example involving both nested loops and nested conditional statements:

```
#!/bin/bash
# Complex nested loops with nested if statements

for i in 1 2 3; do
    echo "Outer loop value: $i"
    for j in 0 1; do
        echo " Inner loop value: $j"
        if [ $i -eq 2 ]; then
            echo " Skipping over subsequent checks as i equals 2"
            continue
        fi
        if [ $j -eq 1 ]; then
            echo " Performing action as j equals 1"
        fi
    done
done
```

The output generated by this script will look like:

```
Outer loop value: 1
  Inner loop value: 0
  Inner loop value: 1
    Performing action as j equals 1
Outer loop value: 2
  Inner loop value: 0
    Skipping over subsequent checks as i equals 2
  Inner loop value: 1
    Skipping over subsequent checks as i equals 2
Outer loop value: 3
  Inner loop value: 0
  Inner loop value: 1
    Performing action as j equals 1
```

In this example, during each iteration of the outer loop, the inner loop executes and checks the values of i and j. If i equals 2, the script skips further actions within the inner loop iteration by using the continue statement. Otherwise, it checks if j equals 1 and performs specific actions based on that condition.

Understanding and effectively utilizing nested loops and conditional statements in shell scripts are critical skills enabling the automation of complex tasks with precision. These constructs form the backbone of sophisticated scripting, increasing the robustness and efficiency of your code.

4.9 Using Logical Operators

Logical operators are critical components in shell scripting, allowing for the evaluation of multiple conditions within a control structure. These operators enable more complex decision-making processes by combining Boolean expressions. In the context of shell scripting, logical operators include AND, OR, and NOT. Understanding their syntax and application is vital for developing robust and efficient scripts.

AND Operator (&&): The AND operator returns true if and only if all the conditions it connects are true. In shell scripting, it is denoted by a double ampersand (&&). When utilizing the AND operator in scripts, both conditions must be satisfied for the whole expression to evaluate to true.

```
if [ $a -gt 5 ] && [ $b -lt 10 ]; then
    echo "Both conditions are true."
else
    echo "One or both conditions are false."
fi
```

In the above example, the script checks if variable $a is greater than 5 **AND** $b is less than 10. Only if both conditions are true will the message

"Both conditions are true." be printed.

OR Operator (||): The OR operator returns true if at least one of the conditions it connects is true. In shell scripting, it is represented by a double vertical bar (||). This operator is useful when a variety of conditions can trigger the same set of commands.

```
if [ $a -gt 5 ] || [ $b -lt 10 ]; then
    echo "At least one condition is true."
else
    echo "Both conditions are false."
fi
```

The example script evaluates whether variable $a is greater than 5 **OR** $b is less than 10. The message "At least one condition is true." will be displayed if either of the conditions holds.

NOT Operator (!): The NOT operator is unary and used to invert the Boolean value of the condition it precedes. In shell scripting, the NOT operator is represented by an exclamation mark (!). It turns a true condition into false and vice versa.

```
if ! [ $a -gt 5 ]; then
    echo "\$a is not greater than 5."
else
    echo "\$a is greater than 5."
fi
```

In this example, the condition $a -gt 5 is negated. Hence, if $a is not greater than 5, the message "$a is not greater than 5." will be printed.

Using logical operators can significantly enhance the decision-making capability of shell scripts. For instance, the combination of AND and OR operators can address more complex conditions. Below is an example that demonstrates their combined usage:

```
if [ $a -gt 5 ] && ([ $b -lt 10 ] || [ $c -eq 20 ]); then
    echo "Condition met: a>5 AND (b<10 OR c==20)"
else
    echo "Condition not met."
fi
```

To interpret this example, the script first checks if $a is greater than 5. If true, it proceeds to check whether $b is less than 10 **OR** $c is equal to 20. The parenthesis grouping ensures correct evaluation sequencing.

Logical operators also play a crucial role in loop control structures. For instance, they can be used in a while loop to continue iterating as long as combined conditions hold true.

```
while [ $a -lt 10 ] && [ $b -gt 0 ]; do
```

```
    echo "a is $a and b is $b"
    a=$((a + 1))
    b=$((b - 1))
done
```

In this looping structure, the while condition evaluates whether $a is less than 10 **AND** $b is greater than 0. The loop will continue executing as long as both conditions remain true.

Logical operators not only aid in writing clearer and more concise shell scripts but also enable the creation of complex condition testing frameworks essential for advanced scripting tasks. Utilizing these operators proficiently is a hallmark of advanced shell scripting proficiency.

4.10 The select Loop for Menus

The select loop is a powerful feature in bash scripting that facilitates the creation of simple, interactive menus. This loop is particularly useful for presenting a list of choices to the user and executing a specific action based on the user's selection. The syntax of the select loop is concise and shares the fundamental structure of other looping constructs.

The basic syntax is:

```
select var in list
do
    commands
done
```

Here, var is the variable that will hold the user's selection, and list represents a space-separated list of items to choose from. The commands block will execute after the user makes a selection.

Example: Basic Menu

To illustrate a basic usage of the select loop, consider the following script that prompts the user to choose a fruit:

```
#!/bin/bash
PS3="Please select a fruit: "
select fruit in Apple Banana Orange Quit
do
    case $fruit in
        Apple)
            echo "You selected Apple."
            ;;
        Banana)
            echo "You selected Banana."
            ;;
        Orange)
```

```
            echo "You selected Orange."
            ;;
        Quit)
            echo "Exiting."
            break
            ;;
        *)
            echo "Invalid option. Please try again."
            ;;
    esac
done
```

Explanation:

- PS3: The prompt string which appears before the user's input.
- select fruit in Apple Banana Orange Quit: The list of items presented to the user.
- case $fruit in: Evaluates the user's selection and executes the corresponding commands.

Output:

```
1) Apple
2) Banana
3) Orange
4) Quit
Please select a fruit:
```

The user can then enter the number corresponding to their choice. If the user selects 4, the script terminates.

Handling Invalid Inputs

The select loop allows easy management of invalid inputs. If a user inputs an invalid number, such as 5 in the example above, the script re-displays the menu and prompts the user to try again. This behavior is managed by the case statement's *) block, which acts as a default case for unexpected inputs.

Additional Features

The select loop permits customization and additional features:

- **Default Behavior**: If the user presses enter without typing a number, the prompt reappears. This can be controlled by checking if $REPLY is empty and handling it accordingly.
- **Dynamic Lists**: The list can be generated dynamically, allowing for flexible scripts that react to changing input data.

Example: Dynamic Menu

Consider a script that dynamically generates a menu from an array:

```
#!/bin/bash
options=("Add User" "Delete User" "Quit")
PS3="Please select an option: "
select opt in "${options[@]}"
do
    case $opt in
        "Add User")
            echo "Adding a new user."
            ;;
        "Delete User")
            echo "Deleting a user."
            ;;
        "Quit")
            echo "Exiting."
            break
            ;;
        *)
            echo "Invalid option."
            ;;
    esac
done
```

Explanation:

- options=("Add User" "Delete User" "Quit"): An array holding the menu items.
- select opt in "${options[]}": The select loop iterates over the array.

Dynamic list generation is particularly useful in scripts integrating with other system components, enabling real-time updates to the presented options.

Practical Applications

The utility of the select loop extends beyond simplistic menus. It can be integrated into larger scripts for:

- **System administration tasks**: Facilitating user interactions during automated setups or maintenance scripts.
- **Configuration utilities**: Guiding users through software configuration steps interactively.
- **Educational tools**: Creating interactive tutorials or quizzes.

Best Practices

When using the select loop:

- Ensure the prompt (PS3) is informative and sets user expectations clearly.
- Always include a mechanism (e.g., a "Quit" option) for the user to exit the loop.
- Validate user inputs to handle unexpected selections gracefully.

By employing these practices, the select loop becomes a robust tool for enhancing shell scripts with user-friendly interfaces, minimizing the complexity of capturing and processing user input.

4.11 Practical Examples of Control Structures

To solidify the understanding of control structures, it is crucial to explore practical examples that integrate various types of control statements. These examples demonstrate how conditional statements, loops, and logical operators can be combined to solve real-world problems efficiently.

Consider the task of processing a list of filenames and performing different actions based on their extensions. This requires the use of conditional statements (if, elif, else), case statements, and loops. The following example script will scan a directory and apply specific commands depending on the file type.

```
#!/bin/bash

# Directory containing the files to be processed
DIRECTORY="/path/to/directory"

# Create directories for each file extension if they don't exist
mkdir -p "$DIRECTORY/images"
mkdir -p "$DIRECTORY/documents"
mkdir -p "$DIRECTORY/archives"
mkdir -p "$DIRECTORY/others"

# Loop through each file in the directory
for FILE in "$DIRECTORY"/*; do
    # Extract file extension
    EXTENSION="${FILE##*.}"

    # Apply actions based on file extensions
    case "$EXTENSION" in
        jpg|png|gif)
            mv "$FILE" "$DIRECTORY/images/"
            ;;
        pdf|docx|txt)
```

```
            mv "$FILE" "$DIRECTORY/documents/"
            ;;
        zip|tar|gz)
            mv "$FILE" "$DIRECTORY/archives/"
            ;;
        *)
            mv "$FILE" "$DIRECTORY/others/"
            ;;
    esac
done
```

This script utilizes a for loop to iterate over all files in the specified directory. It then uses a case statement to check the file extension and move each file to an appropriate subdirectory based on its extension.

Another common scenario involves reading user input in a loop and performing actions based on that input. Consider the example of a simple calculator script that repeatedly prompts the user for two numbers and an operator until the user decides to exit.

```
#!/bin/bash

# Function to perform arithmetic operations
calculate() {
    local NUM1=$1
    local NUM2=$2
    local OPERATOR=$3
    case "$OPERATOR" in
        +)
            echo "$((NUM1 + NUM2))"
            ;;
        -)
            echo "$((NUM1 - NUM2))"
            ;;
        \*)
            echo "$((NUM1 * NUM2))"
            ;;
        /)
            # Ensure not dividing by zero
            if [ "$NUM2" -ne 0 ]; then
                echo "$((NUM1 / NUM2))"
            else
                echo "Error: Division by zero."
            fi
            ;;
        *)
            echo "Invalid operator."
            ;;
    esac
}

while true; do
    # Read user input
    read -p "Enter first number: " NUM1
    read -p "Enter second number: " NUM2
    read -p "Enter operator (+, -, *, /) or 'q' to quit: " OPERATOR

    # Exit the loop if user enters 'q'
    if [ "$OPERATOR" = "q" ]; then
```

```
        break
    fi

    # Call the calculate function and display the result
    RESULT=$(calculate "$NUM1" "$NUM2" "$OPERATOR")
    echo "Result: $RESULT"
done
```

This script showcases the use of a while loop for continuous user interaction, incorporating read statements to gather input and a case statement for handling different arithmetic operations. The break statement is used to exit the loop when the user inputs 'q'.

Next, consider an advanced example that combines nested loops and conditional statements to generate a multiplication table for a given range of numbers. This script demonstrates the ability to nest loops and conditionals to create complex logic.

```
#!/bin/bash

# Read the range from the user
read -p "Enter the starting number: " START
read -p "Enter the ending number: " END

# Generate the multiplication table
for ((i=START; i<=END; i++)); do
    for ((j=START; j<=END; j++)); do
        RESULT=$((i * j))
        printf "%4d" $RESULT
    done
    echo
done
```

This script uses nested for loops to iterate over all possible combinations of the range specified by the user. Each product is calculated and formatted for display using the printf command.

These examples integrate various control structures, conditional statements, and logical operators, providing practical applications that improve understanding and proficiency in shell scripting.

Chapter 5

Working with Variables and User Input

This chapter focuses on the use of variables and managing user input in shell scripts. It covers how to define and use variables, adhere to naming rules, and differentiate between environment and local variables. The chapter explains the handling of positional parameters and special variables, employing the 'read' command for user input, and performing command substitution. Additionally, it provides insights into arithmetic and string operations, exporting and importing variables, and understanding variable scope and lifetime, along with practical examples for effective variable usage.

5.1 Introduction to Variables

In the context of shell scripting within the Linux environment, variables play a crucial role in facilitating dynamic and flexible script execution. Variables are symbolic names that represent values stored in the memory, enabling scripts to handle data efficiently and perform operations on that data. These symbolic names are not merely restricted to storing numbers or textual data; they can encapsulate a broad range of values, including the results of commands or computed expressions.

Variables in shell scripting allow the storage of data that can be modified and retrieved at any point within the script, granting scripts a level of dynamism that is essential for handling varying inputs, conditional logic, and iterative processes.

Creation and Assignment: A variable is created and assigned a value using the assignment operator =. It is important to note that, in shell scripting, there must be no spaces around the = operator. For example:

```
variable_name=value
```

Example:

```
name="Alice"
number=42
```

In these instances, the variable name stores the string "Alice," while the variable number stores the integer 42.

Referencing Variables: To utilize the value stored in a variable, prefix the variable name with a dollar sign ($). For example:

```
echo $name
echo $number
```

Executing the above commands will display:

```
Alice
42
```

Types of Variables: Variables in shell scripting can be categorized into two main types: shell (local) variables and environment variables.

- **Shell (Local) Variables:** These variables are defined within the context of a shell and are only accessible within the shell session where they were created. They remain in existence for the duration of the shell session or until explicitly unset.
- **Environment Variables:** These variables are inherited by any child processes or subshells spawned from the original shell session. They provide a means to influence the behavior of these child processes and stand as a means for communication between the different processes.

To promote a local variable to an environment variable, the export command is used.

```
export variable_name
```

Example:

```
export name
```

The variable name would now be accessible in any child processes of the current shell session.

Variable Names: There are specific rules adhered to in naming variables in shell scripting. Valid variable names begin with a letter (a–z or A–Z) or an underscore (_), followed by any combination of letters, digits (0–9), or underscores.

- Valid names: VAR1, _var, var_123
- Invalid names: 1VAR, var-1, var!name

Using expressive and descriptive names for variables is encouraged to enhance script readability and maintainability.

Unsetting Variables: To delete a variable, the unset command is employed. This removes the variable from the current shell session.

```
unset variable_name
```

Example:

```
unset name
```

This command will remove the variable name from the shell session, rendering it inaccessible.

Command Substitution: Variables in shell scripts can also store the output of a command using command substitution, which is achieved using backticks (`command`) or $(command) syntax.

```
current_date=`date`
# or alternatively
current_date=$(date)
```

This will store the result of the date command in the variable current_date.

Understanding the mechanisms behind variable management is fundamental to developing effective shell scripts. Proper use of variables allows scripts to be more flexible, maintainable, and powerful. The ability to dynamically change values and pass data between different parts of the script enhances the script's capability to manage complex tasks efficiently.

5.2 Defining and Using Variables

In shell scripting, variables are essential for storing data that can be referenced and manipulated throughout the script. A variable in a shell script is a symbolic name that represents the value assigned to it. This section delves into the methodology of defining and utilizing variables within your scripts, enhancing both readability and functionality.

To define a variable in a shell script, use the syntax:

```
VARIABLE_NAME=value
```

Variable names are case-sensitive and by convention, uppercase names are used for environment variables, while lowercase or mixed-case names are typically used for user-defined variables. It is crucial to avoid spaces around the equal sign when assigning a value to a variable; any spaces can result in syntax errors.

Here is an example of defining a variable and assigning a value:

```
greeting=”Hello, World!”
```

To access the value stored in a variable, precede the variable name with a dollar sign ($). For instance, to print the value of the greeting variable defined above, you would use the echo command:

```
echo \$greeting
```

This command outputs:

```
Hello, World!
```

If you wish to include the value of a variable within a string, you can do so by embedding the variable within double quotes:

```
name=”Alice”
echo ”Welcome, \$name!”
```

Executing the script will yield:

```
Welcome, Alice!
```

Variables can also be assigned the result of a command using command substitution. Command substitution can be performed using either backticks (̀) or the $() syntax. The latter is more modern and preferred for its clarity:

```
date_today=\$(date)
echo ”Today’s date is: \$date_today”
```

Running this script might produce:

```
Today's date is: Thu Aug 12 01:23:45 UTC 2023
```

Additionally, variables can store the results of arithmetic operations. Shell scripting supports basic arithmetic operations such as addition, subtraction, multiplication, division, and modulus. The expr command or the $((...)) syntax can be used for arithmetic operations.

Using expr:

```
num1=5
num2=3
sum=\$(expr \$num1 + \$num2)
echo "The sum is: \$sum"
```

Using $((...)) for arithmetic expansion:

```
num1=5
num2=3
sum=\$((num1 + num2))
echo "The sum is: \$sum"
```

Variable values can be dynamic, changing throughout the execution of the script. The scope and lifetime of variables will be discussed later in the chapter. For now, it is essential to understand that a variable's value can be re-assigned as needed:

```
counter=1
counter=\$((counter + 1))
echo "Counter: \$counter"
```

This script will output:

```
Counter: 2
```

When defining variables, it is often useful to know whether the variable is intended for local scope (within a single script or function) or to persist globally (across function calls or scripts). The export command is used to mark a variable for export to the environment or to another script:

```
export PATH=\$PATH:/usr/local/bin
```

By exporting the PATH variable, the defined value persists across subshells and scripts sourced from the current shell.

In certain situations, variables must store multi-line text or the result of complex commands. To correctly handle multi-line strings, use a combination of single quotes for literal strings or double quotes with embedded variables and escape sequences:

```
multi_line_text="This is line one.
```

```
This is line two,
and this is line three."
echo "\$multi_line_text"
```

This script produces:

```
This is line one.
This is line two,
and this is line three.
```

Understanding how to define and use variables effectively is fundamental for creating efficient, readable, and maintainable shell scripts. This foundational knowledge enables the development of more complex scripting functionalities and paves the way for advanced operations and handling techniques presented in subsequent sections.

5.3 Variable Naming Rules

When working with variables in shell scripting, adhering to specific naming conventions is crucial to avoid errors and ensure script readability and maintainability. Here we delve into the detailed rules and best practices for naming variables.

1. Begin with a Letter or Underscore: Variable names in shell scripts must start with a letter (a-z or A-Z) or an underscore (_). This is a strict requirement as starting a variable name with a number or other characters will result in an error.

```
# Valid variable names
username="student"
_age=25

# Invalid variable names and their errors
1username="student" # Error: Variable name cannot start with a number
*user="student" # Error: Variable name cannot start with special characters
```

2. Use Alphanumeric Characters and Underscores: After the initial letter or underscore, variable names can include numbers, letters, and underscores. Special characters such as !, @, #, $, %,^, &, *, (,), and so on are not allowed and will result in an error if used.

```
# Valid variable names
user_name="Alice"
user100="Charlie"

# Invalid variable names
user-name="Dave" # Error: Variable name cannot contain a dash
user@name="Eve" # Error: Variable name cannot contain an at symbol
```

3. Case Sensitivity: Variable names in shell scripts are case-sensitive. This means that VAR and var are considered two distinct variables.

```
VAR="Hello"
var="World"

# Correct usage
echo $VAR # Outputs: Hello
echo $var # Outputs: World
```

4. Avoid Keywords and Built-In Commands: It is essential to avoid naming variables with keywords or names of built-in commands. Using these names can lead to unexpected behaviors and bugs. Keywords consist of reserved words such as if, then, else, fi, etc., while built-in commands include names like echo, read, test, etc.

```
# Avoid using keywords
if="test" # Incorrect
then="test" # Incorrect

# Avoid using built-in commands
echo="output" # Incorrect
read="input" # Incorrect
```

5. Descriptive and Meaningful Names: While not a strict rule, it is highly recommended to use descriptive and meaningful variable names that reflect the stored data or the purpose of the variable. This practice improves the readability and maintainability of the script.

```
# Descriptive names
filename="data.txt"
user_count=10

# Nondescriptive names
x="data.txt" # Not recommended
a=10 # Not recommended
```

6. Consistency and Conventions: Follow consistent naming conventions throughout the script. Common conventions include snake_case (e.g., user_name), camelCase (e.g., userName), and all caps for constants (e.g., MAX_VALUE). Select a convention at the beginning of your scripting project and stick to it throughout.

```
# Snake_case convention
total_users=50

# CamelCase convention
totalUsers=50

# Constants in all caps
MAX_USERS=100
```

7. Length Limitations: While technically there is no fixed length limit for variable names in most modern shell interpreters, it is good practice to keep variable names reasonably short yet descriptive, avoiding excessively long names which can be cumbersome.

```
# Reasonably short and descriptive names
user_age=30
data_file="records.csv"

# Avoid excessively long names
current_user_age_based_on_recorded_data_from_input_file=30 # Not
    recommended
```

Adhering to these variable naming rules will help ensure that scripts are error-free, easy to understand, and maintainable. Through consistent practice and careful attention to these guidelines, scripts will become more reliable and professional.

5.4 Environment Variables

Environment variables in Unix-like operating systems like Linux are a set of dynamic named values that can affect the way running processes will behave on a computer. These variables are part of the environment in which a process runs and can be utilized across different shell sessions and applications. They play a crucial role in configuration settings and in the smooth operation of scripts and programs.

Environment variables are typically inherited from the parent process that created the shell. They are set at the system level and can be exported so that they are available to any subprocesses spawned by the shell. It is essential to grasp how these variables work, how to manipulate them, and understand their scope, as they are vital for scripting and software development.

To list all the current environment variables, use the env or printenv command in your terminal:

```
env
# or
printenv
```

Example output will look like this:

```
PATH=/usr/local/sbin:/usr/local/bin:/usr/sbin:/usr/bin:/sbin:/bin:/usr/games:/usr/local/games
HOME=/home/username
USER=username
SHELL=/bin/bash
```

The critical environment variables and their common usage include:

- **PATH**: Lists directories the shell searches through when looking for commands. Modifying this variable can change where the shell looks for executables.
- **HOME**: Specifies the current user's home directory.
- **USER**: Contains the name of the current user.
- **SHELL**: Indicates the path of the current user's shell.

Setting an environment variable can be done using the export command, which makes the variable available to any child processes of the shell. For instance:

```
export EDITOR=nano
```

This command sets the **EDITOR** variable to nano and ensures that any subsequent commands or scripts run in this session will use nano as the default text editor, provided they check the **EDITOR** variable.

If you want an environment variable assignment to persist across multiple shell sessions, you can place the export statement in one of your shell's startup files, such as ~/.bashrc, ~/.bash_profile, ~/.profile, or equivalent for other shells like zsh or ksh.

To remove an environment variable, use the unset command:

```
unset EDITOR
```

When script files are executed, they inherit the environment variables from the invoking shell. However, if a variable is to be modified or set just for the scope of the script, it can be done without the export keyword, which would then be considered as a local variable. For example:

```
#!/bin/bash
MY_VAR="Hello World"
export ENV_VAR="I am an environment variable"

echo $MY_VAR
echo $ENV_VAR
```

In this script, **MY_VAR** is local to the script, while **ENV_VAR** is an environment variable that would also be accessible by any child processes invoked by the script.

To understand the scope of an environment variable, consider the following example with nested shell calls:

```
#!/bin/bash
```

```
export GLOBAL_VAR="I am a global variable"

function local_scope {
    LOCAL_VAR="I am a local variable"
    echo $LOCAL_VAR
    echo $GLOBAL_VAR
}

local_scope
```

When local_scope is called, it will print both **LOCAL_VAR** and **GLOBAL_VAR**. **GLOBAL_VAR** is accessible within the function because it was exported in the global environment. **LOCAL_VAR** is only available within the function scope and will not persist outside of it.

Understanding and managing environment variables efficiently allows scripts to be more modular, adaptable, and easier to maintain. They also provide a method to pass configuration and settings without hard-coding values into scripts, enhancing the versatility and portability of shell scripting.

5.5 Positional Parameters and Special Variables

Positional parameters and special variables are essential components in shell scripting, offering a means to handle command-line arguments and manipulate script behavior dynamically. This section delves into these parameters and variables, elucidating their roles and usage through precise explanations and practical examples.

Positional parameters provide a mechanism to access arguments passed to a shell script or a function. These parameters are denoted by a sequence of numbers following a dollar sign (e.g., $1, $2, $3, etc.). Each positional parameter corresponds to a specific argument supplied during the invocation of the script.

To illustrate, consider the following example script that accepts three parameters:

```
#!/bin/bash

echo "First argument: $1"
echo "Second argument: $2"
echo "Third argument: $3"
```

When executed with the command:

```
./script.sh arg1 arg2 arg3
```

The output will be:

```
First argument: arg1
Second argument: arg2
Third argument: arg3
```

In this example, $1 corresponds to arg1, $2 to arg2, and $3 to arg3. It is vital to note that $0 holds a special place among positional parameters, representing the name of the script itself.

When a script or function is invoked with more arguments than positional parameters, only the first nine parameters ($1 to $9) are directly accessible. To reference parameters beyond the ninth, curly braces must be utilized (e.g., ${10}, ${11}, etc.).

Special variables in shell scripting are predefined variables that offer additional control and insight into the script's execution environment. Some commonly used special variables include:

- $* and $@
- $#
- $?
- $$
- $_
- $-

$* and $@ both represent all the arguments passed to the script. However, they differ in how they handle quoted strings. $* treats all arguments as a single string, while $@ handles each argument individually. The distinction becomes clear in the following example:

```
#!/bin/bash

echo "\$* output: $*"
echo "\$@ output: $@"

for arg in "$*"; do
    echo "\$* arg: $arg"
done

for arg in "$@"; do
    echo "\$@ arg: $arg"
done
```

Given the command:

```
./script.sh "arg1 arg2" arg3
```

The output will be:

```
$* output: arg1 arg2 arg3
$@ output: arg1 arg2 arg3
$* arg: arg1 arg2 arg3
$@ arg: arg1 arg2
$@ arg: arg3
```

$# provides the total number of arguments passed to the script. It is particularly useful for validation and control within scripts. For instance:

```
#!/bin/bash

if [ $# -ne 3 ]; then
    echo "Usage: $0 arg1 arg2 arg3"
    exit 1
fi

echo "All arguments are present."
```

Executing the script with fewer than three arguments will prompt a usage message and terminate execution with an error code.

$? captures the exit status of the last executed command. An exit status of 0 indicates successful execution, while any non-zero value signifies an error. This variable aids in error handling and debugging. For example:

```
#!/bin/bash

command1
echo "Command 1 exit status: $?"

command2
echo "Command 2 exit status: $?"
```

$$ returns the process ID (PID) of the current shell. This is useful in ensuring unique temporary filenames or managing concurrent processes. Here is an example:

```
#!/bin/bash

temp_file="/tmp/tmpfile.$$"
echo "Creating temporary file: $temp_file"
touch $temp_file
```

$_ holds the absolute path of the last executed command's last argument. This variable is often used in scripts to maintain context or track command execution. For example:

```
#!/bin/bash
```

```
ls -l
echo "Last argument: $_"
```

$- reveals the current shell's flags, providing insight into the various modes or options enabled for the session. Displaying the flags can aid in debugging script environments:

```
#!/bin/bash

echo "Current shell flags: $-"
```

Understanding and leveraging positional parameters and special variables is crucial for effective shell scripting. These tools enable scripts to handle arguments dynamically, perform error-checking, manage processes, and track execution contexts, enhancing script functionality and robustness.

5.6 Using the 'read' Command for User Input

The read command is a fundamental utility in shell scripting that allows a script to receive input from the user during its execution. This user interaction enriches the script by making it dynamic and responsive to variable inputs based on user requirements.

The syntax of the read command is straightforward:

```
read [options] variable_name
```

Upon execution, the read command waits for the user to enter input, which is then stored in the specified variable. If no variable name is supplied, the input is stored in the default REPLY variable.

```
read input_variable
```

This line prompts the user to enter data, storing the provided data in the variable input_variable. Several options can modify the behavior of the read command to tailor its usage to specific needs. Some common options include:

- **-p**: Allows specifying a prompt to display before reading input.
- **-s**: Hides user input, useful for password prompts.

- **-t**: Sets a timeout for input, making the script non-blocking after a specified period.
- **-n**: Limits the number of characters to be read.
- **-r**: Precludes backslashes from being interpreted as escape characters.

```
read -p "Enter your name: " name
```

In this example, the `-p` option specifies a message `"Enter your name: "` that appears before the user input is read. The input is stored in the variable `name`.

```
read -s -p "Enter your password: " password
```

Here, the `-s` option is used so the user input (password) is not echoed on the screen.

Multiple variables can also be specified in a single `read` command, enabling the user to input several values in one line. Each value must be separated by appropriate whitespace:

```
read var1 var2 var3
```

If the user inputs the line `apple banana orange`, `var1` will be `apple`, `var2` will be `banana`, and `var3` will be `orange`. Any excess input will be assigned to the last variable if there are more words than variables.

It is also essential to handle scenarios where the `read` command's input operation might fail due to invalid input or user interruption. For improved robustness, incorporating error-checking mechanisms is advisable.

An advanced use case of the `read` command incorporates the utilization of a timeout:

```
if read -t 10 -p "Enter your username within 10 seconds: " username
then
    echo "Hello, $username"
else
    echo "Timed out waiting for user input."
fi
```

In this script, the `-t` option specifies a timeout of 10 seconds. If the user does not provide input within the allocated time, the conditional block after else will execute. This is a practical way to ensure that the script does not hang indefinitely waiting for input.

By default, the read command reads a single line from standard input. If multi-line inputs are required, one must loop the read command or use other input techniques. The versatility of the read command makes it pivotal in interacting with users in shell scripts, allowing scripts to be prepared dynamically based on user preferences and inputs without pre-hardcoded values. Proper utilization of options and considerations for input capturing nuances ensures that read remains a robust tool in any shell scripter's repertoire.

5.7 Command Substitution

Command substitution is a powerful feature in shell scripting that allows the output of a command to be used as a value within a script. This facilitates dynamic and responsive data handling, enabling scripts to integrate real-time command outputs into variables and other constructs. The syntax for command substitution can be achieved via two primary methods: the backtick (`) and the $() construct.

The older form uses backticks:

```
DATE=`date`
echo "The current date and time is: $DATE"
```

While the modern and preferred method employs the $() syntax:

```
DATE=$(date)
echo "The current date and time is: $DATE"
```

Both of these commands will store the output of the date command into the DATE variable and then echo the contents. However, due to better readability and nesting capability, the $() syntax is generally recommended.

Advantages of $() Over Backticks

- **Improved Readability:** The $() syntax is visually cleaner and easier to discern, especially in scripts that make heavy use of command substitution.

- **Nesting Capabilities:** With the $() syntax, it is straightforward to nest command substitutions, enhancing script complexity management. While nesting backticks is possible, it can become convoluted.

Consider this example using the $() syntax:

```
result=$(echo $(ls))
echo "Files and directories: $result"
```

Attempting the above with backticks:

```
result=`echo \`ls\``
echo "Files and directories: $result"
```

Every additional layer of nesting introduces another set of backticks that could complicate readability.

Command Substitution within Arithmetic Operations

Command substitution can also be applied within arithmetic operations. Here's an example demonstrating its use:

```
files_count=$(ls | wc -l)
echo "The number of files and directories is: $files_count"
```

Here, ls | wc -l counts the number of files and directories, with the result stored in files_count.

Using Command Substitution in Strings

When concatenating the output of a command with other text, command substitution provides a seamless integration. This is particularly useful for generating messages that include dynamic data. For instance:

```
HOSTNAME=$(hostname)
echo "This script is running on host: $HOSTNAME"
```

Multi-line Command Substitution

While often used on single lines, command substitution supports multi-line commands. This capability aids in more complex scripts, for example:

```
file_list=$(ls -1
          echo "end")
echo "$file_list"
```

Differences in Quoted and Unquoted Command Substitution

The output of command substitution can vary depending on whether the substitution is within double quotes. When command substitution is not quoted, the shell performs word splitting and filename expansion on the output, whereas quoted command substitution preserves the literal output without such expansions.

Observe the distinction:

```
unquoted_output=$(echo "a b c")
echo $unquoted_output # output: a b c

quoted_output="$(echo "a b c")"
echo "$quoted_output" # output: a b c
```

In the first example, multiple spaces are reduced to a single space due to word splitting. In contrast, the quoted version maintains exact spacing.

Command substitution is an essential component in shell scripting that allows commands to interact with variables and strings efficiently, facilitating dynamic scripting and immediate incorporation of real-time data. Its proper use, especially with the preferred $() syntax, enhances script maintainability and readability.

5.8 Arithmetic Operations in Shell Scripts

Arithmetic operations in shell scripts are essential for performing calculations and manipulating numerical data. The shell provides several ways to perform arithmetic operations, including using the expr command, the double parentheses syntax (( )), and the let command. Understanding how these operations work and their syntax is crucial for writing efficient and functional scripts.

The primary arithmetic operators available in the shell are addition (+), subtraction (-), multiplication (*), division (/), modulus (%), and exponentiation (**). Here, we will explore each of these methods and demonstrate practical examples to illustrate their usage.

- **Using the expr Command**

The expr command evaluates expressions and prints the result. It supports basic arithmetic operations as shown below:

```
result=$(expr 5 + 3)
echo $result # Output: 8
```

```
result=$(expr 10 \* 2)
echo $result # Output: 20
```

Note that the multiplication operator * must be escaped () to prevent it from being interpreted as a wildcard character by the shell.

- **Using Double Parentheses**

A more modern and convenient way to perform arithmetic operations is using the double parentheses syntax. This method also supports a broader range of operators and has a more intuitive syntax:

```
result=$((5 + 3))
echo $result # Output: 8
```

```
result=$((10 * 2))
echo $result # Output: 20
```

The double parentheses syntax allows for complex expressions and supports operator precedence:

```
result=$((1 + 2 * 3))
echo $result # Output: 7
```

It also supports increment and decrement operations:

```
((value++))
echo $value # Increment value by 1
```

```
((value--))
echo $value # Decrement value by 1
```

- **Using the let Command**

The let command is another way to perform arithmetic operations. It evaluates the expression in a manner similar to the double parentheses syntax:

```
let result=5+3
echo $result # Output: 8
```

```
let result=10*2
echo $result # Output: 20
```

The let command allows direct manipulation of variables:

```
let value++
echo $value # Increment value by 1
```

```
let value--
echo $value # Decrement value by 1
```

- **Example: Calculating Factorial**

A common example of using arithmetic operations in shell scripts is calculating the factorial of a number. Below is a script that calculates the factorial of a given number using a for loop and arithmetic operations:

```
#!/bin/bash

read -p "Enter a number: " num
factorial=1

for (( i=1; i<=num; i++ ))
do
    factorial=$((factorial * i))
done

echo "The factorial of $num is $factorial"
```

When executed, the user is prompted to enter a number, and the script calculates the factorial by multiplying the numbers iteratively from 1 to the entered number.

- **Handling Floating-Point Arithmetic**

The shell natively handles only integer arithmetic. For floating-point operations, bc (Basic Calculator) or other external tools are necessary:

```
result=$(echo "scale=2; 5 / 3" | bc)
echo $result # Output: 1.66
```

By setting the scale parameter, we can specify the number of decimal places.

Arithmetic operations are fundamental in shell scripting due to their wide range of applications in script flow control, data processing, and task automation. Utilizing the various methods and understanding their respective syntaxes ensures the efficient handling of numerical data in scripts.

5.9 String Operations and Manipulations

String operations are an essential part of shell scripting, enabling the manipulation and transformation of text. Mastery of string operations and manipulations is crucial for effective script writing. This section delves into various string operations like concatenation, length calculation, substring extraction, pattern matching, and replacement.

String concatenation is a fundamental operation that combines multiple strings into a single string. In a shell script, this can be performed using simple juxtaposition of variables or strings.

```
#!/bin/bash
str1="Hello"
str2="World"
result="$str1 $str2"
echo "$result" # Outputs: Hello World
```

Calculating the length of a string is another common requirement. This can be achieved in Bash using the parameter expansion syntax $#variable.

```
#!/bin/bash
str="Linux"
length=${#str}
echo "The length of the string is $length" # Outputs: The length of the string is 5
```

Extracting a substring from a given string in Bash is possible using the substring expansion $variable:offset:length. The *offset* specifies the starting position, and *length* is the number of characters to extract.

```
#!/bin/bash
str="LinuxShellScripting"
subStr=${str:5:5}
echo "$subStr" # Outputs: Shell
```

Pattern matching and replacement within strings utilize tools like sed and parameter expansion, allowing for advanced text transformations. For simple replacements, parameter expansion can be employed: $variable//pattern/replacement replaces all occurrences of *pattern* with *replacement*.

```
#!/bin/bash
str="abcabc"
newStr=${str//a/A}
echo "$newStr" # Outputs: AbcAbc
```

For more complex patterns and transformations, sed (Stream Editor) is used. sed is a powerful utility that parses and transforms text using regular expressions.

```
#!/bin/bash
str="Hello World"
newStr=$(echo "$str" | sed 's/World/Linux/')
echo "$newStr" # Outputs: Hello Linux
```

Removing a substring from a string is often required in script operations. This is achievable using parameter expansion in Bash. $variable#pattern and $variable##pattern remove the shortest and longest match of *pattern* from the beginning of *variable*, respectively. $variable%pattern and $variable%%pattern perform similar operations but remove from the end.

```
#!/bin/bash
str="file.tar.gz"
base=${str%.*}
echo "$base" # Outputs: file

extension=${str##*.}
echo "$extension" # Outputs: gz
```

Joining strings with delimiters, splitting strings, and manipulating fields are often necessary in data processing. Using IFS (Internal Field Separator) allows splitting a string into an array based on a delimiter.

```
#!/bin/bash
str="one:two:three"
IFS=':'
read -ra ADDR <<< "$str"
for i in "${ADDR[@]}"; do
    echo "$i"
done
```

```
Outputs:
one
two
three
```

Script robustness can be enhanced by removing whitespaces from strings, which can be achieved using sed or tr (translate).

```
#!/bin/bash
str=" text with whitespace "
cleanedStr=$(echo "$str" | sed 's/^[ \t]*//;s/[ \t]*$//')
echo "Start-$cleanedStr-End"
```

```
Outputs:
Start-text with whitespace-End
```

String operations and manipulations significantly enhance the capabilities and efficiency of shell scripts. Mastering these operations enables the manipulation of textual data with precision and ease.

5.10 Exporting and Importing Variables

Variables in shell scripts can have either local or global scope. By default, variables in a shell script are local to the session or script in which they are defined. However, there might be instances where you would need to share variables across different scripts or make them available to child processes. This is where exporting variables becomes essential.

The export command is used to mark a variable for export to the environment of child processes. This allows the child process to inherit the exported variable and use it in its execution. The syntax for exporting a variable is straightforward:

```
export VARIABLE_NAME=value
```

For example, if we have a variable MY_VAR and we want to make it available to child processes:

```
MY_VAR="Hello, World"
export MY_VAR
```

Once exported, the variable MY_VAR can be accessed by any child process. To demonstrate this, consider a simple example where a parent script exports a variable and a child script accesses it.

First, create the parent script, parent.sh:

```
#!/bin/bash
MY_VAR="Hello, World"
export MY_VAR
./child.sh
```

Next, create the child script, child.sh:

```
#!/bin/bash
echo "Value of MY_VAR in child script: \$MY_VAR"
```

Make both scripts executable using the following commands:

```
chmod +x parent.sh
chmod +x child.sh
```

Now, execute the parent script:

```
./parent.sh
```

The expected output should be:

```
Value of MY_VAR in child script: Hello, World
```

This output confirms that the variable MY_VAR was successfully exported from parent.sh to child.sh.

It is also possible to export a variable at the time it is declared. This can save a line of code and is done as follows:

```
export MY_VAR="Hello, World"
```

When dealing with environments where variables need to be passed back and forth between scripts or processes, importing variables into a script becomes as crucial as exporting them. Importing generally involves making sure that the script has access to the environment where the variables are defined. This can be done using the source command or the dot operator (.).

Consider a file vars.sh where we define and export some variables:

```
#!/bin/bash
MY_VAR="Hello, Universe"
export MY_VAR
```

To use these variables in another script, we can source vars.sh:

```
#!/bin/bash
source vars.sh
echo "Imported MY_VAR: \$MY_VAR"
```

Alternately, the dot operator can be used which is a shorthand for source:

```
#!/bin/bash
. vars.sh
echo "Imported MY_VAR: \$MY_VAR"
```

These techniques of sourcing ensure that the variables defined and exported in vars.sh become available in the current shell session, making them accessible throughout the script execution.

The export/import mechanism is a core part of shell scripting that facilitates more modular and maintainable scripts by allowing variables to be shared across different script files and sub-processes effectively.

5.11 Scope and Lifetime of Variables

In shell scripting, understanding the scope and lifetime of variables is essential for writing robust and maintainable scripts. The scope of a variable refers to the context within which the variable is accessible, while the lifetime of a variable denotes the duration for which the variable exists in memory.

A variable's scope can be categorized into two types: global and local. Global variables are accessible from anywhere within the script after being declared, whereas local variables are confined to the function or block in which they are declared. Shell scripts typically use the export command to define global variables and the local keyword to define local variables within functions.

Global variables are declared outside of any function and are available throughout the script. For instance:

```
#!/bin/bash

global_variable="I am a global variable"

function display_global {
    echo $global_variable
}

display_global
```

In this example, global_variable is defined outside the function display_global, making it a global variable accessible both inside and outside the function.

Conversely, local variables are declared within a function using the local keyword and their scope is limited to that function. Here is an illustrative example:

```
#!/bin/bash

function display_local {
    local local_variable="I am a local variable"
    echo $local_variable
}

display_local
echo $local_variable
```

The variable local_variable is declared within the function display_local using the local keyword, making it inaccessible outside that function. Attempting to use local_variable outside the function results in no value being displayed, as evidenced by the absence of any output from the echo $local_variable command after the function call.

Variable shadowing occurs when a local variable within a function shares the same name as a global variable, effectively overriding the global variable within the function's scope. The global variable remains unaffected outside the function. Consider the following example:

```
#!/bin/bash

my_var="I am a global variable"

function shadow_variable {
    local my_var="I am a local variable"
    echo $my_var
}
```

```
shadow_variable
echo $my_var
```

Running this script outputs:

```
I am a local variable
I am a global variable
```

Within the shadow_variable function, the local variable my_var shadows the global variable of the same name. Once the function completes its execution, the global variable my_var remains unaffected.

The lifetime of a variable is determined by its scope. Global variables persist for the duration of the script's execution, making them suitable for maintaining state information or configuration settings that need to be accessed throughout the script. Local variables, however, only exist for the lifetime of the function execution and are automatically destroyed once the function finishes, ensuring their temporary nature and reducing the risk of unintended side effects elsewhere in the script.

Functions themselves also have scope and lifetime rules. Functions declared within a script are accessible globally, just like global variables, unless otherwise restricted. Here is a script to illustrate:

```
#!/bin/bash

function a_global_function {
    echo "I am a global function"
}

a_global_function

if true; then
    function a_local_function {
        echo "I am a local function"
    }
fi

a_local_function
```

Executing this script results in:

```
I am a global function
I am a local function
```

Both functions a_global_function and a_local_function are accessible globally despite one being declared within a condition. However, defining functions within conditional blocks or loops is not a best practice due to readability and predictability concerns.

To manage the lifetime and scope of variables judiciously, programmers can leverage local variables for temporary computations and utilize global variables sparingly to store essential information that needs to be accessed repeatedly or across different components of the script. By adhering to these principles, the clarity, maintainability, and reliability of shell scripts are significantly enhanced.

5.12 Practical Examples of Variable Usage

To consolidate the theoretical knowledge about variables, it is imperative to analyze their usage through practical examples. This section offers detailed illustrations demonstrating how different types of variables can be employed in various shell scripting scenarios.

Example 1: Calculating the Area of a Rectangle

In this example, we will define variables to store the dimensions of a rectangle and subsequently calculate and display its area.

```
#!/bin/bash

# Define variables for rectangle dimensions
length=5
width=3

# Calculate the area
area=$((length * width))

# Display the result
echo "The area of the rectangle is $area"
```

```
The area of the rectangle is 15
```

The script initializes length and width, then performs an arithmetic operation using the $((...)) syntax to compute the area. The result is stored in the area variable and printed to the terminal.

Example 2: Greeting a User

This script takes the user's name as input and greets them, demonstrating string manipulation and user input.

```
#!/bin/bash

# Prompt the user for their name
echo "Please enter your name:"
read user_name

# Display the greeting
echo "Hello, $user_name! Welcome to the Linux Shell Scripting tutorial."
```

```
Please enter your name:
John
Hello, John! Welcome to the Linux Shell Scripting tutorial.
```

This example uses the read command to capture user input into the user_name variable. It then constructs a greeting message leveraging variable substitution.

Example 3: File Existence Check

This script checks if a file exists within the current directory and echoes an appropriate message. It highlights the use of command substitution and conditional statements.

```
#!/bin/bash

# Define the file name
file_name="example.txt"

# Check if the file exists
if [ -e "$file_name" ]; then
    echo "The file $file_name exists."
else
    echo "The file $file_name does not exist."
fi
```

```
The file example.txt exists.
```

Here, the if [-e "$file_name"] statement evaluates the existence of example.txt. Depending on the file's presence, a corresponding message is displayed.

Example 4: Summing Command Line Arguments

This example demonstrates the use of positional parameters to sum numbers provided as command line arguments.

```
#!/bin/bash

# Initialize sum variable
sum=0

# Loop through all command line arguments
for arg in "$@"
do
    # Add each argument to the sum
    sum=$((sum + arg))
done

# Display the result
echo "The sum of the numbers is $sum"
```

```
./sum_arguments.sh 4 5 6
The sum of the numbers is 15
```

Positional parameters $@ are iterated through a for loop, and each value is added to sum, demonstrating the handling of multiple inputs.

Example 5: Using Environment Variables

This example manipulates environment variables to display the current user's home directory and modify the path temporarily.

```
#!/bin/bash

# Display the current user's home directory
echo "Your home directory is $HOME"

# Temporarily add a directory to the PATH variable
export PATH=$PATH:/my/custom/path

# Display the new PATH
echo "Updated PATH is $PATH"
```

```
Your home directory is /home/username
Updated PATH is /usr/local/sbin:/usr/local/bin:/usr/sbin:/usr/bin:/sbin:/bin:/my/custom/path
```

Using $HOME, the script fetches the home directory of the current user. By modifying $PATH with export, it shows how environment variables can be adjusted within a session.

Example 6: Implementing a Simple Calculator

This interactive script functions as a basic calculator, allowing users to perform arithmetic operations.

```
#!/bin/bash

# Prompt the user for two numbers
echo "Enter first number:"
read num1
echo "Enter second number:"
read num2

# Prompt the user for an operation
echo "Enter operation (+, -, *, /):"
read op

# Perform the calculation
result=0
case $op in
    +) result=$((num1 + num2)) ;;
    -) result=$((num1 - num2)) ;;
    '*') result=$((num1 * num2)) ;;
    '/') result=$((num1 / num2)) ;;
    *) echo "Invalid operation" ;;
esac

# Display the result
if [ "$op" != "" ]; then
    echo "The result is $result"
fi
```

```
Enter first number:
10
Enter second number:
5
Enter operation (+, -, *, /):
*
The result is 50
```

Utilizing case, the script handles different arithmetic operations input by the user.

These practical examples vividly illustrate how variables can be effectively used to perform calculations, interact with users, manage files, and manipulate environment variables in shell scripting.

Chapter 6

File and Directory Management

This chapter covers essential techniques for managing files and directories in Linux. It includes creating, viewing, copying, moving, and deleting files as well as navigating and manipulating directories. It addresses handling hidden files, setting permissions, and changing ownership. The chapter also discusses creating symbolic and hard links, using wildcards, finding files and directories, and managing special file types. Practical script examples are provided to illustrate these concepts in real-world applications.

6.1 Introduction to File and Directory Management

File and directory management form the core of any operating system's functionality, and Linux provides an extensive set of tools and commands to handle these tasks efficiently. Understanding how to manipulate files and directories is fundamental for any user aspiring to gain proficiency in shell scripting and Linux system administration.

The Linux filesystem is a structured hierarchy of directories, starting from the root directory /. Each directory can contain files and subdirectories, enabling an organized placement of data and software components. This hierarchy makes locating and managing resources intuitive and efficient.

In Linux, everything is treated as a file, including hardware devices and processes. Regular files, directories, symbolic links, and special files such as device files, pipes, and sockets all fall under the file category. This unification simplifies the interaction with different system components.

To better understand file and directory management, we will explore several core concepts and commands that facilitate the creation, manipulation, and deletion of these entities. This section lays the groundwork for more advanced topics covered later in the chapter.

Linux provides a rich set of commands for viewing directories and file contents. Some of these commands include the following:

- ls for listing directory contents,
- cat for concatenating and displaying file content,
- less and more for viewing files page by page,
- head and tail for displaying the beginning or end of files.

The ls command is used to list the contents of a directory, and it supports numerous options to display information in various formats. For example, to display all files, including hidden ones, use the -a option. To include detailed information such as file permissions, number of links, owner, group, size, and timestamp, use the -l option. Here is an example command along with its sample output:

```
ls -la
```

```
total 48
drwxr-xr-x  5 user user 4096 Aug 21 12:34 .
drwxr-xr-x 23 root root 4096 Aug 21 12:33 ..
-rw-r--r--  1 user user  220 Aug 21 12:31 .bash_logout
-rw-r--r--  1 user user 3771 Aug 21 12:31 .bashrc
drwxr-xr-x  2 user user 4096 Aug 21 12:32 .config
drwxr-xr-x  3 user user 4096 Aug 21 12:33 .local
-rw-r--r--  1 user user  807 Aug 21 12:31 .profile
drwx------  2 user user 4096 Aug 21 12:34 .ssh
```

Creating files can be achieved using commands such as touch to create empty files or echo to write text to files. For example:

```
touch newfile.txt
echo "Hello, World!" > hello.txt
```

These commands will create newfile.txt as an empty file and hello.txt containing the text "Hello, World!" respectively.

Copying and moving files require the cp and mv commands. The cp command copies files and directories, while mv can both move and rename them. Examples of these commands include:

```
cp sourcefile.txt destinationfile.txt
mv oldname.txt newname.txt
```

Removing files and directories involves the rm and rmdir commands. The rm command is versatile and can delete both files and directories when used with the appropriate options:

```
rm filetoRemove.txt
rm -r directoryToRemove/
```

The first command deletes a file, and the second command recursively deletes a directory and its contents. Note that these operations are generally irreversible, so caution is advised.

Navigating the filesystem relies on the cd (change directory) command. This command changes the current working directory, allowing access to different parts of the filesystem. For example:

```
cd /path/to/directory
```

To return to the home directory, you can simply use:

```
cd ~
```

Similarly, to move up one level in the directory hierarchy, use:

```
cd ..
```

Understanding file permissions is crucial for maintaining security and proper access control. File permissions in Linux consist of read (r), write (w), and execute (x) permissions. These permissions are set for three user classes: the owner, group, and others. The command ls -l can be used to display these permissions. For example:

```
ls -l
```

```
-rw-r--r-- 1 user user 4096 Aug 21 12:31 myfile.txt
```

This output indicates that the file myfile.txt is readable and writable by the owner, readable by the group, and readable by others.

Permission management is achieved using the chmod command,

which alters file permissions. Changes can be specified using symbolic representation (e.g., u+x to add execute permission for the user) or numeric representation (e.g., 755). Ownership changes are handled by the chown and chgrp commands.

This brief overview establishes a foundation for systematically managing files and directories in Linux. The subsequent sections delve deeper into these commands and concepts, providing comprehensive coverage and practical examples to enhance proficiency.

6.2 Working with Files (Creating, Viewing, Copying, Moving, Deleting)

The capability to manage files effectively is fundamental to working within the Linux environment. This section elaborates on creating, viewing, copying, moving, and deleting files, providing a comprehensive understanding of basic file operations.

Creating files in Linux can be accomplished using a variety of commands. One of the simplest methods is using the touch command, which is primarily used to create empty files or update the timestamps of existing files. To create a new file named example.txt, you would use:

```
touch example.txt
```

For adding content to a file upon creation, utilities like echo, cat, or text editors such as nano, vi, and vim can be utilized:

```
echo "Hello World" > example.txt
```

This command directs the string "Hello World" into example.txt, effectively creating the file with the given content if it does not already exist, or overwriting the existing file. To append content to an existing file without overwriting, the » operator is used:

```
echo "Append this line" >> example.txt
```

Viewing the contents of files is another fundamental operation. The cat command is widely employed for this purpose:

```
cat example.txt
```

For larger files, less, more, or head and tail may offer better utility, providing pagination and the ability to view sections of the file:

```
less example.txt
```

less allows scrolling through the file, offering a more flexible viewing experience compared to cat, which displays the entire content at once.

Copying files involves the cp command. The syntax requires specifying the source file and the destination path:

```
cp example.txt copy_of_example.txt
```

For copying directories and their contents, the -r or –recursive option is necessary:

```
cp -r directory_name destination_directory
```

Moving files is handled by the mv command, which also serves to rename files:

```
mv example.txt new_location/example.txt
mv example.txt renamed_example.txt
```

The first command moves example.txt to the specified directory, while the second renames the file within its current directory.

Deleting files is performed using the rm command:

```
rm example.txt
```

Caution must be exercised with rm, as it permanently deletes files. Adding the -i option prompts for confirmation before each file is deleted:

```
rm -i example.txt
```

To remove directories, especially those that contain files, the -r or –recursive option is required:

```
rm -r directory_name
```

Forcing the deletion of files and directories, without confirmation or error prompts, involves the -f (force) option:

```
rm -rf directory_name
```

Each of these operations—creating, viewing, copying, moving, and deleting files—form the core actions for file management in the Linux shell. Understanding these commands in depth allows for proficient and efficient file handling, ensuring that users can manipulate files as required by their workflows.

6.3 Working with Directories (Creating, Navigating, Removing)

Creating Directories

To create directories in Linux, the mkdir (make directory) command is used. The basic syntax for mkdir is straightforward:

```
mkdir <directory_name>
```

For instance, to create a single directory named example:

```
mkdir example
```

If there is a need to create multiple directories at once, this can be achieved by listing each directory name separated by a space:

```
mkdir dir1 dir2 dir3
```

Additionally, creating a nested directory structure can be accomplished with the -p (parents) option, which creates parent directories as needed:

```
mkdir -p parent/child/grandchild
```

This command will create the entire directory path parent/child/grandchild if it does not already exist.

Navigating Directories

Navigating directories in the Linux filesystem is performed with the cd (change directory) command. The basic usage of cd is depicted below:

```
cd <directory_name>
```

To move into a directory named example, the command would be:

```
cd example
```

Different navigational contexts can be addressed as follows:

- Moving up one directory level:

  ```
  cd ..
  ```

- Returning to the previous directory:

```
cd -
```

- Returning to the home directory of the current user:

```
cd ~
```

- Moving to an absolute path, for instance, to /usr/local:

```
cd /usr/local
```

To ascertain the current directory at any given time, the pwd command (print working directory) can be used:

```
pwd
```

Output:

/home/user/example

Removing Directories

The removal of directories can be performed with the rmdir or rm command, depending on whether the directory is empty or not. The rmdir command removes empty directories:

```
rmdir <directory_name>
```

To remove the directory example if it is empty:

```
rmdir example
```

For directories that contain files or other directories, the rm command with the -r (recursive) option needs to be used:

```
rm -r <directory_name>
```

For example, to remove a directory named example and its contents:

```
rm -r example
```

Exercise caution with the rm -r command as it will delete all files and subdirectories within the specified directory. To avoid accidentally removing important files, the -i (interactive) option can be employed to prompt for confirmation before each deletion:

```
rm -ri example
```

Output:

```
rm: descend into directory 'example'? y
rm: remove regular file 'example/file1'? y
rm: remove directory 'example'? y
```

Effective management of directories is foundational in Linux, ensuring organized structure and efficient navigation.

6.4 Handling Hidden Files and Directories

In Linux systems, hidden files and directories are those whose names begin with a dot character ('.'). These files and directories are not displayed by default when listing the contents of a directory using commands such as ls or comparable tools. Hidden files are typically used to store configuration settings and preferences for various applications and services.

To illustrate, consider the following commands and their outputs when executed in a typical home directory:

```
$ ls
Documents Downloads Music Pictures Public
```

The output does not show hidden files or directories. To reveal all files, including hidden ones, use the -a option with the ls command:

```
$ ls -a
. .bashrc Documents Music .profile
.. .cache Downloads Pictures Public
.bash_logout .config .local .ssh
```

This command lists all entries in the current directory, including hidden files (e.g., .bashrc, .profile, .ssh).

To handle hidden files and directories programmatically within shell scripts, the same principles apply as with regular files, with particular attention to ensuring that the dot prefix is included in file manipulation commands.

Creating Hidden Files and Directories

Creating hidden files and directories is straightforward and involves using standard commands such as touch, mkdir, and appropriate naming conventions.

```
$ touch .hiddenfile
$ mkdir .hiddendir
```

These commands create a hidden file named .hiddenfile and a hidden directory named .hiddendir in the current working directory.

Copying and Moving Hidden Files and Directories

Copying and moving hidden files and directories can be done using cp and mv commands, ensuring that the filenames (including the dot) are correctly specified:

```
$ cp .hiddenfile /path/to/destination/.hiddenfile
$ mv .hiddendir /path/to/newlocation/
```

To include hidden files when copying an entire directory, use the -a option or a wildcard pattern that includes hidden files:

```
$ cp -a source_directory/./* destination_directory/
```

Removing Hidden Files and Directories

Removing hidden files and directories requires the same commands used for normal files, with careful inclusion of the filenames:

```
$ rm .hiddenfile
$ rm -r .hiddendir
```

This first command removes the hidden file .hiddenfile, while the second recursively removes the hidden directory .hiddendir.

Using Wildcards to Handle Hidden Files

Wildcards (*, ?, []) offer a powerful way to handle multiple files. However, by default, wildcards do not match hidden files. To include hidden files in operations, prefix the wildcard with a dot:

```
$ rm .* # CAUTION: This will attempt to remove all hidden files, including critical
    ones.
```

For safer usage, specify clear patterns or combine with other options:

```
$ mv .* /path/to/target/ # Move all hidden files
```

Script Example: Backing Up Hidden Files

This example script demonstrates how to back up all hidden files from a user's home directory to a specified backup location:

```
#!/bin/bash
# Script to backup hidden files from home directory

SOURCE_DIR=$HOME
BACKUP_DIR=$SOURCE_DIR/hidden_backup

# Ensure backup directory exists
mkdir -p $BACKUP_DIR
```

```
# Copy hidden files and directories
cp -a $SOURCE_DIR/.[^.]* $BACKUP_DIR/

# Confirmation message
echo "Hidden files backed up to $BACKUP_DIR"
```

This script first sets the source and backup directory paths, creates the backup directory if it does not exist, and then uses the cp command with appropriate wildcards to copy all hidden files and directories from the source to the backup location.

Handling hidden files and directories effectively in Linux requires a firm understanding of their behaviors and implications within file system operations. Mastery of these concepts facilitates robust file management practices, particularly in scripting and automation tasks.

6.5 File Permissions and Ownership

In Linux, the management of file permissions and ownership is crucial to maintaining system security and establishing appropriate access controls. Every file and directory is associated with an owner and a group, and it has specific permissions that determine which actions users can perform on it. Understanding and correctly applying these permission settings is essential for effective system administration and for protecting the integrity and confidentiality of the data.

Linux file permissions are defined for three types of entities: the owner (user), the group, and others. Each entity has three types of permissions: read (r), write (w), and execute (x). These permissions are crucial as they dictate who can view, modify, or execute a file.

Representation of Permissions

Permissions for files and directories are typically viewed using the ls -l command. This command provides a detailed list of files and their associated permissions. An example output of the ls -l command is as follows:

```
-rwxr-xr-- 1 user group 4096 Mar  5 12:34 example.sh
```

In this example, the first character - indicates that it's a regular file (it would be d if it were a directory). Following this, the string rwxr-xr– represents the permissions:

- rwx for the user (owner) - read, write, and execute.

- r-x for the group - read and execute.
- r– for others - read only.

The permissions are broken down into three groups, each consisting of three characters. The characters indicate the permissions that have been granted:

- r (read): Permission to read (view) the contents of the file.
- w (write): Permission to modify the contents of the file.
- x (execute): Permission to execute the file as a program/script.

Changing File Permissions

File permissions can be modified using the chmod command. There are two ways to specify permissions: symbolic and numeric.

Symbolic mode allows permissions to be specified using letters to represent the user categories and permission types. For example, to add execute permissions for the user, one would use:

```
chmod u+x example.sh
```

In this command, u stands for user, + adds a permission, and x stands for execute.

Numeric mode (octal mode) uses a three-digit octal number to specify permissions. Each type of permission is represented by a digit from 0 to 7, where 4 stands for read, 2 for write, and 1 for execute. These values are summed to create the permission digit:

- 7 (4+2+1): read, write, and execute.
- 6 (4+2): read and write.
- 5 (4+1): read and execute.
- 4: read only.

To set permissions using numeric mode, the command would be:

```
chmod 755 example.sh
```

This command sets the file to be readable, writable, and executable by the owner, readable and executable by the group, and readable and executable by others.

File Ownership

Every file and directory in Linux is owned by a user and associated with a group. Ownership can be viewed with the ls -l command, where the ownership is displayed after the permissions string. For instance:

```
-rwxr-xr-- 1 user group 4096 Mar  5 12:34 example.sh
```

In this example, user is the owner of the file, and group is the associated group.

The chown command is used to change the ownership of a file or directory. Only the root user or file owner can change file ownership. To change the owner of a file:

```
chown newuser example.sh
```

To change both the owner and the group:

```
chown newuser:newgroup example.sh
```

Similarly, the chgrp command is used specifically to change the group ownership of a file:

```
chgrp newgroup example.sh
```

Special Permissions

In addition to the standard permissions, Linux also supports special permissions that provide advanced access control features: SUID (Set owner User ID), SGID (Set Group ID), and the sticky bit.

SUID is applied to executable files and allows a program to run with the permissions of the file owner. This can be set with:

```
chmod u+s example.sh
```

SGID can be set on executable files or directories. For executable files, it allows the program to run with the group permissions of the file; for directories, it ensures new files created within the directory inherit the group ID:

```
chmod g+s example_directory
```

The sticky bit, set on directories, ensures that only the file's owner can delete or rename files, even if others have write permissions to the directory. This is often set on shared directories to enhance security:

```
chmod +t shared_directory
```

To remove special permissions, the - symbol is used instead of +.

Understanding and properly managing file permissions and ownership is essential for system security and ensuring that only authorized users can access or modify sensitive data.

6.6 Changing File Permissions (chmod)

In Linux, file and directory permissions are a critical aspect of system security and functionality. Permissions dictate what actions a user can perform on a file or a directory. The chmod command, an abbreviation for "change mode," is used to modify these permissions.

Linux assigns three types of permissions to each file or directory: read (r), write (w), and execute (x). These permissions can be granted or denied to three types of users: the owner (u), the group (g), and others (o).

Permissions are represented as a set of characters in the format rwxrwxrwx, where each triplet corresponds to the owner, the group, and others, respectively. For instance, the permission set rwxr-xr– indicates that the owner has read (r), write (w), and execute (x) permissions, the group has read (r) and execute (x) permissions, and others have read (r) permission only.

Permissions can also be represented numerically using octal values:

- r (read) is represented by 4.
- w (write) is represented by 2.
- x (execute) is represented by 1.

The sum of these values within each triplet defines the permissions:

- 7 (4+2+1) for read, write, and execute permissions.
- 6 (4+2) for read and write permissions.
- 5 (4+1) for read and execute permissions.
- 4 for read only.

The chmod command employs two syntaxes: symbolic and numeric.

Symbolic Syntax: The symbolic syntax specifies the user category (u, g, o, a for all), operation symbols (+ to add permission, - to remove permission, = to set specific permission), and the permissions (r, w, x).

```
# Add execute permission for the owner
chmod u+x filename

# Remove write permission for the group
chmod g-w filename

# Set read permission only for others
chmod o=r filename
```

Numeric Syntax: The numeric syntax involves a three-digit octal number where each digit corresponds to the permissions for the owner, group, and others.

```
# Set permissions to rwxr-xr--
chmod 754 filename

# Set permissions to rw-r-----
chmod 640 filename
```

Executing chmod modifies the file permissions in accordance with the specified instruction. Here are concrete examples to solidify your understanding:

To give the owner read, write, and execute permissions; the group read and execute permissions; and others only read permission, you would use:

```
chmod 754 filename
```

Alternatively, using symbolic syntax:

```
chmod u=rwx,g=rx,o=r filename
```

To remove execute permission from the group using symbolic syntax:

```
chmod g-x filename
```

Verify the changes with the ls -l command:

```
ls -l filename
```

```
# Output
-rwxr-xr--
```

For directories, permissions work similarly but have additional implications:

- Read (r) allows listing directory contents.

- Write (w) permits creating and deleting files within the directory.
- Execute (x) allows entering the directory.

Setting the permission to allow anyone to read and enter the directory but only allowing the owner to make modifications would be:

```
chmod 755 directoryname
```

Be cautious with permissions, especially write and execute permissions, to maintain security: excessively permissive settings can introduce vulnerabilities, while overly restrictive settings can hinder functionality.

Understanding and correctly applying chmod ensures appropriate access control, contributing to a secure and efficient system.

6.7 Changing File Ownership (chown, chgrp)

Ownership of files and directories in Linux is a fundamental concept that determines who has control and access to specific file system objects. Two primary commands facilitate changing file ownership: chown and chgrp. Understanding and properly utilizing these commands enhances the management and security of file systems.

In Unix-like systems, every file and directory has an owner and a group associated with it. The chown command can change both the owner and the group, while the chgrp command is solely for modifying the group ownership. The precise syntax and options for both commands offer flexibility for various operational needs.

The basic usage of chown is as follows:

```
chown [OPTION]... [OWNER][:[GROUP]] FILE...
```

Changing Ownership with chown

To change the ownership of a file, you specify the new owner followed by the file name. For example, to change the owner of example.txt to user alice, you would use:

```
chown alice example.txt
```

Executing this command changes the owner of example.txt to alice. If you need to change both the owner and the group, you can specify both, separated by a colon:

```
chown alice:staff example.txt
```

In this example, the file example.txt will now have alice as the owner and staff as the group.

Recursive Ownership Changes

When dealing with directories, it is often necessary to change the ownership recursively for all files and subdirectories. The -R option achieves this:

```
chown -R alice:staff /path/to/directory
```

This command changes the owner and group of the specified directory and all of its contents to alice and staff, respectively.

Using Numeric IDs

In some cases, you may want to set the owner or the group using their numeric IDs instead of names. The syntax remains similar, using the numeric user ID (UID) and group ID (GID):

```
chown 1001:1001 example.txt
```

Here, both the UID and GID are specified as 1001, accordingly setting the ownership based on these IDs.

Important Options

Several options enhance the functionality of the chown command:

- –reference=RFILE: Change the ownership of files to that of the reference file RFILE.
- -f: Suppress most error messages.
- -v: Output a diagnostic for every file processed.

The chgrp Command

While chown can change both the user and group ownership, chgrp is used exclusively for changing the group ownership. The syntax is straightforward:

```
chgrp [OPTION]... GROUP FILE...
```

To change the group of example.txt to developers, use:

```
chgrp developers example.txt
```

Similar to chown, chgrp also supports recursive changes:

```
chgrp -R developers /path/to/directory
```

Practical Examples

To consolidate understanding, let us consider a practical scenario dealing with a project directory. Suppose we have a directory structure:

```
project/
  src
    script.sh
    main.c
  docs
    README.md
```

Change the ownership of all files and directories within project to user bob and group development. Use:

```
chown -R bob:development project
```

Alternatively, to only change the group ownership to docs, you invoke:

```
chgrp -R docs-group project/docs
```

Maintaining Security

Effective use of chown and chgrp not only aids in organizing file systems but also enhances security. By ensuring that only appropriate users and groups access or modify files, the system's integrity and confidentiality are preserved.

Efficient file and directory ownership management using chown and chgrp equips users and administrators with crucial tools for maintaining structured and secure file systems in a multi-user environment.

6.8 Creating Symbolic and Hard Links

In Linux, symbolic and hard links provide powerful means to manage files and directories efficiently. Understanding their differences and respective use cases is crucial for effective file system management. This section delves into creating both symbolic and hard links, discusses their inherent characteristics, and provides practical examples to illustrate their application.

A **symbolic link**, also known as a soft link, is a special type of file that points to another file or directory. It operates similarly to a shortcut in other operating systems. Creating symbolic links can be advantageous for setting up reference points without duplicating the actual files. This is particularly useful in scenarios where different directories need to access the same file.

A **hard link**, on the other hand, is an additional name for an existing file on the same filesystem. Unlike symbolic links, hard links cannot span across different filesystems. They point directly to the inode (a data structure on a filesystem on Linux and UNIX-like systems that stores information about a file or a directory) of a file rather than the file name.

Creating Symbolic Links

The ln command with the -s option is used to create symbolic links. The syntax is as follows:

```
ln -s <target> <link_name>
```

Here, <target> refers to the file or directory you want to link to, and <link_name> is the name of the symbolic link you wish to create.

Example:

```
ln -s /home/user/important_file.txt /home/user/shortcut_to_important_file.txt
```

Executing the command above creates a symbolic link named shortcut_to_important_file.txt that points to /home/user/important_file.txt. Listing the directory with the ls -l command will show something similar to:

```
lrwxrwxrwx 1 user group    24 Aug 25 12:34 shortcut_to_important_file.txt -> /home/user/important_file.txt
```

The leading l in the file permissions indicates the file is a symbolic link. The arrow (->) points to the target file.

Characteristics of Symbolic Links

Symbolic links possess unique attributes:

- They can link to directories and files across different filesystems.
- Deleting or moving the symbolic link does not affect the original file.
- The link becomes broken if the target file is deleted or moved. Operations on the link will result in a "No such file or directory" error.

Creating Hard Links

To create a hard link, use the ln command without the -s option:

```
ln <target> <link_name>
```

Example:

```
ln /home/user/important_file.txt /home/user/hardlink_to_important_file.txt
```

This command creates a hard link named hardlink_to_important_file.txt pointing to /home/user/important_file.txt. Checking the directory listing with ls -l, you will see:

```
-rw-r--r-- 2 user group  1234 Aug 25 12:34 hardlink_to_important_file.txt
-rw-r--r-- 2 user group  1234 Aug 25 12:34 important_file.txt
```

Both files have the same inode number, indicating they are hard links to the same file.

Characteristics of Hard Links

Hard links have distinct features:

- They cannot link directories (to prevent circular references) and must reside within the same filesystem.
- Deleting the original file does not remove the data as long as one hard link exists; only the link count is decremented.
- Hard links share the inode, meaning any changes to one link will reflect in all linked files.

Practical Example

Consider a scenario to clearly observe the differences between symbolic and hard links:

- Create a file and write some content into it:

```
echo "Sample text for link demonstration" > /home/user/original_file.txt
```

- Create a symbolic link:

```
ln -s /home/user/original_file.txt /home/user/symlink_to_original.txt
```

- Create a hard link:

```
ln /home/user/original_file.txt /home/user/hardlink_to_original.txt
```

- Listing the directory:

```
-rw-r--r-- 2 user group 1234 Aug 25 12:34 original_file.txt
-rw-r--r-- 2 user group 1234 Aug 25 12:34 hardlink_to_original.txt
lrwxrwxrwx 1 user group   20 Aug 25 12:34 symlink_to_original.txt -> /home/user/original_file.txt
```

- Modify original_file.txt:

```
echo "Additional text" >> /home/user/original_file.txt
```

- Verify the content of each link:

```
/home/user/original_file.txt
/home/user/symlink_to_original.txt
/home/user/hardlink_to_original.txt
```

Each file will contain the "Sample text for link demonstration" followed by "Additional text," indicating the shared content.

Understanding the internals of symbolic and hard links can significantly enhance your file management strategies in Linux. These links facilitate efficient storage use and flexible access to files, making them indispensable tools for system administrators and developers.

6.9 Using Wildcards and Globbing

In Linux shell scripting, wildcards and globbing play a crucial role in specifying patterns for filenames and directories, enabling efficient file manipulation with minimal commands. Wildcards are special characters that represent one or more characters in filenames, while globbing is the process by which the shell expands these wildcard characters to match actual filenames. This section delves into the mechanics of wildcards and globbing, providing comprehensive examples to illustrate their practical applications.

The primary wildcard characters used in Linux are the asterisk *, question mark ?, and square brackets []. Each of these wildcards serves a distinct purpose:

- * (Asterisk): Represents zero or more characters in a filename.
- ? (Question mark): Represents a single character in a filename.
- [] (Square brackets): Represents any one of the characters enclosed within the brackets.

To solidify the conceptual understanding, consider the following practical examples demonstrating each of these wildcards.

Wildcard Examples:

1. * (Asterisk)

```
$ ls *txt
document.txt notes.txt report.txt summary.txt
```

   In this example, the *txt pattern matches all files ending with .txt. The shell expands the pattern to include all files that meet the criteria.

2. ? (Question mark)

```
$ ls file?.txt
file1.txt file2.txt file3.txt
```

   Here, the file?.txt pattern matches any file with a single character replacing the ?. This matches file1.txt, file2.txt, and file3.txt but not file10.txt.

3. [] (Square brackets)

```
$ ls file[123].txt
file1.txt file2.txt file3.txt
```

   The file[123].txt pattern matches any file with 1, 2, or 3 as the single character within the square brackets. This pattern does not match files like file4.txt.

Combining these wildcard characters allows for more complex and flexible pattern matching. Consider the following examples:

- Combining * and ?

```
$ ls *?.txt
notes1.txt summary2.txt document3.txt
```

  This pattern matches all files ending with .txt and having at least one character before .txt.

- Combining * and []

```
$ ls project[!1-3]*.txt
project4.txt projectABC.txt
```

The pattern project[!1-3]*.txt matches all files starting with project, followed by any character except 1, 2, or 3, and ending with .txt.

Advanced Globbing Patterns:

Beyond basic wildcards, the shell supports advanced globbing patterns such as brace expansion and extended globbing. Brace expansion involves the use of curly braces { } to generate multiple patterns from a single string:

```
$ ls {file1,file2,file3}.txt
file1.txt file2.txt file3.txt
```

This command lists file1.txt, file2.txt, and file3.txt, as the shell generates each pattern within the braces.

Extended globbing, which can be enabled using the shopt command, offers even more flexibility:

```
$ shopt -s extglob
$ ls +(file|document).txt
file.txt document.txt
```

In this case, the +(pattern) syntax matches one or more occurrences of the specified patterns. The shopt -s extglob command enables these advanced globbing features.

Practical Applications:

Wildcards and globbing have numerous practical applications, especially in scripting. Consider a script that deletes all temporary files in a directory:

```
#!/bin/bash
# Delete all temporary files
rm -v *~ *.bak
```

The script uses rm -v to remove files ending with ~ and .bak. The * and *.bak patterns ensure that all temporary and backup files are targeted.

In another example, imagine a scenario where you need to move all log files older than a certain date to an archive directory:

```
#!/bin/bash
# Move old log files to archive
find /var/log -name "*.log" -mtime +30 -exec mv {} /backup/old_logs/ \;
```

The script uses find with the -name option to match log files (*.log) and the -mtime +30 option to find files modified more than 30 days ago. The

-exec option executes the mv command for each matched file, moving it to the specified archive directory.

Wildcards and globbing provide a robust mechanism for pattern matching in Linux shell scripting. Understanding and utilizing these features enhances the efficiency and flexibility of file and directory management scripts.

6.10 Finding Files and Directories

The ability to locate specific files and directories within the Linux filesystem is an essential skill for proficient shell scripting and system administration. This requires familiarity with several tools and commands that enable efficient searching and filtering based on various criteria. The primary command used for this purpose is find, which provides a comprehensive solution for searching files and directories based on their attributes. This section explores the find command in depth, offering detailed syntax explanations and practical examples.

The basic syntax of the find command is as follows:

```
find [path] [expression]
```

Path Specification: The [path] argument specifies the starting point for the search. If omitted, find defaults to the current directory. Paths can be simple (e.g., "." for the current directory) or absolute (e.g., "/home/user/documents").

Expression: The [expression] parameter determines the criteria for matching files and directories. Expressions can include various tests based on name, type, modification time, size, permissions, and other attributes. Commonly used tests include:

- -name pattern: Matches files and directories according to the specified pattern.
- -type type: Filters by file type (e.g., f for regular files, d for directories).
- -mtime n: Matches files modified *n* days ago.
- -size n: Filters files by size, where *n* can be followed by a unit (e.g., c for bytes, k for kilobytes).
- -perm mode: Selects files with specific permissions.

- -user name: Filters files owned by the specified user.

Suppose you wish to find all files with the extension ".txt" in the current directory and its subdirectories. The following command accomplishes this:

```
find . -name "*.txt"
```

Using the -type option to filter only directories:

```
find /home/user -type d -name "project*"
```

To search for files that were modified in the last 7 days:

```
find /var/log -mtime -7
```

Combining Multiple Expressions: The find command supports combining multiple expressions using logical operators such as -and, -or, and -not. This allows for sophisticated and precise searches. For example, to find all ".log" files in "/tmp" that are larger than 1MB and were last modified more than 30 days ago:

```
find /tmp -name "*.log" -size +1M -mtime +30
```

To exclude certain directories from the search, the prune expression can be used. For example, to search for files in "/home/user" but exclude the "Downloads" directory:

```
find /home/user -path "/home/user/Downloads" -prune -o -name "*.conf" -print
```

Actions on Matched Files: The -exec option allows executing a command on each file that matches the search criteria. The command to be executed is terminated by a semicolon ( ) or a plus sign (+). When using the semicolon, each file is processed one at a time:

```
find /logs -name "*.log" -mtime +30 -exec rm {} \;
```

In this example, all ".log" files older than 30 days in the "/logs" directory are deleted. The {} placeholder represents the current file being processed.

Using the plus sign (+) groups the matched files and passes them as arguments to the given command:

```
find /images -name "*.jpg" -exec ls -lh {} +
```

This lists detailed information for all ".jpg" files in the "/images" directory and its subdirectories.

Finding by File Permissions: The -perm option helps in locating files with specific permissions. For instance, to find files with the permission set to 644:

```
find /usr/share -perm 644
```

To locate files with executable permissions for the owner, you can use:

```
find /usr/local/bin -perm /u=x
```

The /u=x specifies that the owner of the file has execute permissions.

Finding Files by User and Group: The -user and -group options filter files owned by a specific user and group, respectively. To find files owned by the user "alice":

```
find /home -user alice
```

Similarly, to find files belonging to the group "developers":

```
find /projects -group developers
```

Print Results: By default, find prints the path of each matched file or directory. The -print0 option can be used to handle files names with special characters or spaces, producing null-terminated strings suitable for processing with xargs:

```
find /media -type f -print0 | xargs -0 ls -lah
```

This generates a detailed listing for files in the "/media" directory.

Permissions	Links	Owner	Group	File Name
drwxr-xr-x	3	user	user	.
drwxr-xr-x	24	root	root	..
drwxr-xr-x	2	user	user	public
lrwxrwxrwx	1	user	user	symbolic_link -> public

Table 6.1: File Listing Example

This powerful and versatile command, when combined with its numerous options and expressions, provides an indispensable tool for effective and efficient file and directory management within the Linux environment.

6.11 Handling Special File Types

Special file types in Linux include symbolic links, hard links, device files, named pipes (FIFOs), and sockets. Understanding how to manage these file types is critical in comprehensive Linux file system management. This section delves into the creation, usage, and characteristics of these special file types.

Symbolic and Hard Links

Symbolic links, often referred to as symlinks or soft links, are references to another file or directory in the filesystem. Hard links are direct pointers to the inode of a file, implying that both the original file and the hard link access the same data blocks on disk.

To create a symbolic link:

```
ln -s target_link_name link_name
```

To create a hard link:

```
ln target_file link_name
```

Example of creating a symbolic link:

```
$ ln -s /home/user/original_file /home/user/link_to_original
```

Example of creating a hard link:

```
$ ln /home/user/original_file /home/user/hardlink_to_original
```

Device Files

Device files provide an interface to interact with hardware devices. These are generally found in the /dev directory. Two types of device files exist: character device files and block device files.

Character device files, denoted by c, allow for sequential data transfers. Examples include /dev/tty for terminals and /dev/zero or /dev/null.

Block device files, denoted by b, manage data in blocks. Examples include the entries for disks such as /dev/sda and /dev/sdb.

To create device files, use:

```
mknod device_name type major minor
```

For instance, to create a character device file:

```
$ sudo mknod /dev/mydevice c 89 1
```

Here, 89 and 1 represent the major and minor numbers, which uniquely identify device drivers and device instances respectively.

Named Pipes (FIFOs)

Named pipes enable inter-process communication (IPC). Unlike ordinary pipes, named pipes are persistent and exist as filesystem objects, allowing unrelated processes to communicate.

To create a named pipe:

```
$ mkfifo my_pipe
```

Writing to and reading from a named pipe:

```
$ echo "Hello, World!" > my_pipe
$ cat my_pipe
```

Sockets

Sockets facilitate IPC, primarily in network communication, but can also be used locally. They enable communication between processes running on the same or different hosts.

Creating a socket:

```
$ socat UNIX-LISTEN:/tmp/mysocket,fork EXEC:/bin/cat
```

This command sets up a Unix socket file /tmp/mysocket and binds it to the execution of cat.

Summary of Key Commands

```
$ ln -s target_link_name link_name    # Symbolic link
$ ln target_file link_name            # Hard link
$ sudo mknod /dev/mydevice c 89 1     # Character device file
$ mkfifo my_pipe                      # Named pipe
$ socat UNIX-LISTEN:/tmp/mysocket,fork EXEC:/bin/cat # Socket
```

Examining the properties of these special files often leverages the ls -l command to provide detailed information about file types and permissions.

```
$ ls -l
```

Output interpretation:

```
lrwxrwxrwx 1 user group   18 Mar  5 12:00 link_to_original -> /home/user/original_file
brw-rw---- 1 root disk 8,  0 Mar  5 12:00 /dev/sda
crw-rw-rw- 1 root tty  5,  0 Mar  5 12:00 /dev/tty
prw------- 1 user group    0 Mar  5 12:00 my_pipe
srw-rw-rw- 1 user group    0 Mar  5 12:00 /tmp/mysocket
```

The initial character in the listing output (l, b, c, p, s) identifies the file type.

Exercising precision in handling these file types and understanding their behavior within the Linux filesystem infrastructure is essential for advanced system administration and scripting purposes.

6.12 Practical Script Examples for File Management

Practical scripting is central to effective file and directory management in Linux. This section demonstrates various real-world examples of shell scripts that automate and streamline these tasks. Each script illustrates the application of commands covered in previous sections. These examples can be adapted to suit specific needs, enhancing both understanding and practical competence.

Example 1: Backup Script

The following script creates a backup of a specified directory. It leverages the tar command to archive and compress the directory contents.

```
#!/bin/bash

# Variables
SOURCE_DIR="$1"
BACKUP_DIR="$2"
TIMESTAMP=$(date +"%Y%m%d%H%M%S")
BACKUP_FILE="${BACKUP_DIR}/backup_${TIMESTAMP}.tar.gz"

# Check if source and backup directories are provided
if [ -z "$SOURCE_DIR" ] || [ -z "$BACKUP_DIR" ]; then
  echo "Usage: $0 <source_directory> <backup_directory>"
  exit 1
fi

# Create backup
tar -czf "$BACKUP_FILE" -C "$SOURCE_DIR" .

# Verify if the backup was successful
if [ $? -eq 0 ]; then
  echo "Backup of $SOURCE_DIR completed successfully to $BACKUP_FILE"
else
  echo "Backup of $SOURCE_DIR failed"
fi
```

To execute this script:

```
$ chmod +x backup.sh
$ ./backup.sh /path/to/source /path/to/backup
```

Example 2: Log File Rotation

This script manages log file rotation, which is crucial for maintaining system performance and storage management. It renames the current log file by appending a timestamp and then creates a new, empty log file.

```
#!/bin/bash

# Variables
LOG_FILE="/var/log/myapp.log"
TIMESTAMP=$(date +"%Y%m%d%H%M%S")

# Rotate log file
mv "$LOG_FILE" "${LOG_FILE}_${TIMESTAMP}"
touch "$LOG_FILE"

# Set appropriate permissions
chmod 644 "$LOG_FILE"

echo "Log file rotation completed. Old log saved as ${LOG_FILE}_${TIMESTAMP}"
```

To execute this script:

```
$ chmod +x rotate_log.sh
$ ./rotate_log.sh
```

Example 3: Directory Cleanup

This script cleans up a specific directory by deleting files older than a specified number of days. It uses the find command to locate old files and remove them securely.

```
#!/bin/bash

# Variables
TARGET_DIR="$1"
DAYS_OLD="$2"

# Check if target directory and days old are provided
if [ -z "$TARGET_DIR" ] || [ -z "$DAYS_OLD" ]; then
  echo "Usage: $0 <target_directory> <days_old>"
  exit 1
fi

# Find and delete old files
find "$TARGET_DIR" -type f -mtime +"$DAYS_OLD" -exec rm {} \;

echo "Files older than $DAYS_OLD days in $TARGET_DIR have been deleted."
```

To execute this script:

```
$ chmod +x cleanup.sh
$ ./cleanup.sh /path/to/directory 30
```

Example 4: Directory Synchronization

This script synchronizes the contents of two directories, useful for mirroring directories on different servers. It uses the rsync command for efficient file transfer and synchronization.

```
#!/bin/bash

# Variables
SOURCE_DIR="$1"
DEST_DIR="$2"

# Check if source and destination directories are provided
if [ -z "$SOURCE_DIR" ] || [ -z "$DEST_DIR" ]; then
  echo "Usage: $0 <source_directory> <destination_directory>"
  exit 1
fi

# Synchronize directories
rsync -av --delete "$SOURCE_DIR/" "$DEST_DIR/"

# Verify if the synchronization was successful
if [ $? -eq 0 ]; then
  echo "Synchronization from $SOURCE_DIR to $DEST_DIR completed successfully"
else
  echo "Synchronization from $SOURCE_DIR to $DEST_DIR failed"
fi
```

To execute this script:

```
$ chmod +x sync.sh
$ ./sync.sh /path/to/source /path/to/destination
```

Each of these scripts improves efficiency and accuracy in file and directory management. They are designed to handle various scenarios, from routine backups to meticulous log file rotation, ensuring system administrators and users maintain a well-organized and optimized file system. By executing these examples and understanding their components, one develops key scripting skills applicable across diverse Linux environments.

Chapter 7

Processing Text Using Filters and Regular Expressions

This chapter provides a comprehensive guide to processing text in Linux using various filters and regular expressions. It explains the use of commands like 'cat', 'grep', 'cut', 'sort', 'uniq', 'tr', and 'sed' for text display, searching, extraction, sorting, removing duplicates, translating characters, and stream editing. The chapter also introduces regular expressions, covering basic syntax and advanced usage with tools like 'grep' and 'sed'. Techniques for advanced text processing using 'awk' are included, along with practical examples to demonstrate their application.

7.1 Introduction to Text Processing

Text processing is an essential aspect of working with data in the Linux environment. The ability to manipulate and transform text data is fundamental for a vast array of tasks, ranging from simple file manipulation to complex data analysis pipelines. This section introduces the fundamental concepts and commands used in text processing, setting the stage for deeper exploration in subsequent sections.

In the Linux ecosystem, text processing typically involves using a series of commands and utilities designed to read, manipulate, and output text. These tools are often stringed together in pipelines to perform complex operations efficiently. Key commands that form the backbone of text processing include cat, grep, cut, sort, uniq, tr, sed, and awk. Each of these commands has unique functionalities and can be combined to perform robust text manipulations.

The cat command is often one of the first tools introduced to newcomers. It stands for "concatenate" and is used to display the content of files, combine multiple files into one, or create new files. Its simplicity belies its power, as it forms the foundation for more advanced pipelines.

The grep command is indispensable for searching within text files. It uses regular expressions to locate patterns, making it a powerful tool for finding specific strings within large datasets. The basic syntax is intuitive, yet it supports a wide array of options that enhance its functionality, including recursive searching and color highlighting of matches.

The cut command is used to extract specific sections from each line of a file, such as columns of a spreadsheet stored in a text file. This command can operate on both character and delimiter-based fields, providing flexibility in handling structured text data.

Sorting is a common task in text processing, and the sort command is tailored for this purpose. It sorts lines of text alphabetically or numerically, with options for handling case sensitivity, removing duplicates, and sorting based on specific fields within the lines.

The uniq command works hand-in-hand with sort. After sorting data, uniq can be used to remove duplicate lines or count occurrences of repeated lines, which is particularly useful for data summarization.

Character translation and deletion are tasks suited for the tr command. It replaces or deletes characters in text, which is essential for cleaning and preparing data for further analysis. For example, removing whitespace or converting text to uppercase can be achieved efficiently with tr.

Stream editing with the sed command brings a whole new level of text processing capabilities. sed can perform complex modifications on text by using scripts to automate edits, such as substitution, insertion, and deletion of text. This makes it a powerful tool for batch processing of files.

The awk command stands apart due to its programming language design. It is used for pattern scanning and processing, allowing for the execution of complex data manipulations based on specified rules. Its versatility and power make it ideal for tasks ranging from simple field extraction to elaborate data reporting.

Each of these commands will be explored in detail in subsequent sections, with practical examples provided to demonstrate their usage in real-world scenarios. By mastering these tools, users can significantly enhance their productivity and efficiency in handling text data on the Linux command line.

Understanding regular expressions is pivotal, as they are integral to the functionality of many text processing commands. Regular expressions provide a concise and flexible means to search and manipulate text based on patterns, making them a cornerstone of text processing mastery.

In text processing, the combination of these tools enables the execution of complex tasks that go beyond the capabilities of individual commands. Pipelines, where the output of one command serves as the input for the next, exemplify the power of text processing on Linux. This modular approach not only simplifies complex tasks but also enhances script readability and maintainability.

This foundational knowledge equips readers to delve deeper into each command's specifics, thereby expanding their text processing toolkit. Through systematic exploration and practice, users will be able to construct efficient and sophisticated text processing solutions tailored to their specific needs.

7.2 Using cat for Text Display

The cat command in Linux stands for "concatenate" and is one of the most frequently used commands for viewing the contents of files. It can display text files, join them together, and redirect output into new files. The fundamental operation of cat is to read files sequentially, writing them to the standard output. Consequently, its simplicity and versatility make cat an indispensable tool in shell scripting and text processing.

To display the contents of a file using cat, you can invoke the command followed by the filename. For example, to display the content of file.txt, the following command is used:

```
cat file.txt
```

If the file file.txt contains the following lines:

```
Hello World
This is a text file.
```

The output of the above command will be:

```
Hello World
This is a text file.
```

- **Concatenating Multiple Files:** The cat command can concatenate multiple files into a single output. If you have two files, file1.txt and file2.txt, the command:

```
cat file1.txt file2.txt
```

- will output the contents of file1.txt followed by file2.txt. This can be redirected to a new file using the > operator. For instance:

```
cat file1.txt file2.txt > combined.txt
```

Now, combined.txt will contain the contents of both file1.txt and file2.txt.

- **Appending to Files:** To append the contents of one file to another, you can use the » operator. For example:

```
cat file2.txt >> file1.txt
```

This appends the content of file2.txt to file1.txt.

- **Displaying Line Numbers:** The -n option with cat displays line numbers in the output. To show line numbers along with the content of a file, use:

```
cat -n file.txt
```

For a file file.txt containing:

```
Hello World
This is a text file.
```

The output will be:

```
1 Hello World
2 This is a text file.
```

- **Displaying Non-Printing Characters:** The -v option can be used to display non-printing characters (excluding tabs and the end of line character). For example, if file.txt contains a tab or other special characters, they will be represented in a visible format.

- **Squeezing Blank Lines:** The -s option can be employed to squeeze multiple consecutive blank lines into a single blank line in the output. Consider file.txt with multiple blank lines:

```
Hello World


This is a text file.


Another line.
```

Running:

```
cat -s file.txt
```

will produce:

```
Hello World

This is a text file.

Another line.
```

- **Combining Options:** You can combine multiple options in a single cat command. For instance:

```
cat -ns file.txt
```

will display file.txt with line numbers and suppressed consecutive blank lines.

- **Use in Shell Scripting:** In shell scripting, cat is often used in conjunction with other commands via pipes. For example, to search for a string within a file and display the number of matches with line numbers:

```
cat file.txt | grep -n "search_string"
```

This pipes the output of cat file.txt to grep, which then searches for search_string and displays matched lines with their numbers.

- **Example Script:** Consider a simple shell script that concatenates the contents of all .txt files in the current directory and saves them into a combined.txt file:

```
#!/bin/bash
cat *.txt > combined.txt
```

This script uses globbing (*.txt) to match all .txt files in the directory and concatenates their contents into combined.txt.

The cat command is a fundamental tool in text processing and plays a crucial role in the Unix philosophy of using simple, single-purpose tools to perform complex tasks by combining them. By understanding its various options and how they integrate with other tools, users can leverage cat for efficient and effective text manipulation in a variety of contexts.

7.3 Using grep for Text Searching

The grep command, an acronym for "Global Regular Expression Print," is a powerful utility that allows users to search through text or search the content of files and directories for patterns specified through regular expressions. It is an indispensable tool in the arsenal of a Linux user, particularly for those engaged in text processing, scripting, and system administration.

The basic syntax of grep is as follows:

```
grep [OPTIONS] PATTERN [FILE...]
```

Where:

- OPTIONS are additional parameters that modify the behavior of grep.
- PATTERN is the regular expression pattern to search for.
- FILE... are the files to be searched (if no files are specified, grep searches standard input).

A fundamental example of using grep involves searching a single pattern within a file. Assume we have a text file named sample.txt:

```
Hello World
This is a sample file
Containing multiple lines
And several words
Including Hello again
```

Searching for the term "Hello" in sample.txt can be done as follows:

```
grep "Hello" sample.txt
```

The output would be:

```
Hello World
Including Hello again
```

Commonly Used Options

- -i: Ignore case distinctions in patterns and inputs.

  ```
  grep -i "hello" sample.txt
  ```

  This would match both "Hello" and "hello".

- -v: Invert the sense of matching, to select non-matching lines.

  ```
  grep -v "Hello" sample.txt
  ```

  This option outputs lines that do not contain the pattern "Hello".

- -c: Count the number of matches instead of printing the matching lines.

  ```
  grep -c "Hello" sample.txt
  ```

  This would output:

  ```
  2
  ```

- -n: Prefix each line of output with the line number within its input file.

  ```
  grep -n "Hello" sample.txt
  ```

  This outputs:

  ```
  1:Hello World
  5:Including Hello again
  ```

Searching Multiple Files

grep can search across multiple files, outputting the filename where the match is found. Assume we have another file named example.txt:

```
Example text
Another line with Hello
And more text
```

Executing:

```
grep "Hello" sample.txt example.txt
```

Outputs:

```
sample.txt:Hello World
sample.txt:Including Hello again
example.txt:Another line with Hello
```

-l: List filenames with matching lines (suppresses normal output).

```
grep -l "Hello" sample.txt example.txt
```

This would list:

```
sample.txt
example.txt
```

Using Regular Expressions with grep

grep's true power lies in its ability to utilize regular expressions for pattern matching. By default, grep uses Basic Regular Expressions (BRE). If Extended Regular Expressions (ERE) are required, the -E (or egrep) option should be used.

Wildcard and Anchors: Consider . for matching any single character and ^ and $ for matching the start and end of a line, respectively.

```
grep "^Hello" sample.txt
```

Matches lines starting with "Hello".

```
grep "again$" sample.txt
```

Matches lines ending with "again".

Character Classes and Ranges: Using [] to denote a character class.

```
grep "[Hh]ello" sample.txt
```

Matches "Hello" and "hello".

Repetition Operators: * matches zero or more occurrences of the preceding character.

```
grep "He*llo" sample.txt
```

Matches "Hllo", "Hello", "Heello", etc.

For more complex pattern matching:

```
grep -E "(Hello|Hi)" sample.txt
```

Matches either "Hello" or "Hi".

Practical Usage and Advanced Options

-R or -r: Recursively search directories.

```
grep -r "Hello" /path/to/directory
```

Searches for "Hello" in all files within the specified directory and its subdirectories.

-A, -B, -C: Display lines of context around the matches. -A specifies the number of lines to show after a match, -B before a match, and -C for both.

```
grep -A 2 "Hello" sample.txt
```

Displays two lines after each match.

Performance Considerations

For extensive searches, employing the –binary-files=text option can help when working with files that might be mistakenly identified as binary:

```
grep --binary-files=text "search_term" file
```

Encapsulating text processing tasks with grep optimizes data retrieval for scripts and enhances system diagnostics by filtering relevant log entries.

Combining grep with other Linux commands in pipelines further elevates its utility:

```
cat sample.txt | grep "pattern" | sort | uniq
```

This command sequence first concatenates and displays the text, filters lines matching the pattern, sorts them, and removes duplicate entries.

7.4 Using cut to Extract Portions of Text

The cut command in Unix/Linux is used for cutting out sections from each line of files and writing the result to standard output. It is a powerful and versatile tool, particularly useful for extracting specific columns or fields from text. It works by dividing the input based on defined delimiters and then selecting specified segments (fields or characters).

The syntax for the cut command is as follows:

```
cut OPTION... [FILE]...
```

Where OPTION denotes various flags that determine how cut operates.

Important Options and Their Usage:

- -b, –bytes=LIST Select only the listed bytes from each line. For instance, cut -b 1-3,5 extracts bytes 1, 2, 3, and 5.
- -c, –characters=LIST Select only the listed characters. For example, cut -c 1-4 selects characters one through four.
- -d, –delimiter=DELIM Use the specified delimiter instead of the default TAB character. Commonly used when dealing with fields separated by characters like commas or colons.
- -f, –fields=LIST Select only the listed fields; fields are separated by the designated delimiter. For example, cut -d':' -f1,3 selects the first and third fields in a colon-separated file.
- –complement Complement the selection, which picks everything except the identified portions.
- –output-delimiter=STRING Use STRING as the output delimiter. The default is to use the input delimiter.

Example Usage:

1. Extracting specific columns from a CSV file:

```
cut -d',' -f2,4 students.csv
```

If students.csv contains:

ID,Name,Grade,Score
001,John Doe,B,85
002,Jane Smith,A,90
003,Jim Brown,C,70

The command above extracts the Name and Score columns:

```
Name,Score
John Doe,85
Jane Smith,90
Jim Brown,70
```

Usage with Byte and Character Options:

2. Extracting characters from fixed-width data:

```
echo "abcdefghij" | cut -c 1-4,8-
```

Output:

```
abcdhij
```

This command selects characters 1 through 4 and then from character 8 to the end.

Handling Delimiters:

3. Changing the output delimiter:

```
cut -d':' -f1,3 --output-delimiter=',' /etc/passwd
```

For a line in /etc/passwd:

```
root:x:0:0:root:/root:/bin/bash
```

The output would be:

```
root,0
```

cut is a fundamental tool in text processing, enabling efficient extraction of data segments for further processing or analysis. The alignment of fields using delimiters or extracting specific characters makes it adaptable to various data formats encountered in log files, CSV data, and configuration files.

7.5 Using sort for Text Sorting

The sort command in Linux is a powerful utility used for arranging the lines of text files in a particular order. The default behavior of sort is to arrange the lines in ascending order based on the standard ASCII collating sequence. This section delves into the various options and functionalities provided by sort, and includes practical examples to elucidate its usage.

sort can handle a variety of data sorting requirements such as numerical sorting, reverse sorting, sorting by specific fields, and handling non-unique entries efficiently. Below are the most commonly used options with sort:

- -n: Sort numerically.
- -r: Sort in reverse order.
- -k: Sort based on a specific field (or column).
- -c: Check if a file is sorted.
- -u: Suppress duplicate lines.
- -t: Specify a field delimiter.

To elucidate the conceptual and practical significance of these options, consider the following examples.

Example 1: Basic Text Sorting

Assume a text file named names.txt with the following contents:

```
Charlie
Alice
Bob
David
```

Executing the basic sort command on this file can be done as follows:

```
sort names.txt
```

The output will be:

```
Alice
Bob
Charlie
David
```

Example 2: Numerical Sorting

Consider a file named numbers.txt that contains a list of numbers:

```
10
3
55
23
4
```

Using the -n option, we can sort the numbers in ascending numerical order:

```
sort -n numbers.txt
```

The output will appear as follows:

```
3
4
10
23
55
```

Example 3: Reverse Order Sorting

Applying the -r option, one can sort the contents in reverse order. For the file names.txt, the command and resulting output will be:

```
sort -r names.txt
```

```
David
Charlie
Bob
Alice
```

Example 4: Sorting by a Specific Field

Suppose we have a file students.txt with student names and their scores:

```
Alice 85
Bob 92
Charlie 87
David 78
```

To sort this file by the scores (second field), the -k option is used:

```
sort -k 2 -n students.txt
```

The output will be:

```
David 78
Alice 85
Charlie 87
Bob 92
```

Example 5: Using a Field Delimiter

Taking another similar file employees.txt where fields are separated by colons:

```
Alice:85
Bob:92
Charlie:87
David:78
```

To sort based on the second field using colon as the delimiter:

```
sort -t ':' -k 2 -n employees.txt
```

Resulting output:

```
David:78
Alice:85
Charlie:87
Bob:92
```

Example 6: Checking if a File is Sorted

To verify whether a file is already sorted, use the -c option. For example:

```
sort -c names.txt
```

If the file is sorted, no output is produced; otherwise, it outputs information about the disorder.

Example 7: Suppressing Duplicate Lines

Suppose fruits.txt contains:

```
Apple
Orange
Banana
Apple
Grape
Banana
```

Using the -u option to produce a sorted list with duplicates removed:

```
sort -u fruits.txt
```

The output will be:

```
Apple
Banana
Grape
Orange
```

Integrating these commands efficiently into your workflows can significantly streamline text processing tasks. By mastering sort and its numerous options, you can handle diverse data sorting requirements with precision and ease.

7.6 Using uniq for Removing Duplicates

The uniq command in Linux is used to filter out or detect duplicate lines in a text file. This command is especially useful when working with sorted data since uniq assumes that repeated lines are adjacent to each other. Therefore, to effectively utilize uniq, the input data should typically be pre-sorted using the sort command.

The basic syntax for using uniq is as follows:

```
uniq [OPTIONS] [INPUT [OUTPUT]]
```

To better understand uniq, consider a sample text file named sample.txt with the following content:

```
apple
banana
apple
orange
banana
apple
apple
orange
```

To remove duplicate lines and display the unique lines, the file must first be sorted. This can be achieved using a pipeline with the sort command:

```
sort sample.txt | uniq
```

The output of the above command will be:

```
apple
banana
orange
```

The uniq command provides several useful options to control its behavior. Some of the commonly used options are detailed below:

- -c, –count Precedes each output line with the number of times it occurs in the input.
- -d, –repeated Only prints lines that are repeated in the input.
- -u, –unique Only prints lines that are not repeated in the input.
- -i, –ignore-case Ignores differences in case when comparing lines.
- -f N, –skip-fields=N Ignores the first N fields (fields are sequences of non-space non-tab characters separated by spaces or tabs).
- -s N, –skip-chars=N Ignores the first N characters of each line.
- –help Displays help information.

To illustrate these options, consider the sorted version of sample.txt:

```
apple
apple
apple
apple
banana
banana
orange
orange
```

Using the -c option:

```
sort sample.txt | uniq -c
```

The output will be:

```
4 apple
2 banana
2 orange
```

This output indicates the number of occurrences of each line. The -d option can be used to display only the repeated lines:

```
sort sample.txt | uniq -d
```

The output will be:

```
apple
banana
orange
```

To display only the unique lines that are not repeated, the -u option is used:

```
sort sample.txt | uniq -u
```

Since every line in sample.txt is repeated, the output will be empty. However, if the input file was:

```
apple
banana
kiwi
orange
```

Then using -u after sorting would display:

```
kiwi
```

In some cases, it may be necessary to ignore case differences when detecting duplicates. The -i option provides this functionality. For instance:

```
Apple
apple
Banana
banana
```

Using the following command:

```
sort sample.txt | uniq -i
```

will output:

```
Apple
Banana
```

To ignore the first few fields or characters of each line, the -f and -s options respectively can be used. Consider the file fields.txt with the following contents:

```
1 apple
2 apple
2 banana
1 orange
```

To ignore the first field when detecting duplicates:

```
sort fields.txt | uniq -f 1
```

The output will be:

```
1 apple
2 banana
1 orange
```

Alternatively, to ignore the first two characters:

```
sort fields.txt | uniq -s 2
```

The output will be:

```
1 apple
2 banana
1 orange
```

Utilizing these options with uniq allows for flexible and powerful text processing workflows, particularly in combination with sorting and other text manipulation commands. Mastering uniq and its various options expands the capabilities of text processing in complex scripts and data analysis tasks.

7.7 Using tr for Translating Characters

The tr command in Linux is a powerful utility used for translating or deleting characters from standard input and writing the results to standard output. Unlike some of the other commands discussed earlier which often operate on lines, tr operates on individual characters, making it particularly useful for character-level text processing.

The fundamental syntax for tr is as follows:

```
tr [options] SET1 [SET2]
```

Here, SET1 represents the characters to be transformed, while SET2 represents the characters to which SET1 should be mapped. If SET2 is omitted, tr removes the characters in SET1.

Consider an example to better understand the basic usage of tr:

```
echo "hello world" | tr 'a-z' 'A-Z'
```

This command would transform the input string "hello world" by mapping all lowercase letters to their corresponding uppercase letters:

```
HELLO WORLD
```

One of the most common use-cases for tr is case conversion as demonstrated above. The specification of ranges (a-z and A-Z) allows for concise representation of the sets of characters involved. It is crucial to ensure that SET1 and SET2 have the same length when specifying ranges or individual characters; otherwise, tr will not perform the translation.

- **Deleting Characters**

The -d option allows tr to delete characters in SET1 from the input. For instance, to remove digits from the input text:

```
echo "h3ll0 w0rld" | tr -d '0-9'
```

This produces:

```
hll wrld
```

- **Squeezing Repeated Characters**

Another useful option is -s, known as –squeeze-repeats. This collapses sequences of repeated characters into a single character. For example, converting multiple spaces to a single space:

```
echo "hello world" | tr -s ' '
```

The output will be:

```
hello world
```

- **Complementing Sets**

The -c option complements SET1, essentially meaning that it will operate on all characters except those specified in SET1. For example, to keep only alphabetic characters and delete all other characters:

```
echo "hello123 world!" | tr -cd 'a-zA-Z'
```

This results in:

```
helloworld
```

- **Mappings and Equivalence Classes**

A more advanced feature of tr is the use of character classes or equivalence classes. For instance, the [:upper:] and [:lower:] classes can be used to switch between uppercase and lowercase:

```
echo "Hello World" | tr '[:upper:]' '[:lower:]'
```

This command converts all uppercase letters to lowercase:

```
hello world
```

Equivalence classes, represented by [=c=], equate characters that are deemed equivalent by the current locale. For example, the Nordic languages have several characters that are considered equivalent in sorting if specific collating sequences are used.

- **Using tr with Shell Scripts**

In practice, tr is often combined with other commands in shell scripts to perform complex text transformations. One common scenario is reading text files, processing them line by line, and applying character translations. Consider the following simple script:

```
#!/bin/bash
# Script to convert spaces to underscores in filenames
for file in *
do
    newfile=$(echo $file | tr ' ' '_')
    mv "$file" "$newfile"
done
```

This script iterates over all files in the current directory, converts spaces in filenames to underscores, and renames the files accordingly.

Overall, the tr command provides a versatile toolkit for character-level operations in text processing. By mastering its options and combinations, one can handle a wide array of text transformation tasks efficiently.

7.8 Using sed for Stream Editing

The sed command, short for *stream editor*, is a powerful tool used for parsing and transforming text in a data stream or a file. It interprets a script and applies specified transformations to the input data, allowing automation of repetitive editing tasks.

The basic syntax of sed is as follows:

```
sed [options] 'script' [input-file]
```

Where *[options]* are command-line options, *'script'* is the sequence of editing commands, and *[input-file]* is the file to be processed. If no input file is specified, sed reads from the standard input (stdin).

A typical sed script comprises a series of commands that specify text operations. Each command in sed typically consists of an optional address or address range followed by a command and its arguments. The following are some common editing commands:

- s/pattern/replacement/ - Substitutes occurrences of the *pattern* with *replacement*.
- d - Deletes lines that match a specified condition.
- p - Prints lines that match a specified condition.
- a text - Appends *text* after a line.
- i text - Inserts *text* before a line.
- c text - Changes the lines specified by an address to *text*.

Basic Usage Examples

1. **Substitution**
To replace all occurrences of the word 'apple' with 'orange' in a file:

```
sed 's/apple/orange/g' input.txt
```

The s command performs substitution. The g at the end signifies a global replacement on each line.

2. **Deletion**
To delete all lines containing the word 'banana':

```
sed '/banana/d' input.txt
```

The d command deletes those lines where the regular expression /banana/ matches.

3. **Printing**
To print only lines that contain the word 'cherry':

```
sed -n '/cherry/p' input.txt
```

Here, the -n option suppresses automatic printing of pattern space, and the p command prints only the matching lines.

4. **Appending Text**
To append the line 'END' after each line containing 'date':

```
sed '/date/a END' input.txt
```

5. **Inserting Text**
To insert the line 'START' before each line containing 'fig':

```
sed '/fig/i START' input.txt
```

6. **Changing Lines**
To change lines matching 'grape' to 'FRUIT':

```
sed '/grape/c FRUIT' input.txt
```

Advanced Usage Examples

1. **Multiple Commands**
Using the -e option allows the execution of multiple commands. For instance, to replace 'apple' with 'orange' and delete lines containing 'banana':

```
sed -e 's/apple/orange/g' -e '/banana/d' input.txt
```

2. **Using a Script File**
If the number of commands becomes large, it is more manageable to store them in a script file, say commands.sed, and execute them as follows:

```
sed -f commands.sed input.txt
```

3. **Conditional Processing**

Nested if-else conditions are not straightforward in sed, but they can be achieved with labels and branching. Consider the following example that changes 'yes' to 'no' if 'maybe' precedes it:

```
sed '/maybe/{
  :loop
  n
  /yes/s//no/
  p
  /yes/!b loop
}' input.txt
```

Here, :loop is a label, n reads the next line, p prints the line, and b loop branches back to the loop label if the condition is not met.

4. **Transforming Data Streams**
To convert a list of names from 'first last' to 'last, first':

```
sed 's/^\(.*\) \(.*\)$/\2, \1/' input.txt
```

This uses back-references ... to capture parts of the matching text and rearrange them.

The sed utility, with its extensive command set and scripting capabilities, is indispensable for stream editing and automating text processing tasks in Linux. Its syntax, though compact, can be intricate, demanding precision and practice to master effectively.

7.9 Introduction to Regular Expressions

Regular expressions, often abbreviated as regex or regexp, are powerful tools used for pattern matching within strings. In the context of Linux shell scripting, regular expressions enable users to search, edit, or manipulate text and data in an efficient way. They form the backbone of many text processing utilities like grep, sed, and awk that are pivotal in Linux environments.

Regular expressions can be employed to perform a variety of tasks from the simplest search operations to complex text manipulations. They define search patterns based on character sequences. These patterns, when matched against text, allow for identifying, replacing, or extracting substrings that conform to specified criteria.

Basic Components of Regular Expressions:
Regular expressions are constructed using a combination of literal characters and special characters, also known as metacharacters. The primary components include:

- **Literal Characters:** Literal characters match the exact characters in a string. For instance, the regex 'abc' would match occurrences of the substring 'abc' in the target text.

- **Metacharacters:** Metacharacters have special meanings and can be used to build complex patterns. The key metacharacters include:
  - . (dot): Matches any single character except a newline.
  - * (asterisk): Matches zero or more occurrences of the preceding element.
  - + (plus): Matches one or more occurrences of the preceding element.
  - ? (question mark): Matches zero or one occurrences of the preceding element.
  - ^ (caret): Matches the beginning of a line.
  - $ (dollar sign): Matches the end of a line.
  - [] (brackets): Defines a character class. Matches any one of the characters within the brackets.
  - \ (backslash): Escapes a metacharacter, providing it with no special meaning.
  - {} (curly braces): Specifies an exact number of occurrences or a range of occurrences for the preceding element.
  - | (pipe): Acts as a logical OR operator between multiple patterns.
  - () (parentheses): Groups multiple tokens together and remembers the matched text, often used for capturing groups.

Consider the following example to illustrate immediate application:

```
# Example of basic metacharacter usage
echo "The rain in Spain" | grep -E 'S.*n'
```

The pattern 'S.*n' employs:

- S which matches the character 'S'.
- .* which matches any number of any characters.
- n which matches the character 'n'.

Thus, it will match the substring 'Spain'.

Greedy and Non-Greedy Matching:
Regex is inherently greedy, meaning it tries to match as much text as possible. To illustrate, consider the string 'abc 123 def'. The greedy pattern '.*' will match the entire string. To change to non-greedy (or minimal) matching, the modifier ? is used following the quantifier like so: '.*?'.

```
# Greedy vs Non-Greedy Matching
echo "abababab" | grep -o 'a.*b' # Output: abababab
echo "abababab" | grep -o 'a.*?b' # Output: ab, ab, ab
```

```
# Output of the commands:
# First grep command: abababab
# Second grep command: ab, ab, ab
```

The output of the first grep command is 'abababab', matching the entire string. The second command outputs 'ab' three times, as it matches the shortest possible text (non-greedy).

Character Classes and Ranges:
Character classes allow for specifying a set of characters to match. [abc] matches any one of 'a', 'b', or 'c'. Ranges within character classes simplify patterns: [a-z] matches any lowercase letter.

```
# Character classes usage
echo "hello123" | grep -E '[a-z]'
echo "hello123" | grep -E '[0-9]'
```

The first command matches any lowercase letters in "hello123", while the second matches any digits.

Negation in Character Classes:
Placing a caret ^ at the beginning of a character class negates it, matching any character not listed:

```
# Negated character class usage
echo "hello123" | grep -E '[^a-z]'
```

This command matches any characters in "hello123" that are not lowercase letters.

Anchors:
Anchors like ^ and $ are vital for enforcing position-specific matches. ^ ensures the pattern starts at the beginning of the line, while $ ensures it ends at the end of the line.

```
# Using anchors
echo "start middle end" | grep -E '^start'
echo "start middle end" | grep -E 'end$'
```

In these examples, the first command matches lines starting with "start", and the second matches lines ending with "end".

The structured and thoughtful use of regular expressions can greatly simplify text processing tasks. Understanding and mastering their components and behavior sets a solid foundation for efficiently managing textual data in Linux.

7.10 Basic Regular Expression Syntax

Regular expressions, often abbreviated as regex or regexp, are sequences of characters that define a search pattern. They are used for string matching within texts, which is fundamental for text processing tasks. Here, we cover the essential components and symbols of basic regular expression syntax to provide a foundation for their application in tools like grep and sed.

Literal Characters

Literal characters are the simplest form of regular expressions. They match themselves directly. For instance, the pattern abc will match the string "abc" in the text.

Metacharacters

Metacharacters have special meanings. The most commonly used metacharacters are:

- . (dot): Matches any single character except a newline.
- * (asterisk): Matches zero or more occurrences of the preceding element.
- + (plus): Matches one or more occurrences of the preceding element.
- ? (question mark): Makes the preceding element optional, matching zero or one occurrence.
- ^ (caret): Anchors the match at the beginning of a line.
- $ (dollar): Anchors the match at the end of a line.
- | (pipe): Acts as a logical OR between patterns.

- \ (backslash): Escapes the following character, allowing it to be treated as a literal instead of a special character.
- [] (square brackets): Denote a character class, matching any one character within the brackets.
- () (parentheses): Group patterns and capture submatches for back-referencing.

Character Classes

Character classes allow the matching of any one character from a set. Common usages include:

- [abc]: Matches any one of the characters 'a', 'b', or 'c'.
- [a-z]: Matches any character from 'a' to 'z'.
- [^a-z]: Matches any character except those in the range 'a' to 'z'.

Predefined character classes are shortcuts for common sets of characters:

- \d: Matches any digit, equivalent to [0-9].
- \D: Matches any non-digit.
- \w: Matches any word character (alphanumeric plus underscore), equivalent to [a-zA-Z0-9_].
- \W: Matches any non-word character.
- \s: Matches any whitespace character (spaces, tabs, newlines).
- \S: Matches any non-whitespace character.

Repetition

Repetition allows specifying the exact number of occurrences of a character or group:

- a{3}: Matches exactly three 'a' characters.
- a{3,5}: Matches between three and five 'a' characters.
- a{3,}: Matches three or more 'a' characters.

Anchors

Anchors are used to ensure patterns match at specific positions in the text:

- ^pattern: Matches if the pattern occurs at the beginning of a line.
- pattern$: Matches if the pattern occurs at the end of a line.
- \b: Matches a word boundary.
- \B: Matches a position that is not a word boundary.

Groups and Back-references

Parentheses are used for grouping and capturing purposes, which is useful for back-referencing:

- (abc): Matches the exact sequence "abc" and captures it for back-referencing.
- a(bc)d: Matches "abcd" and "bc" can be referenced for further processing.

A back-reference allows referring to the previously matched group:

- \1: Refers to the first captured group.
- \2: Refers to the second captured group, and so on.

Example Usage

Consider the following example to illustrate the use of basic regular expression syntax:

```
$ echo "abc123xyz" | grep 'abc[0-9]{3}xyz'
```

This command uses grep to search for the pattern abc[0-9]{3}xyz within the string abc123xyz. The pattern indicates:

- abc: Matches the literal sequence "abc".
- [0-9]{3}: Matches exactly three digits.
- xyz: Matches the literal sequence "xyz".

The output is:

```
abc123xyz
```

This command demonstrates the fundamental application of concatenation, character classes, and repetition in basic regular expression syntax.

By mastering these basic building blocks of regular expressions, users can develop complex patterns to match, search, and manipulate text effectively within the Linux environment.

7.11 Using Regular Expressions with grep

The grep command is one of the most powerful and versatile tools available in Unix-like operating systems. It allows for searching through text using patterns, often referred to as regular expressions (regex). By understanding how to integrate regular expressions with grep, users can perform sophisticated text searches that go beyond simple substring matching.

Regular expressions are patterns that describe sets of strings. There are several key elements and operators that can be used to create complex regex patterns, such as character classes, quantifiers, anchors, and grouping.

Basic Usage

The general syntax for using grep with regular expressions is:

```
grep [options] pattern [file...]
```

For example, to search for the word "Linux" in a file called example.txt, you would use:

```
grep "Linux" example.txt
```

Special Characters and Escape Sequences

Regular expressions make extensive use of special characters. These characters must often be "escaped" (preceded by a backslash) to be interpreted as literal characters rather than special operators. Some of these characters include: ., *, +, ?, [,], ^, $, (,).

For instance, to find lines containing the period character '.' in a file, you need to escape the period:

```
grep "\." example.txt
```

Character Classes

Character classes allow you to define a set of characters that you want to match. The most common character class syntax uses square brackets. For example:

```
grep "[aeiou]" example.txt
```

This matches any line containing a vowel. Other important character class constructs include:

- [0-9]: Matches any digit.
- [A-Z]: Matches any uppercase letter.
- [^...]: Matches any character not in the set.

Quantifiers

Quantifiers specify the number of times a character or group can occur. These include:

- *: Matches 0 or more occurrences of the preceding element.
- +: Matches 1 or more occurrences of the preceding element.
- ?: Matches 0 or 1 occurrence of the preceding element.
- {n}: Matches exactly n occurrences.
- {n,}: Matches n or more occurrences.
- {n,m}: Matches between n and m occurrences.

For example, to search for lines containing 'a' followed by one or more 'b':

```
grep "ab+" example.txt
```

Anchors

Anchors are used to specify the position of the match within a line:

- ^: Matches the start of a line.
- $: Matches the end of a line.

To find lines that start with "Hello":

```
grep "^Hello" example.txt
```

To find lines that end with "world":

```
grep "world\$" example.txt
```

Grouping and Alternation

Parentheses () are used for grouping parts of the regex, while the pipe | represents alternation (logical OR).

For example, to match either "cat" or "dog":

```
grep "\(cat\|dog\)" example.txt
```

Using Grep with Extended Regular Expressions

The grep command also supports extended regular expressions (ERE) through the -E option or egrep.

```
grep -E "expression" example.txt
egrep "expression" example.txt
```

With ERE, there is no need to escape the special characters, making the regex syntax more readable. For instance, the previous alternation example can be written as:

```
grep -E "(cat|dog)" example.txt
```

Practical Examples

Consider a file named data.txt with the following content:

Name	Age	Height
Alice	24	5.9
Bob	22	6.0
Charlie	25	5.7

Table 7.1: Sample data in data.txt

To find lines where age is 24 or more:

```
grep -E "[[:digit:]]{2}" data.txt
```

Note that [[:digit:]]{2} matches two digits, assuming the age is two digits long.

To match lines that contain a height of 6.0:

```
grep "6\.0" data.txt
```

By combining various elements of regular expressions with the grep command, users can perform highly specific and efficient text searches across files.

7.12 Using Regular Expressions with 'sed'

The 'sed' command, short for stream editor, is a powerful tool for text processing that utilizes regular expressions. 'sed' performs its operations as commands on the given input streams, which can be files or piped input. Regular expressions (regex) enhance the capabilities of 'sed', enabling complex text manipulations with concise patterns.

'sed' operates on each line by applying the specified command or set of commands. The most common and versatile 'sed' command is the 's' command for substitution. This section delves into applying regular expressions within 'sed' to perform substitution and other operations.

```
$ sed 's/old_pattern/new_pattern/' inputfile
```

The old_pattern represents the regex for the text to be replaced, while new_pattern denotes the replacement text. The single quotes encapsulate the 'sed' command to treat it as a single argument. This command substitutes the first occurrence of old_pattern with new_pattern in each line of inputfile.

For example, to replace the word foo with bar in a file:

```
$ sed 's/foo/bar/' example.txt
```

To replace all occurrences of a pattern within a line, the 'g' (global) flag is appended to the substitute command:

```
$ sed 's/foo/bar/g' example.txt
```

```
Input:   foo foo foo
Output:   bar bar bar
```

'sed' supports a rich set of regex features, such as character classes, anchoring, and grouping.

Anchoring

Anchoring specifies positions in the text. ^ asserts the start of a line, and $ asserts the end of a line.

```
$ sed 's/^foo/bar/' example.txt # Replaces 'foo' at the start of a line
$ sed 's/foo$/bar/' example.txt # Replaces 'foo' at the end of a line
```

Character Classes

Character classes match any character within the brackets. For example, $[abc]$ matches 'a', 'b', or 'c'.

```
$ sed 's/[abc]/d/' example.txt # Replaces 'a', 'b', or 'c' with 'd'
```

Ranges can also be specified within character classes:

```
$ sed 's/[a-z]/X/' example.txt # Replaces any lowercase letter a-z with 'X'
```

Grouping and Alternation

Grouping is achieved with parentheses, and alternation (logical OR) uses $|$. Grouping allows operations on a subset of the pattern.

```
$ sed 's/\(foo\|bar\)/baz/' example.txt # Replaces 'foo' or 'bar' with 'baz'
```

The backslash escapes special characters within the regex.

Backreferences

Backreferences use the previous matched expressions in the replacement string. A parenthesized pattern is assigned a number, starting with one.

```
$ sed 's/\(.\)\1/yy/' inputfile
```

This replaces any doubled character (e.g., aa, bb) with yy. $(.)$
1 captures a character and matches it again.

Here is a comprehensive example illustrating several regex capabilities in 'sed':

```
$ sed 's/^\([a-z]\):\([0-9]*\)/\2-\1/' example.txt
```

For an input line such as:

```
a:1234
```

This 'sed' command performs:

- $[a-z]$ matches a lowercase letter at the beginning and captures it.
- : matches the colon character.
- $[0-9]*$ matches any sequence of digits and captures them.

The replacement string
2-
1 rearranges and inserts a hyphen between the captured sequences. Output:

```
1234-a
```

Care must be taken with delimiters in the substitute command. Although /, by default, can be replaced with any character for specific use cases, ensuring readability:

```
$ sed 's|/usr/local/bin|/usr/bin|g' example.txt
```

Using | as the delimiter here avoids confusion with the path separators /. Regular expressions in 'sed' provide flexible and comprehensive text transformation tools essential for efficient Linux text processing.

7.13 Advanced Text Processing with awk

The awk utility in Unix/Linux serves as a powerful tool used for pattern scanning and processing. Beyond basic tasks, awk is capable of handling complex text transformations and data extraction with ease due to its scripting capabilities. This section explores advanced awk functionalities that enable efficient text processing and data manipulation.

The fundamental concept in awk involves reading input line by line, splitting each line into fields or columns, and performing actions based on patterns and conditions. We start with the general syntax of an awk command:

```
awk 'pattern {action}' inputfile
```

The pattern specifies the conditions under which awk performs the subsequent action. Patterns can involve regular expressions, relational expressions, or logical combinations of these.

One of the pivotal features in awk is its ability to handle field and record separators. By default, awk splits each input line into fields using whitespace as the field separator and treats each line as a record. However, awk provides options to customize these behaviors using built-in variables such as FS (Field Separator), RS (Record Separator), OFS (Output Field Separator), and ORS (Output Record Separator).

```
awk 'BEGIN { FS=","; OFS="\t" } { print $1, $2, $3 }' input.csv
```

In this example, the BEGIN block initializes the input field separator FS to a comma and the output field separator OFS to a tab, facilitating the extraction and formatting of fields from a CSV file.

Advanced awk usage often involves complex expressions and control flow mechanisms similar to structured programming languages. awk supports arithmetic operations, string manipulations, and user-defined functions.

Consider a scenario where we need to calculate the average of numerical values in a specific column. This can be achieved using awk as follows:

```
awk '{ sum += $1; count++ } END { if (count > 0) print sum / count }' input.txt
```

Here, awk iterates over each line of input.txt, accumulating the sum of the values in the first column ($1) and counting the number of records. The END block executes after processing all input lines, calculating and printing the average.

String operations in awk enable sophisticated text processing tasks. Built-in functions such as length, sub, gsub, and split provide robust mechanisms for string manipulation.

awk also supports associative arrays (also known as hash tables), allowing efficient storage and retrieval of key-value pairs. This feature is particularly useful for tasks involving frequency counting or data aggregation.

```
awk '{ count[$1]++ } END { for (word in count) print word, count[word] }' input.txt
```

In this script, awk reads each word from the first column of input.txt and increments its occurrence count in the count array. The END block iterates over the array, printing each word and its count.

Functions in awk can be user-defined to encapsulate reusable code, making scripts modular and easier to maintain. The following example demonstrates defining and using a function to check if a number is prime:

```
awk '
function is_prime(num) {
    if (num < 2) return 0
    for (i = 2; i <= int(sqrt(num)); i++) {
        if (num % i == 0) return 0
    }
    return 1
}

{
```

```
    if (is_prime($1)) print $1 " is prime"
    else print $1 " is not prime"
}' input.txt
```

The is_prime function calculates whether the number provided as an argument is a prime number. Within the main loop, awk uses this function to evaluate each number in the first column of input.txt and prints an appropriate message.

The awk language also supports regular expressions, enabling pattern-based processing within its powerful text manipulation toolkit.

```
awk '/pattern/ { print $0 }' input.txt
```

This command prints all lines from input.txt that match the specified regular expression pattern.

By combining these advanced features, awk scripts can perform complex text processing tasks with efficiency and precision.

7.14 Practical Examples of Text Processing

One of the most enriching ways to enhance your understanding of text processing in Linux is through practical examples. In this section, we will explore several scenarios where text processing tools are used to solve real-world problems. These examples will build on the concepts previously discussed, including the use of commands like cat, grep, cut, sort, uniq, tr, sed, and awk.

Consider a directory of log files containing system events. Each log file's content needs to be processed to find specific information, extract useful data, and reformat it for better readability.

```
$ ls -1 /var/log/*.log
```

Imagine one of these log files, syslog.log, contains entries in the following format:

```
Jan 10 10:00:01 server1 CRON[12345]: (root) CMD (run-parts /etc/cron.hourly)
Jan 10 10:01:22 server1 kernel: [123456.789012] usb 1-1: new high-speed USB
device number 2 using xhci_hcd
Jan 10 10:02:33 server1 sshd[12346]: Accepted password for user1 from
192.168.1.10 port 22 ssh2
```

To count the number of entries, we can use the wc command:

```
$ wc -l /var/log/syslog.log
```

To find all instances related to SSH connections, use grep:

```
$ grep 'sshd' /var/log/syslog.log
```

If we need only the IP addresses from these SSH entries, awk becomes useful:

```
$ grep 'sshd' /var/log/syslog.log | awk '{print $11}'
```

We may also be interested in counting unique IP addresses that have accessed the SSH service:

```
$ grep 'sshd' /var/log/syslog.log | awk '{print $11}' | sort | uniq -c
```

To generate a summary report, we can integrate several commands in a shell script. This script counts total log entries, identifies SSH connections, and counts unique IP addresses. Here is the script:

```
#!/bin/bash

LOGFILE="/var/log/syslog.log"
TOTAL_ENTRIES=$(wc -l < $LOGFILE)
SSH_ENTRIES=$(grep -c 'sshd' $LOGFILE)
UNIQUE_IPS=$(grep 'sshd' $LOGFILE | awk '{print $11}' | sort | uniq -c)

echo "Log Analysis Report"
echo "===================="
echo "Total log entries: $TOTAL_ENTRIES"
echo "SSH connection attempts: $SSH_ENTRIES"
echo "Unique IP addresses:"
echo "$UNIQUE_IPS"
```

To execute this script and observe the output:

```
$ chmod +x log_analysis.sh
$ ./log_analysis.sh
```

```
Log Analysis Report
====================
Total log entries: 5000
SSH connection attempts: 150
Unique IP addresses:
10 192.168.1.10
8 192.168.1.11
...
```

Another practical example involves processing a CSV file containing user data. Assume we have a file named users.csv with the following format:

```
id,name,email,age
1,John Doe,john.doe@example.com,30
2,Jane Smith,jane.smith@example.com,25
3,Bob Johnson,bob.johnson@example.com,40
```

To extract the names and emails of users over the age of 30, we first filter and then format the output using awk:

```
$ awk -F, '$4 > 30 {print $2, $3}' users.csv
```

```
Bob Johnson bob.johnson@example.com
```

Often, we need to create a formatted list with names and corresponding emails. awk allows for custom formatting:

```
$ awk -F, '$4 > 30 {printf "Name: %s, Email: %s\n", $2, $3}' users.csv
```

```
Name: Bob Johnson, Email: bob.johnson@example.com
```

Consider a task to anonymize email addresses by replacing the domain with example.com. We use sed:

```
$ sed 's/@[a-zA-Z0-9.-]*/@example.com/' users.csv
```

```
id,name,email,age
1,John Doe,john.doe@example.com,30
2,Jane Smith,jane.smith@example.com,25
3,Bob Johnson,bob.johnson@example.com,40
```

Thus, these examples present a concise guide on applying text processing techniques for practical tasks, demonstrating the flexibility and efficacy of Linux text processing tools.

Chapter 8

Working with Functions and Libraries

This chapter explores the creation and use of functions in shell scripts to enhance modularity and reusability. It covers defining and calling functions, passing arguments, and handling return values. The chapter addresses function scope, local variables, and recursive functions. It also delves into best practices for writing functions, creating shell script libraries, organizing functions within libraries, and sourcing them in scripts. Additionally, error handling within functions and practical examples of function and library usage are provided.

8.1 Introduction to Functions in Shell Scripts

Functions in shell scripting are fundamental constructs that enable the development of modular, maintainable, and reusable code. By encapsulating a series of commands within a function, script developers can simplify complex tasks, reduce redundancy, and enhance script readability. This section will provide a comprehensive overview of functions in shell scripting, focusing on their definition, usage, and the advantages they offer.

A function in shell scripting is essentially a named block of code that performs a specific task. Once defined, a function can be invoked directly by its name, allowing the same block of code to be executed multiple times throughout the script. This avoids code duplication and makes scripts more organized. The basic syntax for defining a function in a shell script is as follows:

```
function_name() {
    # Commands
}
```

Here, function_name is the name of the function, and the commands within curly braces are executed whenever the function is called. It is important to place the function definition before any call to the function within the script to avoid errors.

Consider the following simple example where a function named greet is defined and called:

```
#!/bin/bash

greet() {
    echo "Hello, $1!"
}

greet "World"
```

In this script, the greet function takes one argument and prints a greeting message. The output of the above script is:

```
Hello, World!
```

Functions not only make scripts easier to read and maintain but also contribute to better error handling and debugging. By isolating specific tasks within functions, it becomes easier to identify and fix issues in a controlled manner. Additionally, functions promote code reuse, as commonly used functionalities can be defined once and used across different parts of a script or even in different scripts.

Unlike some programming languages, shell functions do not have explicit return types. Instead, they return an exit status, an integer value with a convention that 0 indicates success, and any non-zero value indicates an error. This exit status can be captured using the special variable $?. Here is an illustrative example:

```
#!/bin/bash

check_file_existence() {
    if [ -f "$1" ]; then
        return 0
    else
        return 1
```

```
    fi
}

check_file_existence "/path/to/file"
if [ $? -eq 0 ]; then
    echo "File exists."
else
    echo "File does not exist."
fi
```

In this script, the function check_file_existence checks if a file exists and returns 0 if it does, or 1 otherwise. The exit status is then used to print an appropriate message. The conditional check [-f "$1"] uses the test command to determine if the file specified by the function argument exists and is a regular file.

Functions can also utilize local variables to prevent namespace conflicts and accidental modification of variables that may have the same name but are used in different parts of the script. Local variables can be declared within functions using the local keyword:

```
#!/bin/bash

name="GlobalName"

print_names() {
    local name="LocalName"
    echo "Function name: $name"
}

print_names
echo "Global name: $name"
```

The output of this script will be:

```
Function name: LocalName
Global name: GlobalName
```

Here, the global variable name remains unaffected by the local variable declared within the function, demonstrating the use of local scope to mitigate variable naming conflicts.

Additionally, shell functions can call other functions, enhancing modularity. Function calls within other functions enable the creation of intricate and layered scripts while maintaining each function's simplicity and focused purpose.

Understanding the essential structure and utility of functions in shell scripts equips script developers with the ability to write efficient, modular, and reusable code. These principles form the foundation for more advanced topics such as passing arguments, handling return values, and creating shell script libraries, all of which will be discussed in subsequent sections.

8.2 Defining and Calling Functions

In shell scripting, functions are fundamental building blocks that enable programmers to create modular, reusable, and more readable code. Functions make it easier to manage complexity, reduce redundancy, and maintain scripts. This section explains how to define and call functions in a shell script, utilizing syntax and examples to illustrate these concepts.

A function in a shell script is defined using the following syntax:

```
function_name() {
    # Commands to be executed
}
```

Alternatively, the function keyword can be used, although it is not obligatory:

```
function function_name {
    # Commands to be executed
}
```

The function name must be unique within the script or sourcing environment to avoid conflicts. By convention, function names should be descriptive, using underscores (_) to separate words for readability.

Once a function is defined, it can be called by simply using its name followed by any required arguments:

```
function_name argument1 argument2
```

Let us consider a practical example to solidify our understanding. Suppose we need a function to display a greeting message:

```
greet_user() {
    echo "Hello, \$1!"
}
```

In this script, greet_user is the function name, and it accepts a single argument represented by $1, which is the first positional parameter. To call this function and pass an argument to it, we can write:

```
greet_user "Alice"
```

The output will be:

```
Hello, Alice!
```

This example demonstrates the simplicity of defining and calling functions, as well as passing arguments to them.

Another key aspect of functions in shell scripts is their ability to encapsulate logic. Consider a function that calculates and prints the factorial of a given number:

```
factorial() {
    local num=\$1
    local result=1

    while [ \$num -gt 1 ]; do
        result=\$((result * num))
        num=\$((num - 1))
    done

    echo \$result
}
```

In this case, the factorial function calculates the factorial of num, which is passed as the first argument. The local keyword is used to ensure that the variables num and result are confined to the function scope, preventing unintended side effects.

To call this function and calculate the factorial of 5, we use:

```
factorial 5
```

The output will be:

```
120
```

Multiple functions can be defined within a single script. To illustrate, let us create a script with two functions: one to add two numbers and another to multiply two numbers:

```
add_numbers() {
    local sum=\$(( \$1 + \$2 ))
    echo \$sum
}

multiply_numbers() {
    local product=\$(( \$1 * \$2 ))
    echo \$product
}
```

Calling these functions as follows:

```
add_numbers 3 4
multiply_numbers 3 4
```

Produces the respective outputs:

```
7
12
```

The examples provided highlight various aspects of defining and calling functions, demonstrating how functions can encapsulate logic, manage inputs, and control outputs effectively. Proper use of functions in a shell script promotes modularity, readability, and maintainability.

8.3 Passing Arguments to Functions

In shell scripting, passing arguments to functions allows for the creation of more versatile and reusable commands. By utilizing arguments, a function can operate on various data inputs, rather than relying on hard-coded values. This capability enhances the general applicability and robustness of scripts.

When a function is called, any arguments provided during the call are accessible within the function using positional parameters. These parameters are referenced by the syntax $1, $2, $3, and so forth, where $1 represents the first argument, $2 the second, and so on. The following example demonstrates a basic function that takes two arguments and prints them:

```
#!/bin/bash

print_arguments() {
    echo "Argument 1: $1"
    echo "Argument 2: $2"
}

print_arguments "Hello" "World"
```

Executing this script yields the output:

```
Argument 1: Hello
Argument 2: World
```

It is crucial to understand that if a function is called without the expected number of arguments, the positional parameters within the function will be empty. This can be managed via default value assignments or explicit checks for argument presence. Consider the following example, which checks for argument presence:

```
#!/bin/bash

print_arguments_with_check() {
    if [ -z "$1" ] || [ -z "$2" ]; then
        echo "Two arguments are required."
        return 1
    fi
```

```
    echo "Argument 1: $1"
    echo "Argument 2: $2"
}

print_arguments_with_check "Hello"
```

In this script, the output is:

```
Two arguments are required.
```

Implicitly, this highlights the importance of verifying argument expectations to prevent unintended script behavior.

Another consideration when working with arguments is the handling of multiple or an unknown number of arguments. The special variable $# stores the number of arguments passed to a function, while $* and $ provide access to all passed arguments. Here is an example demonstrating the nuances between $* and $:

```
#!/bin/bash

print_all_arguments() {
    echo "Using \$*: $*"
    echo "Using \$@: $@"
    for arg in "$*"; do
        echo "Arg with \$*: $arg"
    done
    for arg in "$@"; do
        echo "Arg with \$@: $arg"
    done
}

print_all_arguments "Hello" "World" "Welcome"
```

Executing this script produces the following output:

```
Using $*: Hello World Welcome
Using $@: Hello World Welcome
Arg with $*: Hello World Welcome
Arg with $@: Hello
Arg with $@: World
Arg with $@: Welcome
```

The key difference illustrated here is that $* treats all arguments as a single entity, whereas $ treats each argument as a separate entity, facilitating iterative processing.

In cases where argument parsing and validation grow complex, leveraging getopts enhances maintainability and readability. This utility allows for sophisticated command-line argument parsing, akin to getopt in C. Below is an example employing getopts within a function:

```
#!/bin/bash

parse_arguments() {
```

```
    while getopts "a:b:" opt; do
        case $opt in
            a) echo "Option a with value $OPTARG";;
            b) echo "Option b with value $OPTARG";;
            \?) echo "Invalid option";;
        esac
    done
}

parse_arguments -a "Hello" -b "World"
```

The output of this script is:

```
Option a with value Hello
Option b with value World
```

By employing getopts, script functions can handle named arguments with options, enhancing clarity and user experience.

In summary, passing arguments to functions in shell scripting extends their flexibility and adaptability. By understanding positional parameters, handling multiple arguments, and utilizing tools like getopts, scripts can be made more dynamic and robust. This foundational knowledge is crucial for writing advanced shell scripts that are both modular and maintainable.

8.4 Returning Values from Functions

In shell scripting, functions can return values to the calling context, enabling more complex operations and data manipulations. Unlike in some programming languages, shell functions do not explicitly return values using a return statement with a value; instead, they rely on exit status or variable scope to convey results. Understanding these mechanisms is crucial for effective function utilization in shell scripts.

Shell functions return an exit status, which is a numeric value between 0 and 255 that indicates the success or failure of the function. By convention, an exit status of 0 denotes success, whereas any non-zero value indicates an error. The exit status of a function can be set using the return command followed by a numeric value. If no explicit return statement is used, the exit status of a function is the exit status of the last command executed within the function.

```
#!/bin/bash

function check_file_exists() {
    if [ -e "$1" ]; then
        return 0 # Success: file exists
    else
```

```
        return 1 # Failure: file does not exist
    fi
}

check_file_exists "/etc/passwd"
echo "Exit status: $?" # Output the exit status
```

Here, the function check_file_exists sets the exit status to 0 if the file exists and 1 if it does not. The special variable $? captures the exit status of the last executed command, which is used here to output the result.

In many scenarios, numeric exit statuses are insufficient to convey complex data. Therefore, shell functions often use positional parameters or global variables to return more detailed information. This method allows the function to set values directly in variables or output data that can be captured using command substitution.

```
#!/bin/bash

result=""

function add_numbers() {
    local sum=$(( $1 + $2 ))
    result=$sum # Set the global variable to the result
}

add_numbers 10 20
echo "Sum: $result" # Output the result
```

In this example, the global variable result is used to return the sum of two numbers calculated by the add_numbers function. The use of a global variable ensures that the calling context can access the computed value after the function has executed.

Another approach to returning values from functions is to leverage command substitution. A function can output its result using the echo command, and the caller can capture this output using the syntax $(...) or backticks `...`.

```
#!/bin/bash

function add_numbers() {
    local sum=$(( $1 + $2 ))
    echo $sum # Output the result to be captured
}

result=$(add_numbers 10 20) # Capture the output
echo "Sum: $result" # Output the result
```

The add_numbers function outputs the sum via echo, and the calling context captures that output using $(...). This method is particularly useful for capturing function results without affecting global or environment variables.

While returning values using command substitution or global variables offers flexibility, it is important to manage variable scope carefully. Utilizing local variables within functions ensures that temporary values do not inadvertently affect the global environment, thus preventing hard-to-debug errors.

When capturing multiple values, functions can output data in a structured format, such as delimited strings or arrays. The caller can then parse this output as needed.

```
#!/bin/bash

function get_date_components() {
    local date_str=$(date +%Y-%m-%d)
    local year=${date_str:0:4}
    local month=${date_str:5:2}
    local day=${date_str:8:2}
    echo "$year $month $day" # Output space-delimited values
}

read year month day < <(get_date_components) # Capture and split the output
echo "Year: $year, Month: $month, Day: $day"
```

In this script, the function get_date_components outputs the current date components as space-delimited values. The calling context uses the read command with process substitution < <(...) to capture and split these values into separate variables.

Correct handling of return values from functions enhances the modularity and robustness of shell scripts. Understanding these techniques allows scriptwriters to implement more sophisticated logic and data processing within their scripts, adhering to best practices of clarity and maintainability.

8.5 Function Scope and Local Variables

In shell scripting, understanding function scope and the use of local variables is crucial for writing modular and maintainable code. Scope determines the visibility and lifetime of variables within a script, and by defining variables with appropriate scope, we can control where they can be accessed and modified. This is particularly important when dealing with functions, as it prevents unintended side effects and enhances the readability and reliability of the script.

Variables in shell scripts can either have a global scope or a local scope. A variable with global scope is accessible from anywhere within the script, including inside functions. On the other hand, a variable with local scope is only accessible within the function or block of code where it is defined, and it does not affect nor is affected by variables with the same name outside of that scope.

```
#!/bin/bash

global_var="I am a global variable"

example_function() {
    local local_var="I am a local variable"
    echo "Inside function: global_var = $global_var"
    echo "Inside function: local_var = $local_var"
    global_var="I have been modified within the function"
    local_var="I am a modified local variable"
}

echo "Before function call: global_var = $global_var"
example_function
echo "After function call: global_var = $global_var"
echo "Trying to access local_var outside function: local_var = $local_var"
```

```
Before function call: global_var = I am a global variable
Inside function: global_var = I am a global variable
Inside function: local_var = I am a local variable
After function call: global_var = I have been modified within the function
./script.sh: line 17: local_var: unbound variable
```

In this example:

- global_var is declared outside any function, thus it has a global scope.
- local_var is declared with the local keyword within example_function, giving it local scope.

Within example_function, both global_var and local_var are accessible, but modifying local_var only affects the variable within the function. When example_function is called, global_var is modified globally, while local_var ceases to exist after the function execution.

Shadowing and Isolating Variables

It's important to note that local variables can shadow global variables. If a local variable within a function has the same name as a global variable, the local variable will temporarily overshadow the global variable within that function's scope.

```
#!/bin/bash

var="I am a global variable"
```

```
shadow_example() {
    local var="I am a local variable"
    echo "Inside function: var = $var"
}

echo "Before function call: var = $var"
shadow_example
echo "After function call: var = $var"
```

```
Before function call: var = I am a global variable
Inside function: var = I am a local variable
After function call: var = I am a global variable
```

In this scenario, the local variable var within shadow_example shadows the global variable var only within the function's scope. Once the function exits, the global variable var is unaffected and retains its original value.

Best Practices for Variable Scope

- Always use local variables within functions unless there is an intentional need to modify a global variable.
- Use clear and distinct variable names to avoid unintended shadowing.
- Avoid using the same variable name in different scope levels without a valid reason to prevent confusion and potential bugs.
- Document your code to specify when and why a variable is intended to have a certain scope.

Examples of applying these principles:

```
#!/bin/bash

config_file="/etc/config_file" # Global variable for configuration file

load_configuration() {
    local file="$1" # Local variable for function argument
    if [[ -f "$file" ]]; then
        source "$file"
    else
        echo "Configuration file not found: $file"
        return 1
    fi
}

main() {
    echo "Loading configuration from $config_file"
    if ! load_configuration "$config_file"; then
        echo "Failed to load configuration."
        exit 1
```

```
    fi
    # Further processing after loading configuration
}

main
```

In this example, the global variable config_file is used to store the path to a configuration file. Within the load_configuration function, a local variable file is used to handle the passed argument, ensuring that the global variable is protected from accidental modification. The main function coordinates the script execution, calling load_configuration with the global config_file.

Through careful management of variable scope and the use of local variables, shell scripts become more reliable, easier to debug, and more maintainable. This approach minimizes the risk of side effects caused by inadvertent variable modifications.

8.6 Recursive Functions

Recursion is a powerful programming technique where a function calls itself to solve a problem. In shell scripting, recursive functions can be particularly useful for tasks that involve repetitive processes or hierarchical data structures. Understanding the mechanics of recursion and its application in shell scripting enhances the capability to handle complex tasks with elegance and efficiency.

A recursive function must have a base case to terminate the recursion. Without a base case, the function would call itself indefinitely, leading to a stack overflow error. The general structure of a recursive function in a shell script involves:

- Defining the base case(s)
- Defining the recursive case(s)

To illustrate the concept, consider a factorial calculation. The factorial of a non-negative integer n (denoted as $n!$) is defined recursively as:

$$n! = \begin{cases} 1 & \text{if } n = 0 \\ n \times (n-1)! & \text{if } n > 0 \end{cases}$$

The following script demonstrates a recursive function to calculate the factorial of a given number:

```
#!/bin/bash

# Function to calculate factorial
factorial() {
    local n=$1
    if [ $n -le 1 ]; then
        echo 1
    else
        local temp=$(( n - 1 ))
        local res=$(factorial $temp)
        echo $(( n * res ))
    fi
}

# Read input
read -p "Enter a number: " num
if [ $num -lt 0 ]; then
    echo "Factorial is not defined for negative numbers"
    exit 1
fi

# Call the factorial function
result=$(factorial $num)
echo "Factorial of $num is: $result"
```

Upon execution, this script performs the following steps:

- Prompts the user to enter a number.
- If the number is negative, an error message is displayed, and the script exits.
- For non-negative numbers, the script calls the factorial function, which recursively computes the factorial.

The recursive function factorial first checks if the input number n is less than or equal to 1 (base case). If true, it returns 1. Otherwise, it reduces the number by 1, calls itself with the reduced number, and multiplies the result by n.

Recursive functions can also handle more complex tasks such as directory traversal. Consider a scenario where we need to list all files in a directory and its subdirectories:

```
#!/bin/bash

# Function to traverse directories
traverse_directory() {
    local dir="$1"
    echo "Listing files in directory: $dir"

    for entry in "$dir"/*; do
        if [ -d "$entry" ]; then
            traverse_directory "$entry"
```

```
        else
            echo "$entry"
        fi
    done
}

# Start traversal from the specified directory
start_dir="."
traverse_directory "$start_dir"
```

In this script, the function traverse_directory takes a directory path as an argument. It iterates over each entry within the directory. If an entry is a subdirectory, it recursively calls itself to traverse the subdirectory. If an entry is a file, it prints the file path.

By understanding how recursion operates within shell scripts, we can solve problems that require hierarchical processing. The key points to remember when crafting recursive functions are ensuring the presence of a base case to terminate recursion and managing resources effectively to avoid excessive memory consumption.

Recursion in shell scripting, while less common compared to traditional programming languages, provides a versatile toolset for approaching tasks involving nested or repeated structures. Learning how to effectively implement and optimize recursive algorithms broadens the scope of problems that can be tackled using shell scripts.

8.7 Best Practices for Writing Functions

Writing efficient and maintainable functions is crucial for developing robust shell scripts. This section provides guidelines and best practices to optimize the modularity and reusability of your code while maintaining readability and ensuring effective error handling.

First, always begin with a clear and concise function name. The name should accurately describe the function's purpose. For instance, if a function calculates the sum of two numbers, a suitable name might be calculate_sum. Clarity in naming conventions promotes better understanding and ease of maintenance.

```
# Good example of naming convention:
calculate_sum() {
    local num1=$1
    local num2=$2
    echo $(( num1 + num2 ))
}
```

Next, include comments within your function to describe its parameters, return values, and any non-obvious logic. This documentation helps other developers (and your future self) to understand the function's operation without extensive code review.

```
# Function: calculate_sum
# Description: Calculates the sum of two numbers.
# Parameters:
# num1 - The first number.
# num2 - The second number.
# Returns:
# The sum of num1 and num2.
calculate_sum() {
    local num1=$1
    local num2=$2
    echo $(( num1 + num2 ))
}
```

Functions should generally avoid producing output directly unless it is their primary purpose. Instead, use return values or established shell conventions. For example, the following function illustrates returning values rather than printing them directly.

```
# Function to add two numbers and return the result
add_numbers() {
    local num1=$1
    local num2=$2
    local sum=$(( num1 + num2 ))
    return $sum
}
```

In scenarios where complex output is necessary, consider using echo or printf to deliver formatted results.

Error checking in functions is indispensable. Verify the validity of function arguments and ensure correct operation every step of the way. For example, checking if the correct number of arguments has been supplied can prevent unexpected script failures.

```
# Function to subtract two numbers with basic error checking
subtract_numbers() {
    if (( $# != 2 )); then
        echo "Error: Two arguments required"
        return 1
    fi

    local num1=$1
    local num2=$2
    local difference=$(( num1 - num2 ))
    echo $difference
}
```

Use local variables to avoid unexpected behavior due to variable scope. Local variables are confined to the function's scope, ensuring that they do not interfere with variables outside the function.

```
# Using local variables to avoid scope issues
multiply_numbers() {
    local num1=$1
    local num2=$2
    local product=$(( num1 * num2 ))
    echo $product
}
```

Keep functions focused on a single task. Functions that try to perform multiple unrelated tasks are more difficult to reuse and test. Instead, modular functions that perform specific tasks are easier to compose into more complex operations.

```
# Example of a function performing a specific task
convert_to_uppercase() {
    local input_string="$1"
    echo "${input_string^^}"
}
```

Avoid hardcoding values within functions. Instead, pass values as parameters. This practice enhances the function's flexibility and reusability.

```
# Function to append a string to a file
append_to_file() {
    local file="$1"
    local string_to_append="$2"

    if [[ -z "$file" || -z "$string_to_append" ]]; then
        echo "Error: Both file and string_to_append are required"
        return 1
    fi

    echo "$string_to_append" >> "$file"
}
```

Adopt a consistent function structure, including a prototype or the use of standard sections such as error handling, core logic, and finalizing steps. Consistency helps in maintaining and debugging the code.

```
# Structured function example
divide_numbers() {
    # Error Handling
    if (( $# != 2 )); then
        echo "Error: Two arguments required"
        return 1
    fi

    local dividend=$1
    local divisor=$2

    if (( divisor == 0 )); then
        echo "Error: Division by zero"
        return 1
```

```
    fi

    # Core Logic
    local quotient=$(( dividend / divisor ))

    # Final Step
    echo $quotient
}
```

Integrate logging mechanisms within your functions for better trackability and debugging. Logging can include informational messages, error messages, or warnings about unexpected behavior.

```
# Function with logging
log_message() {
    local message="$1"
    local log_file="/var/log/my_script.log"

    echo "$(date): $message" >>"$log_file"
}
```

Finally, thoroughly test your functions to ensure they perform as expected. Testing should cover valid and invalid input, edge cases, and the function's interaction with other parts of the script. Regular testing aids in early detection of defects and inconsistencies.

Following these best practices ensures that the functions you write in shell scripts are efficient, maintainable, and robust. By adhering to these guidelines, you enhance the modularity and reliability of your scripts, facilitating easier debugging and collaboration.

8.8 Creating Shell Script Libraries

A well-constructed shell script library enables reuse, modularity, and maintainability of your code. When frequent tasks or functions are encapsulated into libraries, it becomes easier to manage and reuse them across different scripts. This section describes the principles and methods for creating shell script libraries.

To create a shell script library, begin by organizing related functions into a single file. Such a file should use a .sh extension and contain only function definitions and necessary variable declarations, avoiding standalone executable statements unless required for initialization.

File Structure and Conventions:

Naming and structuring your library files are crucial for maintainability and clarity. It is advisable to use a naming convention that reflects the functionality of the library. For example, a library that deals with string manipulations could be named string_utils.sh.

A typical library file structure is as follows:

```
# string_utils.sh

# Function to check if a string is empty
is_empty() {
    [ -z "$1" ]
}

# Function to convert a string to uppercase
to_uppercase() {
    echo "$1" | tr '[:lower:]' '[:upper:]'
}

# Function to replace a substring
replace_substring() {
    local str="$1"
    local search="$2"
    local replace="$3"
    echo "${str//$search/$replace}"
}
```

Function Definitions:

Functions within a library should follow best practices such as using local variables to avoid conflicts and providing clear, concise comments for each function. This improves both readability and usability:

```
# string_utils.sh

# Function to check if a string is empty.
# Arguments:
# $1 - The string to check.
# Returns:
# 0 if the string is empty, 1 otherwise.
is_empty() {
    [ -z "$1" ]
}

# Function to convert a string to uppercase.
# Arguments:
# $1 - The string to convert.
# Outputs:
# The uppercase version of the string.
to_uppercase() {
    echo "$1" | tr '[:lower:]' '[:upper:]'
}

# Function to replace a substring in a string with another substring.
# Arguments:
# $1 - The original string.
# $2 - The substring to search for.
# $3 - The substring to replace with.
# Outputs:
# The modified string with the replacements.
replace_substring() {
    local str="$1"
```

```
    local search="$2"
    local replace="$3"
    echo "${str//$search/$replace}"
}
```

Loading Libraries:

To use the functions defined in a shell script library in another script, the source command is employed. This allows the importing script to execute the functions as if they were part of its own codebase:

```
#!/bin/bash

source ./string_utils.sh

# Example usage of the string_utils library

if is_empty "$1"; then
    echo "The input string is empty"
else
    uppercase=$(to_uppercase "$1")
    echo "Uppercase version: $uppercase"
fi

modified_str=$(replace_substring "hello world" "world" "shell")
echo "Modified string: $modified_str"
```

The source command (or the synonym .) incorporates the library file into the current script, making all its functions available. The path to the library file can be relative or absolute, depending on the script's execution context.

Using Global and Local Variables:

When using variables inside functions within a library, it is important to understand the scope of these variables. Local variables should be confined to the function to prevent conflicts, while global variables can be used for constants or configuration settings that need to be accessible across multiple functions.

```
# string_utils.sh

# Global constant
readonly VOWELS="aeiou"

# Function to count the number of vowels in a string.
# Arguments:
# $1 - The string to analyze.
# Outputs:
# The count of vowels in the string.
count_vowels() {
    local str="$1"
    local count=0
    for (( i=0; i<${#str}; i++ )); do
        if [[ "$VOWELS" == *"${str:$i:1}"* ]]; then
            ((count++))
```

```
        fi
    done
    echo $count
}
```

Handling Dependencies:

If a library depends on another library or external command, it is best to declare these dependencies at the beginning of the script. This practice ensures that all required resources are available before any function begins execution:

```
# main_script.sh

# Import libraries
source ./string_utils.sh

# Ensure dependent commands are available
command -v tr >/dev/null 2>&1 || { echo "tr command is required but it's not
    installed. Exiting."; exit 1; }

# Example usage
uppercase=$(to_uppercase "hello")
echo "Uppercase: $uppercase"
```

Dependencies can include other libraries or essential command-line utilities. Checking for their existence and providing meaningful error messages helps prevent runtime issues.

A well-structured library simplifies code management, promotes reuse, and enhances maintainability. Through careful encapsulation of functionality and adherence to best practices, shell script libraries become valuable assets in any scripter's toolkit.

8.9 Organizing Functions in Libraries

When developing shell scripts, one often encounters recurring tasks that necessitate the reuse of code. To promote maintainability and reduce redundancy, it is advisable to organize these reusable code segments into libraries. This section discusses the principles and techniques for structuring shell script functions within libraries, ensuring clarity and facilitating ease of maintenance.

In Unix-like systems, a shell script library is typically a file containing a collection of functions, which can be sourced by other scripts. This file conventionally ends with the .sh extension, although this is not mandatory. The principal task is to logically categorize functions and systematically define them within the library file.

- **Naming Conventions and File Structure**: A well-organized library begins with consistent naming conventions. Function names should be descriptive yet concise, reflecting their purpose. Additionally, prefixes can be used to avoid name collisions, especially when multiple libraries are employed. For instance, functions in a mathematics-related library might all start with math_, e.g., math_add, math_subtract.

  Organizing functions into directories based on their functionality can further enhance clarity. A directory structure for a shell script project might look like this:

  ```
  project-root/
    bin/
    lib/
      math.sh
      string.sh
      file.sh
    scripts/
  ```

  In this structure, the lib directory houses various libraries, each addressing distinct functionalities such as mathematical operations, string manipulations, or file handling.

- **Example Library Structure**: Consider a library file named math.sh, containing various arithmetic functions:

  ```
  #!/bin/bash

  # math_add: Adds two numbers
  # Usage: math_add num1 num2
  math_add() {
      local num1=$1
      local num2=$2
      echo $(( num1 + num2 ))
  }

  # math_subtract: Subtracts the second number from the first
  # Usage: math_subtract num1 num2
  math_subtract() {
      local num1=$1
      local num2=$2
      echo $(( num1 - num2 ))
  }

  # Additional mathematical functions can be defined here
  ```

  Each function should be documented with comments indicating its purpose and usage, aiding other developers or future referential needs. The shebang (#!/bin/bash) at the top ensures that the script is executed with the correct interpreter.

- **Handling Dependencies**: Functions within a library might depend on other functions or external tools. It is essential to handle such dependencies gracefully. Dependencies should be clearly documented, and all necessary checks should be performed to ensure the presence of required tools or functions before execution.

```
#!/bin/bash

# check_dependency: Checks if a command exists
# Usage: check_dependency command
check_dependency() {
    command -v "$1" &> /dev/null
}

# math_divide: Divides the first number by the second
# Usage: math_divide num1 num2
math_divide() {
    local num1=$1
    local num2=$2
    if ! check_dependency "bc"; then
        echo "Error: bc is not installed." >&2
        return 1
    fi
    if [ "$num2" -eq 0 ]; then
        echo "Error: Division by zero is not allowed." >&2
        return 1
    fi
    echo "scale=2; $num1 / $num2" | bc
}
```

  In this example, math_divide depends on the bc utility for floating-point division. The check_dependency function first verifies if bc is available, and the script handles errors by providing informative messages.

- **Modularity and Reusability**: Functions should be designed with modularity and reusability in mind. Avoid hardcoding values within functions; instead, parameters should be passed, and defaults should be documented where applicable. This ensures that functions can cater to a wide range of use cases without modification.

  Moreover, each function should perform a single, well-defined task. This adheres to the principle of single responsibility, making the function easier to test, debug, and maintain.

- **Example Integration**: To use the functions defined in a library such as math.sh, other scripts need to source the library file. This is done using the source command (or . for brevity). A script that utilizes the math.sh library might look like this:

```
#!/bin/bash

source ../lib/math.sh

num1=15
num2=5

sum=$(math_add $num1 $num2)
difference=$(math_subtract $num1 $num2)
division=$(math_divide $num1 $num2)

echo "Sum: $sum"
echo "Difference: $difference"
echo "Division: $division"
```

This script sources math.sh and calls its functions, demonstrating a clear method for integrating and utilizing functions from libraries. The output of executing the script would be:

```
Sum: 20
Difference: 10
Division: 3
```

In a collaborative environment, documenting your library is crucial. Documentation can be provided inline with comments or as separate markdown or text files accompanying the library. This practice significantly enhances readability and helps to onboard new developers efficiently.

By adhering to these principles and techniques, one can organize shell script functions into well-structured, maintainable libraries. This not only fosters code reuse and reduces redundancy but also supports scalable and collaborative software development.

8.10 Sourcing and Using Libraries in Shell Scripts

Using libraries in shell scripts is a powerful technique to promote code reuse and maintainability. This section discusses how to effectively source and use library files in your shell scripts. It assumes familiarity with creating and organizing shell script functions, covered earlier in the chapter.

When we source a library file in a shell script, we essentially include and execute the contents of that file in the current shell environment. This allows us to access functions and variables defined in the library without having to replicate the code.

To source a library file, we use the source command or the shorthand . operator. The syntax is straightforward:

```
source /path/to/library.sh
# or equivalently
. /path/to/library.sh
```

Here is a detailed example to illustrate the process of sourcing and using libraries in shell scripts.

First, let's create a simple library file named mylib.sh containing a few utility functions.

```
#!/bin/bash

# Function to print a greeting
greet() {
    echo "Hello, $1!"
}

# Function to calculate the square of a number
square() {
    echo $(( $1 * $1 ))
}
```

Next, we write a shell script that sources mylib.sh and utilizes its functions:

```
#!/bin/bash

# Source the library file
source ./mylib.sh

# Use the functions from the library
greet "World"
result=$(square 4)
echo "The square of 4 is $result"
```

When executed, this script will source mylib.sh, making the greet and square functions available for use. The output of running the script will be:

```
Hello, World!
The square of 4 is 16
```

It is crucial to ensure the library file is executable and has the correct path specified. Relative paths like ./mylib.sh imply the library is in the same directory as the script. For more complex directory structures, absolute paths or environment variables like $HOME or $PATH can be used to locate libraries dynamically.

Additionally, it is good practice to handle errors gracefully while sourcing files. For instance, you might want to check if the file exists before attempting to source it:

```
#!/bin/bash

LIB_PATH="./mylib.sh"

if [[ -f $LIB_PATH ]]; then
    source $LIB_PATH
else
    echo "Library file $LIB_PATH not found!"
    exit 1
fi

greet "World"
result=$(square 4)
echo "The square of 4 is $result"
```

In cases where the library is critical to the operation of the script, using an appropriate error message and exiting can prevent subsequent errors and ensure smoother script execution.

When developing more extensive scripts that source multiple libraries or large library files, it becomes essential to prevent function name collisions. Using unique prefixes for each function name or employing namespaces can mitigate such issues. For example, prefixing all function names in mylib.sh with mylib_:

```
#!/bin/bash

# Function to print a greeting
mylib_greet() {
    echo "Hello, $1!"
}

# Function to calculate the square of a number
mylib_square() {
    echo $(( $1 * $1 ))
}
```

And calling these namespaced functions in the main script:

```
#!/bin/bash

LIB_PATH="./mylib.sh"

if [[ -f $LIB_PATH ]]; then
    source $LIB_PATH
else
    echo "Library file $LIB_PATH not found!"
    exit 1
fi

mylib_greet "World"
result=$(mylib_square 4)
echo "The square of 4 is $result"
```

Further, appropriately organizing your libraries and scripts into well-defined directory structures can enhance clarity and ease of maintenance. For instance, you could have a directory named libs to store all your library files:

myproject/
libs/
mylib.sh
anotherlib.sh
scripts/
mainscript.sh

Table 8.1: Directory Structure Example

With this structure, the sourcing in mainscript.sh would look like:

```
#!/bin/bash

LIB_PATH="../libs/mylib.sh"

if [[ -f $LIB_PATH ]]; then
    source $LIB_PATH
else
    echo "Library file $LIB_PATH not found!"
    exit 1
fi

mylib_greet "World"
result=$(mylib_square 4)
echo "The square of 4 is $result"
```

Following these practices ensures that your use of libraries in shell scripts remains effective, organized, and maintainable. Properly sourced libraries provide a robust foundation to build complex scripts with reusable components, promoting efficiency and reducing redundancy in your shell scripting projects.

8.11 Error Handling in Functions

Error handling plays a crucial role in writing robust shell scripts. By effectively managing errors within functions, scripts become more resilient and easier to debug. This section outlines various techniques and strategies for handling errors in shell functions, ensuring that any deviations from the expected workflow are detected and properly addressed.

Exit Status and Conditional Constructs

In shell scripting, every command returns an exit status, which can be checked to determine whether the command executed successfully or encountered an error. The exit status of a command is stored in the special variable $?. A status of 0 indicates success, while any non-zero value denotes an error.

To handle errors, one can use conditional constructs such as if, elif, else, and case. These constructs evaluate the exit status and execute appropriate code based on whether a command succeeded or failed.

```
my_function() {
    # Attempt to create a directory
    mkdir /some/directory

    if [ $? -ne 0 ]; then
        echo "Error: Failed to create directory."
        return 1 # Return non-zero status to indicate an error
    fi

    echo "Directory created successfully."
    return 0 # Return zero status to indicate success
}
```

In this example, the function my_function attempts to create a directory. If the mkdir command fails, an error message is printed and the function returns 1, indicating an error. Otherwise, a success message is printed and the function returns 0.

Using set -e **and** trap

The set -e command can be used to make a script exit immediately if any command within it returns a non-zero status. While this is useful for catching errors early, it might not be desirable in all scenarios. Selective error trapping can be implemented using the trap command, which allows the execution of a specified command if a particular signal is received.

```
my_function() {
    trap 'echo "Error: Command failed."; return 1' ERR

    # Commands that might fail
    cp /some/nonexistent/file /another/location

    # Reset the trap to avoid catching subsequent errors
    trap - ERR

    echo "File copied successfully."
    return 0
}
```

In this example, if any command within the my_function fails, the trap command prints an error message and returns 1. The trap - ERR command resets the trap, ensuring that subsequent commands outside this context don't trigger the error handling trap.

Custom Error Handlers

For more complex error handling, custom error-handling functions can be defined and invoked whenever an error is detected. This approach provides a clean and centralized way to manage errors.

```
# Custom error handler function
error_handler() {
    echo "An error occurred in function: $1"
    echo "Error message: $2"
    return 1
}

copy_file() {
    cp "$1" "$2" || error_handler "copy_file" "Failed to copy $1 to $2"
}

my_function() {
    copy_file "/some/nonexistent/file" "/another/location"

    # Further processing...
}
```

Here, the error_handler function takes two arguments: the name of the function where the error occurred and a custom error message. The copy_file function demonstrates how to use the custom error handler in conjunction with the cp command. If the cp command fails, the error handler is invoked with relevant information.

Returning Error Codes and Messages

Sometimes, it's beneficial to return specific error codes and messages from functions to indicate the nature of the error. This practice helps in diagnosing issues and taking corrective actions.

```
download_file() {
    local url="$1"
    local destination="$2"

    curl -o "$destination" "$url"
    if [ $? -ne 0 ]; then
        echo "Error: Unable to download file from $url"
        return 2 # Custom error code for download failure
    fi

    echo "File downloaded successfully."
    return 0
}

my_function() {
    download_file "http://example.com/file.zip" "/path/to/destination"
    local status=$?

    if [ $status -ne 0 ]; then
        if [ $status -eq 2 ]; then
            echo "Download failed, please check the URL or network connection."
        fi
```

```
        return $status
    fi

    # Further processing...
}
```

In this example, the download_file function returns 2 if the download fails. The calling function, my_function, checks the return status and provides a specific message if the error code matches the custom error code for download failure.

Logging Errors

Logging errors to a file helps in tracking issues over time and facilitates debugging. A logging function can be created to append error messages to a log file.

```
log_error() {
    echo "$(date '+%Y-%m-%d %H:%M:%S') - $1" >> error_log.txt
}

delete_file() {
    rm "$1"
    if [ $? -ne 0 ]; then
        log_error "Failed to delete file: $1"
        return 1
    fi

    echo "File deleted successfully."
    return 0
}

my_function() {
    delete_file "/some/nonexistent/file"

    # Further processing...
}
```

In this example, the log_error function appends an error message with a timestamp to the error_log.txt file. The delete_file function uses log_error to record any errors encountered while attempting to delete a file.

Effective error handling in shell scripts, especially within functions, ensures the creation of reliable and maintainable scripts. By incorporating these techniques, one can gracefully manage unexpected situations, providing meaningful feedback to users and facilitating debugging processes.

8.12 Practical Examples of Using Functions and Libraries

Practical application is paramount in mastering shell scripting functions and libraries. This section provides robust examples that illustrate the creation, usage, and organization of functions and libraries, enhancing your script modularity and maintainability.

First, consider a scenario where we need to manage user accounts in a Linux system. We will create a shell script library, user_management.sh, and then demonstrate its usage in a script.

```
#!/bin/bash
# Library for User Management Functions

# Function to add a new user
add_user() {
    local username=$1
    if id "$username" &>/dev/null; then
        echo "User '$username' already exists."
    else
        sudo useradd -m "$username"
        echo "User '$username' has been added."
    fi
}

# Function to delete an existing user
delete_user() {
    local username=$1
    if id "$username" &>/dev/null; then
        sudo userdel -r "$username"
        echo "User '$username' has been deleted."
    else
        echo "User '$username' does not exist."
    fi
}

# Function to list all users
list_users() {
    cut -d: -f1 /etc/passwd
}
```

The above shell script, user_management.sh, defines three essential functions for managing users: add_user, delete_user, and list_users.

To use these functions in a shell script, we source the library and call the functions as needed. Here is an example script that utilizes this library:

```
#!/bin/bash
# Script to manage users using user_management.sh library

# Source the user management library
source ./user_management.sh
```

```
# Add a user
add_user "john_doe"

# Delete a user
delete_user "john_doe"

# List all users
list_users
```

When executed, manage_users.sh will produce output similar to the following, assuming appropriate permissions:

```
User 'john_doe' has been added.
User 'john_doe' has been deleted.
root
daemon
bin
sys
...
```

Next, let's create a more complex example involving mathematical operations. This example demonstrates leveraging recursion in a shell function library, math_operations.sh.

```
#!/bin/bash
# Library for Mathematical Operations Functions

# Recursive function to calculate factorial
factorial() {
    local n=$1
    if [ "$n" -le 1 ]; then
        echo 1
    else
        local temp=$((n - 1))
        local result=$(factorial $temp)
        echo $((n * result))
    fi
}

# Function to calculate the greatest common divisor (GCD) using Euclid's algorithm
gcd() {
    local a=$1
    local b=$2
    if [ "$b" -eq 0 ]; then
        echo $a
    else
        gcd "$b" "$((a % b))"
    fi
}
```

The math_operations.sh library includes two functions: factorial and gcd. The factorial function calculates the factorial of a number recursively, while the gcd function computes the greatest common divisor using Euclid's algorithm.

Utilizing these mathematical functions in a script is straightforward.

Consider the following script, compute_math.sh, which uses the math_operations.sh library:

```
#!/bin/bash
# Script to compute mathematical operations using math_operations.sh library

# Source the math operations library
source ./math_operations.sh

# Calculate factorial of 5
factorial_result=$(factorial 5)
echo "Factorial of 5 is $factorial_result"

# Calculate GCD of 48 and 18
gcd_result=$(gcd 48 18)
echo "GCD of 48 and 18 is $gcd_result"
```

Running compute_math.sh delivers the following output:

```
Factorial of 5 is 120
GCD of 48 and 18 is 6
```

By now, it should be evident that organizing functions into libraries enhances script readability and maintenance. Libraries promote reusability across multiple scripts, allowing you to build more complex and precise solutions.

Consider another practical scenario where we need date and time operations encapsulated in a library, date_operations.sh.

```
#!/bin/bash
# Library for Date and Time Operations

# Function to get current date and time
current_datetime() {
    echo $(date '+%Y-%m-%d %H:%M:%S')
}

# Function to get the number of days until a specified date
days_until() {
    local future_date=$1
    local current_date=$(date +%s)
    local target_date=$(date -d "$future_date" +%s)
    local difference=$(( (target_date - current_date) / 86400 ))
    echo $difference
}
```

The date_operations.sh library includes functions to obtain the current date and time and to compute the number of days until a specified date. Employ this library in a script as illustrated in date_info.sh:

```
#!/bin/bash
# Script to demonstrate date operations using date_operations.sh library

# Source the date operations library
source ./date_operations.sh
```

```
# Get current date and time
current_time=$(current_datetime)
echo "Current date and time: $current_time"

# Calculate number of days until a specified date
future_date="2024-12-31"
days_until_date=$(days_until "$future_date")
echo "Days until $future_date: $days_until_date"
```

Executing date_info.sh results in:

```
Current date and time: 2023-10-07 12:34:56
Days until 2024-12-31: 450
```

These extensively detailed examples demonstrate the practical application of functions and libraries in shell scripting. They underline the advantages of modular design, making scripts more manageable and function-specific operations readily reusable.

Chapter 9

Advanced Shell Scripting Techniques

This chapter delves into advanced shell scripting techniques to enhance script functionality and efficiency. It covers using arrays, processing command-line arguments with 'getopts', and managing file descriptors and redirection. The chapter includes background and parallel execution, named pipes for inter-process communication, and advanced pattern matching with regular expressions. It also discusses signal handling with 'trap', job control, creating and using temporary files, handling large data sets, and optimizing script performance. Practical examples illustrate these advanced techniques in action.

9.1 Introduction to Advanced Techniques

An in-depth understanding of advanced shell scripting techniques is essential for creating robust, efficient, and scalable scripts. This section aims to provide a clear and comprehensive overview of these advanced techniques, facilitating mastery and confident application. We will cover several critical areas, including the use of arrays, handling command-line arguments, managing file descriptors, and various optimization strategies.

- Arrays are powerful data structures that offer a flexible way to handle sequences of data. Unlike scalar variables, arrays can store multiple values under a single name, significantly simplifying data handling and manipulation. We will explore how to define arrays, access array elements, and perform common operations such as iteration and element substitution. Mastering arrays is crucial for improving script organization and efficiency.

- Command-line argument processing in shell scripting is refined with the getopts built-in command, which provides a standard way to handle options and arguments passed to scripts. getopts supports parsing arguments, both with and without options, allowing for more sophisticated command-line interfaces. We will examine the syntax and usage of getopts, including practical examples to illustrate how to handle optional and required arguments.
- File descriptors and redirection are fundamental for controlling input and output streams in shell scripts. Understanding how to manage standard input, output, and error streams enables more precise control over script execution and logging. In addition to the default file descriptors (0 for stdin, 1 for stdout, and 2 for stderr), we will discuss how to utilize custom file descriptors for more complex input/output requirements, including examples of redirection and pipelining.
- Background and parallel execution are critical for optimizing script performance, particularly when dealing with time-consuming tasks. Shell scripting allows multiple processes to run concurrently, improving efficiency and resource utilization. We will cover techniques for running commands in the background using the ampersand (&) operator, monitoring background processes, and employing the wait command to manage process synchronization.
- Named pipes, or FIFOs (First In, First Out), enable inter-process communication by allowing data to be passed between processes through a temporary file. Named pipes are useful for scenarios where data needs to be transferred between scripts or processes that cannot be directly connected. We will demonstrate the creation and use of named pipes in shell scripting, highlighting their practical applications and advantages.
- Advanced pattern matching with regular expressions (regex) is indispensable for extracting and processing text data. Shell scripting supports regex in various commands, such as grep, sed, and

awk, providing powerful mechanisms for pattern matching and text substitution. We will delve into the syntax and usage of regex, along with examples that illustrate common patterns and techniques for matching and transforming text data.

- Signal handling with the trap command allows scripts to respond to specific signals, such as interruptions or termination requests. Properly handling signals ensures that scripts can clean up resources, save state, or perform other necessary actions before exiting. We will explore the use of trap to define custom signal handlers, providing examples of common scenarios and best practices for robust signal handling.

- Job control in shell scripts offers mechanisms for managing and controlling multiple jobs within a single script. This includes starting, stopping, resuming, and backgrounding jobs, as well as querying their status. Job control is particularly useful in long-running scripts that require multitasking. We will cover the relevant commands and techniques for effective job control, ensuring reliable and efficient script execution.

- Creating and using temporary files is essential for storing intermediate data or state information during script execution. Temporary files are often necessary when working with large datasets or when the script needs to pass data between stages. We will discuss methods for securely creating temporary files, including the use of built-in utilities such as mktemp, and best practices for handling temporary file cleanup.

- Handling large datasets efficiently is a common challenge in shell scripting. Techniques such as stream processing, buffering, and utilizing powerful text processing tools like awk and sed can significantly improve performance. We will explore strategies for managing and processing large datasets, with examples that demonstrate efficient data manipulation and transformation.

- Optimizing shell script performance is an ongoing process that involves profiling, identifying bottlenecks, and applying appropriate optimization strategies. This may include reducing overhead, minimizing unnecessary operations, and employing more efficient algorithms. We will discuss various tools and techniques for profiling and optimizing shell scripts, providing practical tips to enhance script performance.

By integrating these advanced techniques into your shell scripting repertoire, you will be well-equipped to create highly efficient, reliable, and maintainable scripts. This comprehensive approach to advanced shell scripting ensures a thorough understanding of each concept, empowering you to tackle complex scripting challenges with confidence.

9.2 Using Arrays in Shell Scripts

An array is a data structure that allows storing multiple values within a single variable. Shell scripting supports arrays, which enhance the capability to process and manipulate collections of data efficiently. Unlike regular variables that hold a single value, arrays can hold multiple values, each of which can be accessed using an index.

In shell scripting, arrays are typically indexed with integers and can be declared, initialized, and manipulated using syntax and commands supported by the shell environment.

Declaring and Initializing Arrays

Arrays in shell scripts can be declared explicitly or implicitly. Explicit declaration involves specifying the values at the time of array creation, whereas implicit declaration occurs when you assign values to specific indices of an undeclared array.

For explicit declaration, you can use the following syntax:

```
array_name=("value1" "value2" "value3")
```

Alternatively, implicit declaration can be achieved by assigning values to indices individually:

```
array_name[0]="value1"
array_name[1]="value2"
array_name[2]="value3"
```

Accessing Array Elements

Array elements are accessed using the array name followed by the index within square brackets. Indexing starts at 0. To retrieve an element from an array, use the following syntax:

```
echo ${array_name[index]}
```

For example, to access the first element of the array named array_name, you would use:

```
echo ${array_name[0]}
```

Modifying Array Elements

You can modify array elements by assigning a new value to a specific index:

```
array_name[1]="new_value"
```

Array Length

The length of an array, i.e., the number of elements it contains, can be determined using the following syntax:

```
length=${#array_name[@]}
echo $length
```

Iterating Over an Array

Looping through array elements allows performing operations on each element. The for loop is commonly used for this purpose:

```
for element in "${array_name[@]}"
do
    echo $element
done
```

Alternatively, you can iterate using indices:

```
for index in "${!array_name[@]}"
do
    echo "Index: $index, Value: ${array_name[$index]}"
done
```

Associative Arrays

While indexed arrays use integers as indices, bash version 4.0 and later support associative arrays, where the indices can be arbitrary strings. To declare an associative array, use the declare -A syntax:

```
declare -A assoc_array
assoc_array[key1]="value1"
assoc_array[key2]="value2"
```

Accessing elements in associative arrays involves using the string keys:

```
echo ${assoc_array[key1]}
```

Iterating over associative arrays typically involves looping through keys:

```
for key in "${!assoc_array[@]}"
```

```
do
    echo "Key: $key, Value: ${assoc_array[$key]}"
done
```

Multi-dimensional Arrays

Shell scripts do not natively support multi-dimensional arrays, but you can achieve similar functionality using associative arrays. For example:

```
declare -A matrix
matrix[0,0]=1
matrix[0,1]=2
matrix[1,0]=3
matrix[1,1]=4

for i in 0 1
do
    for j in 0 1
    do
        echo ${matrix[$i,$j]}
    done
done
```

Practical Example: Storing and Processing File Lines

Consider a scenario where you read lines from a file into an array and process each line. Here is an example script:

```
#!/bin/bash

# Read the file into an array
mapfile -t lines < input.txt

# Process each line
for line in "${lines[@]}"
do
    # Performing operations on each line
    echo "Processing line: $line"
done
```

Array use in shell scripts enhances handling sequences of data, enabling complex operations to be carried out efficiently and effectively. Implementing arrays helps maintain code clarity and scalability, essential for advanced scripting tasks.

9.3 Processing Command Line Arguments with getopts

Command-line arguments are fundamental in scripting, enabling users to provide input to a script dynamically at runtime. The getopts built-in command facilitates the parsing of these command-line options systematically and efficiently, particularly for complex scripts requiring multiple options and arguments.

The getopts command allows scripts to handle options and parse them with an intuitive syntax. At its core, getopts iterates over command-line arguments systematically, allowing script authors to define expected options and handle conditions of their presence or absence accordingly.

The basic syntax for getopts is as follows:

```
getopts optstring varname
```

In this context:

- optstring is a string containing the option characters the script recognizes. If an option character is followed by a colon (:), the option is expected to have an argument.
- varname is the name of the variable where getopts places the option character it finds.

Let's consider a practical example to illustrate the usage of getopts:

```
#!/bin/bash

while getopts "u:p:h" opt; do
  case $opt in
    u) user=$OPTARG ;;
    p) pass=$OPTARG ;;
    h) echo "Usage: $0 [-u user] [-p pass]"; exit 1 ;;
    \?) echo "Invalid option: -$OPTARG" >&2; exit 1 ;;
  esac
done

echo "User: $user"
echo "Password: $pass"
```

In this script:

- The options u and p expect arguments (indicated by the colon following each option letter).
- The option h does not expect an argument and is used to display usage information.
- The variable OPTARG automatically stores the argument provided for any option that expects one.
- The case statement branches based on the option detected, facilitating the handling of each specified option.

When executed, the script parses command-line options and sets variables user and pass based on the provided arguments. If the -h option is detected, it displays usage information and exits.

A crucial aspect is considering how options and arguments are provided:

```
./script.sh -u alice -p secret -h
```

In this command:

- The -u option sets user to alice.
- The -p option sets pass to secret.
- The -h triggers the usage information.

It's essential to handle incorrect or unexpected options gracefully. The getopts command places '¿ in the variable (here opt) for unrecognized options, facilitating error handling within the script.

```
\?) echo "Invalid option: -$OPTARG" >&2; exit 1 ;;
```

This snippet within the case statement covers invalid options, providing clear feedback to the user and terminating the script with an appropriate error code.

The use of OPTIND is also noteworthy. OPTIND keeps track of the index of the next argument to be processed and is initialized to 1 by the shell. It's good practice to reset OPTIND when invoking getopts in a script to rerun the option parsing loop or if multiple option parsing is required within the same script execution context.

```
OPTIND=1
```

In the context of multiple invocations or nested loops, careful management of OPTIND ensures the correct parsing flow without skipping or erroneously interpreting arguments.

When transitioning from basic to advanced shell scripting, understanding getopts is crucial for creating flexible, user-friendly scripts that handle a variety of input scenarios cleanly and predictably.

9.4 Working with File Descriptors and Redirection

In Unix-like operating systems, file descriptors are an integral part of the system's I/O (input/output) mechanism. Each process is provided with a set of file descriptors that it uses to communicate with various resources such as files, terminals, or even other processes. Understanding how to manage these file descriptors is essential for advanced shell scripting, enabling more precise control over input and output streams.

Every process starts with three default file descriptors:

- **Standard Input (stdin)**: file descriptor 0, used for input operations.
- **Standard Output (stdout)**: file descriptor 1, used for output operations.
- **Standard Error (stderr)**: file descriptor 2, used for outputting error messages.

By default, stdin, stdout, and stderr are associated with the terminal. However, redirection allows these descriptors to be associated with other files or processes.

Basic Redirection Syntax

Redirection is achieved using the following basic syntax:

```
command > file # Redirects stdout to a file
command < file # Redirects stdin from a file
command 2> file # Redirects stderr to a file
command &> file # Redirects both stdout and stderr to a file (bash-specific)
```

Appending Output

Instead of overwriting a file, you may want to append the output:

```
command >> file # Appends stdout to a file
command 2>> file # Appends stderr to a file
command &>> file # Appends both stdout and stderr to a file (bash-specific)
```

Combining Output Streams

It is often required to combine the output of stdout and stderr into a single stream.

```
command > file 2>&1 # Directs both stdout and stderr to the same file
```

```
command 2>&1 | tee output.log # Directs both stdout and stderr to a file and the
    console
```

The 2>&1 expression tells the shell to redirect stderr (2) to the current location of stdout (1).

Using Custom File Descriptors

In addition to the standard descriptors, custom file descriptors can be created and used for more complex redirection tasks. The syntax is as follows:

```
exec 3>output.txt # Creates a new file descriptor 3 for writing
exec 4<input.txt # Creates a new file descriptor 4 for reading

command 3>&2 4<&0 # Redirects fd 3 to stderr and fd 4 to stdin
```

These custom descriptors can subsequently be closed when no longer needed:

```
exec 3>&- # Closes file descriptor 3
exec 4<&- # Closes file descriptor 4
```

Practical Example

To illustrate how these concepts come together in a practical context, consider a script that logs both command output and errors, while also appending a custom message to a global log file.

```
#!/bin/bash

log_file="my_log_file.txt"
global_log="/var/log/global_script.log"

{
  echo "Starting script at $(date)"

  # Redirect stdout to log_file and stderr to the same log_file
  exec >$log_file 2>&1

  # Simulate a command's output and error message
  echo "This is standard output"
  ls /nonexistent_directory

  echo "Script completed successfully at $(date)"
} &>> $global_log

echo "Log will be appended to $global_log"
```

In this example, the use of exec allows redirection of command output and errors to my_log_file.txt, while the block is also appending to the global log file. This approach ensures all relevant output is captured, facilitating effective debugging and auditing.

File descriptors and redirection techniques form a powerful toolkit within shell scripting, enabling more precise manipulation of input and output streams. This capability is essential for creating robust, maintainable scripts capable of handling complex tasks efficiently.

9.5 Background and Parallel Execution

A critical skill in advanced shell scripting involves efficiently using background and parallel execution. These concepts allow scripts to perform multiple tasks concurrently, enhancing performance, especially for time-consuming or I/O-bound operations.

Executing commands in the background can be accomplished using the ampersand (&) operator. When appended to a command, this operator sends the process to the background, allowing the shell to continue with subsequent commands immediately without waiting for the background process to complete.

```
$ ./long_running_task.sh &
[1] 12345
$ echo "This command runs immediately after initiating the background task."
```

In the above example, long_running_task.sh starts in the background. The shell assigns it a job number [1] and a process ID (12345). The echo command executes without waiting for long_running_task.sh to complete.

To manage background jobs, the jobs, fg, and bg built-in commands are essential. The jobs command lists active jobs:

```
$ jobs
[1]+ Running ./long_running_task.sh &
```

To bring a background job to the foreground, use fg followed by the job number:

```
$ fg %1
./long_running_task.sh
```

For sending a paused job back to the background, use the bg command:

```
$ bg %1
[1]+ ./long_running_task.sh &
```

Parallel execution involves running multiple commands or scripts simultaneously. This technique is vital when scripts incorporate independent tasks that can execute concurrently to save time.

The wait command plays a crucial role, halting the script until all specified background jobs complete. This synchronization enables orderly completion and proper handling of background processes. Below is an example of executing multiple tasks in parallel and waiting for their completion:

```
#!/bin/bash
task1 &
task2 &
task3 &
wait
echo "All tasks completed."
```

In the script above, task1, task2, and task3 initiate concurrently. The wait command ensures the script pauses until all background tasks finish before proceeding to the echo statement.

GNU parallel is a powerful tool facilitating more advanced parallel execution. It distributes tasks across multiple CPU cores, optimizing performance. To use GNU parallel, it must be installed:

```
$ sudo apt-get install parallel # Debian/Ubuntu
$ sudo yum install parallel # Red Hat/CentOS
```

The following example demonstrates using GNU parallel to run a command on multiple files concurrently:

```
$ ls *.txt | parallel -j 4 gzip
```

Here, parallel processes up to four .txt files concurrently with the gzip command, leveraging multi-core systems efficiently.

Incorporating these techniques requires awareness of potential pitfalls such as race conditions, resource exhaustion, and managing inter-process communication. Ensuring appropriate synchronization, handling job outputs, and balancing system load are essential practices for robust parallel execution in shell scripts.

9.6 Using Named Pipes for Inter-Process Communication

Named pipes, known as FIFOs (First In, First Out), provide an effective mechanism for inter-process communication (IPC) in Linux. They enable processes to communicate with each other by reading and writing to a named pipe file. Unlike anonymous pipes, named pipes exist as persistent files in the filesystem and can be used by unrelated processes.

To create a named pipe in a shell script, use the mkfifo command. This command creates a special file that behaves like a pipe, allowing processes to read from and write to it.

```
mkfifo /tmp/my_fifo
```

The above command creates a named pipe at /tmp/my_fifo. Processes can then read from and write to this pipe using standard file operations.

To demonstrate the usage of named pipes, let's construct an example where one process writes to the pipe and another process reads from it. First, create a named pipe:

```
mkfifo /tmp/my_fifo
```

In one terminal, initiate the writer process:

```
echo "Hello from the writer process!" > /tmp/my_fifo
```

In another terminal, start the reader process:

```
cat /tmp/my_fifo
```

The reader process will block until the writer process sends data through the pipe. When the writer writes data to the pipe, the reader will output:

```
Hello from the writer process!
```

This simple example demonstrates blocking behavior, where the reader waits until data is available. Named pipes are incredibly useful for scenarios requiring synchronization between processes.

- Consider a more complex example involving a producer-consumer scenario. We'll create a script where a producer generates numbers and writes them to a named pipe. A consumer script will read these numbers from the named pipe and process them.

Create the named pipe:

```
mkfifo /tmp/num_fifo
```

The producer script (producer.sh):

```
#!/bin/bash

for i in {1..10}; do
    echo $i > /tmp/num_fifo
    sleep 1
done
```

The consumer script (consumer.sh):

```
#!/bin/bash

while true; do
    if read line < /tmp/num_fifo; then
        echo "Consumer read: $line"
    fi
done
```

Run both scripts in separate terminals:

```
# In one terminal
./producer.sh
# In another terminal
./consumer.sh
```

The output of the consumer.sh script would be:

```
Consumer read: 1
Consumer read: 2
Consumer read: 3
Consumer read: 4
Consumer read: 5
Consumer read: 6
Consumer read: 7
Consumer read: 8
Consumer read: 9
Consumer read: 10
```

In this scenario, the producer generates numbers with a delay of one second between each number and writes them to the named pipe. The consumer continuously reads from the pipe and processes the numbers, showing an effective use of named pipes for IPC.

- It is essential to handle cleanup of named pipes to avoid cluttering the filesystem with unused pipe files. This can be done using the rm command:

```
rm /tmp/my_fifo
```

In practice, including cleanup commands in your scripts ensures that named pipes are appropriately removed after use. For example, you can modify the producer script to clean up:

```
#!/bin/bash

# Create named pipe
mkfifo /tmp/num_fifo

# Generate numbers
for i in {1..10}; do
    echo $i > /tmp/num_fifo
    sleep 1
done

# Clean up
rm /tmp/num_fifo
```

By handling the creation and deletion of named pipes within scripts, users ensure efficient resource management and maintain a clean working environment.

Integrating named pipes into your shell scripts allows for sophisticated inter-process communication and can significantly enhance the functionality and efficiency of your scripts.

9.7 Advanced Pattern Matching with Regular Expressions

Regular expressions provide a powerful means for pattern matching and text manipulation within shell scripts. This section covers advanced regular expression techniques to enhance text processing capabilities in shell scripting. Regular expressions (regex) are sequences of characters defining a search pattern, widely used in tools like grep, sed, awk, and within many programming languages.

When dealing with regular expressions in shell scripts, it is important to distinguish between various flavors and their nuances. The most common types include Basic Regular Expressions (BRE), Extended Regular Expressions (ERE), and Perl-Compatible Regular Expressions (PCRE). Here, we focus on ERE and PCRE, which provide more powerful pattern matching capabilities compared to BRE.

Extended Regular Expressions (ERE) are supported by the grep -E or egrep commands, as well as sed -r and awk, among others. Key elements of ERE include:

- *Character Classes:* Sets of characters can be defined using square brackets, e.g., [a-z] matches any lowercase letter. Pre-

defined character classes include
d for digits and
w for word characters.

- *Anchors:* ^ and $ denote the start and end of a line, respectively.
- *Repetition Operators:* Quantifiers like *, +, and ? denote zero or more, one or more, and zero or one occurrences, respectively. Additionally, curly braces specify exact occurrence counts, such as a{3} matching exactly three 'a' characters.
- *Alternation and Grouping:* The vertical bar | provides an OR operation, and parentheses () group patterns or capture substrings.

Perl-Compatible Regular Expressions (PCRE), utilized in tools like perl, grep -P, and advanced text editors, offer extended features beyond ERE. Examples include:

- *Lookahead and Lookbehind Assertions:* Lookaheads (e.g., ?=) and lookbehinds (e.g., ?<=) specify conditions on the surrounding text without including it in the match.
- *Non-capturing Groups:* Parentheses with a ?: prefix define groups without capturing, aiding complex regex management.
- *Backreferences:* Matched groups can be referenced later in the expression, using
  1,
  2, etc.

Below are practical examples demonstrating advanced regex techniques:

```
# Match lines starting with 'Error' followed by a timestamp (YYYY-MM-DD):
grep -E '^Error [0-9]{4}-[0-9]{2}-[0-9]{2}' logfile.txt
```

In this example, ^Error [0-9]{4}-[0-9]{2}-[0-9]{2} matches lines beginning with 'Error' followed by a date.

```
# Match a word and ensure it appears twice consecutively in the text:
grep -oP '(\b\w+\b) \1' document.txt
```

Here, (
b
w+

b)
1 uses the backreference
1 to ensure the same word appears twice consecutively.

```
# Match 'error' only if preceded by 'critical' and followed by '!':
grep -oP '(?<=critical )error(?=!)' log.txt
```

This example showcases lookbehind (?<=critical) and lookahead (?=!) assertions to precisely match 'error' within specific contexts.

Utilizing regular expressions within shell scripts enhances text processing and parsing capabilities, facilitating complex data extraction, validation, and modification tasks. Mastery of ERE and PCRE syntax is crucial for efficient and effective shell scripting, providing robust tools for sophisticated pattern matching scenarios.

9.8 Using 'trap' for Signal Handling

Signal handling is a critical aspect of robust shell scripting, allowing scripts to manage or mitigate the impact of unexpected interruptions. Signals are software interrupts sent to a process to indicate that an event has occurred. The shell provides a built-in command, trap, to capture and handle these signals.

trap is utilized to specify how the shell should respond when it receives certain signals. With trap, scripts can execute a cleanup procedure or perform other tasks before terminating, thereby enhancing stability and reliability.

```
trap COMMAND SIGNAL
```

In this command:

- COMMAND is the command or a set of commands to be executed when the specified signal is received.
- SIGNAL is the signal number or name to be trapped.

Consider a shell script designed to clean up temporary files when interrupted by a SIGINT (signal number 2, typically generated by pressing Ctrl+C). The following example demonstrates setting up a trap for SIGINT:

```
#!/bin/bash
```

```
# Temporary file
tempfile=$(mktemp /tmp/tempfile.XXXXXX)

# Define a cleanup function
cleanup() {
    echo "Caught SIGINT signal!"
    rm -f "$tempfile"
    echo "Temporary file deleted."
    exit 0
}

# Set the trap
trap cleanup SIGINT

# Main script logic
echo "Script is running. Press Ctrl+C to trigger SIGINT signal."
sleep 30

# Clean up in case script completes without interruption
cleanup
```

This script creates a temporary file and defines a cleanup function to delete the file and exit gracefully when the script receives a SIGINT signal. The trap command associates the cleanup function with the SIGINT signal, ensuring the cleanup function is executed if the user interrupts the script with Ctrl+C.

In addition to SIGINT, the shell recognizes various signals such as:

- SIGHUP (1) - Hangup detected on controlling terminal or death of controlling process.
- SIGQUIT (3) - Quit from keyboard.
- SIGTERM (15) - Termination signal.
- SIGKILL (9) - Kill signal (cannot be caught or ignored).
- SIGUSR1 (10) and SIGUSR2 (12) - User-defined signals.

For example, to handle the SIGTERM signal, which is typically sent to request program termination, one can modify the above script as follows:

```
#!/bin/bash

tempfile=$(mktemp /tmp/tempfile.XXXXXX)

cleanup() {
    echo "Caught SIGTERM signal!"
    rm -f "$tempfile"
    echo "Temporary file deleted."
    exit 0
```

```
}

trap cleanup SIGTERM

echo "Script is running. Send SIGTERM signal to trigger cleanup."
sleep 30

cleanup
```

To test the above script, it can be executed and terminated using the kill command from another terminal:

```
kill -SIGTERM <pid_of_the_script>
```

where <pid_of_the_script> is the process ID of the running script.

Multiple signals can be trapped by specifying them in a space-separated list:

```
trap cleanup SIGINT SIGTERM
```

This ensures the cleanup function is called if either SIGINT or SIGTERM is received.

Traps can also be set to execute commands before the script exits normally, either explicitly via exit or implicitly when the script finishes executing:

```
trap "echo Exiting; rm -f \"$tempfile\"" EXIT
```

In this scenario, the specified commands are executed upon script termination, ensuring final cleanup operations are always performed.

To remove a previously set trap, one can use:

```
trap - SIGNAL
```

For instance:

```
trap - SIGINT
```

This command restores the default action for the SIGINT signal.

Utilizing trap enables scripts to react appropriately to various signals, thus allowing predictable and safe termination or interruption handling. By ensuring important cleanup operations are performed, trap significantly enhances the reliability and maintainability of shell scripts.

9.9 Job Control in Shell Scripts

Job control in shell scripts encompasses the mechanisms for managing multiple processes. This is vital when running multiple commands concurrently, ensuring resources are allocated efficiently. Shell scripting facilitates job control through various commands and constructs, including '&', 'jobs', 'fg', 'bg', and 'wait'.

The '&' symbol is used to run a command in the background, detaching it from the terminal. This allows the terminal to accept new commands while the background process continues execution. For instance, the following script runs 'command1' in the background while 'command2' runs in the foreground:

```
#!/bin/bash
command1 &
command2
```

The 'command1' runs asynchronously with the '&' at the end, allowing 'command2' to execute without waiting for 'command1' to complete.

To monitor background jobs, the 'jobs' command is utilized. It lists all jobs initiated during the current session, providing their job IDs, statuses, and commands. For example:

```
#!/bin/bash
sleep 30 &
jobs
```

Executing this script will display the background job initiated, typically outputting something like:

```
[1]+  Running                 sleep 30 &
```

Bringing jobs to the foreground is achieved with the 'fg' command, followed by the job ID. If no job ID is specified, the shell defaults to the most recent job. Conversely, the 'bg' command resumes suspended jobs in the background. For instance:

```
#!/bin/bash
sleep 30 &
sleep 60 &
jobs
fg %1
bg %2
```

This script will start two 'sleep' commands in the background. The 'jobs' command lists these jobs, 'fg %1' moves the first 'sleep' command to the foreground, and 'bg %2' resumes the second 'sleep' command in the background.

In scenarios requiring synchronization, the 'wait' command is employed. It pauses the script's execution until specified background jobs complete. Without any arguments, 'wait' waits for all background jobs. The following example demonstrates this:

```
#!/bin/bash
sleep 30 &
job1=$!
sleep 60 &
job2=$!
wait $job1
wait $job2
echo "Both jobs have completed."
```

Here, 'sleep 30' and 'sleep 60' run in the background, with their process IDs stored in 'job1' and 'job2' respectively. The 'wait' command halts the script until both 'sleep' commands finish, ensuring the subsequent 'echo' command only executes once both jobs are done.

Advanced job control might involve trapping signals like 'SIGCHLD' to catch child process termination. This technique ensures proper cleanup and handling of terminated background processes. For example, the following script traps the 'SIGCHLD' signal:

```
#!/bin/bash

trap 'echo "A child process has terminated."' SIGCHLD

sleep 30 &
wait
```

When the 'sleep 30' command terminates, the 'SIGCHLD' signal triggers the trap, executing the associated echo command.

Job control is not limited to managing asynchronous tasks. Shells support stopping (suspending) and resuming processes using 'Ctrl-Z' and 'bg'/'fg' commands respectively. By sending 'SIGSTOP' or 'SIGTSTP' to a process, it can be suspended, and later resumed with 'SIGCONT':

```
#!/bin/bash

# Start the sleep command and stop it immediately
sleep 300 &
sleep_pid=$!

kill -SIGSTOP $sleep_pid
echo "sleep 300 has been stopped."

# Resume the sleep command
kill -SIGCONT $sleep_pid
echo "sleep 300 has been resumed."
```

```
wait $sleep_pid
echo "sleep 300 has completed."
```

This script starts a background 'sleep 300' process, stops it with 'SIGSTOP', and later resumes it with 'SIGCONT'. The 'wait' command ensures the script waits until the 'sleep' command completes.

Understanding job control is fundamental for writing efficient and responsive shell scripts. Employing these techniques ensures that scripts can manage multiple processes, react to their statuses, and handle their execution flow programmatically.

9.10 Creating and Using Temporary Files

Temporary files are frequently used in shell scripts to store intermediate data which needs to be used across various stages of script execution. Proper handling of temporary files is crucial for ensuring data integrity and script reliability, as well as for preventing potential resource leaks.

Creating temporary files in Unix-like systems can be done in several ways, each with its own implications for security and portability. The mktemp command is a robust and preferred method to safely create temporary files or directories.

mktemp generates a unique filename and securely opens it for reading and writing. The basic usage of mktemp is illustrated below:

```
temp_file=$(mktemp)
```

This command assigns the name of the newly created temporary file to the variable temp_file. By default, mktemp creates the file in the /tmp directory. The created temporary file is accessible only by the user who created it, having the permissions set to 600.

To create a temporary directory, use the -d option:

```
temp_dir=$(mktemp -d)
```

This command creates a new directory in /tmp and assigns its path to the variable temp_dir.

Temporary files should be removed once they are no longer needed to free up system resources. This can be done using the rm command for files and the rmdir command for directories:

```
rm -f "$temp_file"
```

```
rmdir "$temp_dir"
```

However, it is highly recommended to ensure that temporary files are always cleaned up even if the script exits unexpectedly. Using a trap statement to handle script termination signals enhances the reliability:

```
trap 'rm -f "$temp_file"; rmdir "$temp_dir"' EXIT
```

This command ensures that the specified actions (removing the temporary file and directory) are executed when the script exits, regardless of the exit status.

Sometimes, manually specifying a template for the temporary filename or directory may be desirable. The template must end with at least six 'X's, which mktemp replaces with random characters. For example:

```
temp_file=$(mktemp /tmp/mytempfile.XXXXXX)
temp_dir=$(mktemp -d /tmp/mytempdir.XXXXXX)
```

The security of temporary files is paramount. Avoiding temporary files with predictable names is essential to prevent malicious users from exploiting race conditions. The mktemp utility mitigates such risks by ensuring unique and secure filenames.

Another common method to create temporary files uses the system's built-in facilities via the ${TMPDIR} environment variable. If TMPDIR is not defined, the fallback directory is typically /tmp:

```
temp_file=$(mktemp "${TMPDIR:-/tmp}/mytempfile.XXXXXX")
```

This approach ensures compatibility with systems configured with a custom TMPDIR path.

When working with larger data sets or multi-stage pipelines, temporary files enable significant performance improvements by avoiding extensive in-memory operations. Here is a script example demonstrating a practical use case for temporary files in processing:

```
#!/bin/bash

# Create a temporary file
temp_file=$(mktemp)
trap 'rm -f "$temp_file"' EXIT

# Simulate data processing
for i in {1..1000}; do
    echo "Processing item $i" >> "$temp_file"
done

# Read and manipulate the temporary file's content
while read -r line; do
```

```
    echo "$line - processed"
done < "$temp_file"
```

This script stores intermediate data in a temporary file during looping operations to process a large number of items. The file is read back and manipulated before deletion on script exit.

Integration of temporary files into shell scripts enhances efficiency, security, and reliability by providing a controlled scope for intermediate data storage. Removing temporary files promptly preserves system resources and maintains operational integrity.

9.11 Handling Large Data Sets

Handling large data sets in shell scripting requires a blend of efficient processing techniques and understanding the limitations of the environment. This section presents strategies for managing and processing large data sets, ensuring scripts perform efficiently without running into memory or performance bottlenecks.

Processing large data sets can be challenging due to constraints posed by the shell environment. Importantly, shell scripts operate within the confines of system resources such as CPU, memory, and file descriptors. The shell also follows a linear processing model which may introduce inefficiencies for large-scale data processing tasks. To efficiently handle large data sets, we will utilize various tools and techniques.

- **Stream Processing with awk, sed, and cut:** One effective way to process large data sets is through stream processing tools. Tools like awk, sed, and cut can process data line-by-line, minimizing the amount of data held in memory at any one time.

```
awk '{ print $1, $2 }' large_data_file.txt > processed_data.txt
```

In the above example, awk processes each line of large_data_file.txt, extracting and printing the first two fields, and writes the output to processed_data.txt. This stream processing approach ensures that only a small portion of the file is in memory at any given time.

- **Utilizing sort and uniq for Large Data Sets:** Sorting and removing duplicates from large data sets can be efficiently performed using the sort and uniq commands. These commands are optimized for handling large volumes of data.

```
sort large_data_file.txt | uniq > sorted_unique_data.txt
```

The sort command sorts the entire data set, while uniq removes adjacent duplicate lines. This combination handles large files efficiently as both commands are implemented to work with data streams leveraging effective memory management techniques.

- **Splitting Large Files with split:** When dealing with extremely large files, splitting them into smaller chunks can simplify processing. The split command can divide a large file into smaller, more manageable parts.

```
split -l 10000 large_data_file.txt chunk_
```

The above command splits large_data_file.txt into smaller files, each containing 10,000 lines, with filenames prefixed by chunk_. This approach helps in processing each chunk independently, avoiding memory overload.

- **Employing Parallel Processing with GNU Parallel:** Parallel processing can significantly reduce processing time. The GNU Parallel tool allows multiple operations to run concurrently, leveraging multi-core processors.

```
cat file_list.txt | parallel -j 4 process_script.sh {}
```

Here, file_list.txt contains a list of files to be processed. The parallel command runs process_script.sh on each file concurrently, with up to four jobs (-j 4) running in parallel. This takes advantage of multicore processors to speed up data processing tasks.

- **Memory-Efficient Data Processing with buffer:** The buffer tool can wrap around data streams to control the flow of data, thereby optimizing memory usage during processing.

```
cat large_data_file.txt | buffer -s 1M | processing_script.sh
```

In this example, buffer is set with a buffer size of 1 megabyte (-s 1M), balancing memory usage and processing speed by controlling the flow of data to processing_script.sh.

- **Efficient Text Processing with rg and jq:** Tools like ripgrep (rg) for text search and jq for JSON processing are optimized for handling large data sets efficiently.

```
rg 'pattern' large_data_file.txt > matched_lines.txt
```

```
jq '.[] | {id: .id, name: .name}' large_data.json > processed_data.json
```

rg performs faster searches compared to grep, making it suitable for large files. jq efficiently parses and processes JSON data, ensuring minimal memory usage.

- **Reducing Memory Footprint with shuf and head:** For large data sets where sampling or previewing is necessary, commands like shuf and head come in handy.

```
shuf -n 10000 large_data_file.txt > sampled_data.txt
head -n 10 large_data_file.txt
```

shuf selects a random sample of 10,000 lines, and head previews the first 10 lines. These commands help manage large data efficiently by limiting the amount of data loaded into memory.

These techniques and tools, when applied appropriately, enable efficient handling and processing of large data sets in shell scripts. By leveraging stream processing, parallel execution, and memory management strategies, one can ensure that scripts remain performant and scalable.

9.12 Optimizing Shell Script Performance

Performance optimization in shell scripting is crucial for handling large-scale processes efficiently. Through careful selection of commands, minimizing unnecessary operations, and harnessing efficient programming constructs, one can significantly enhance script performance. This section emphasizes several strategies and best practices for optimizing shell scripts.

Firstly, prefer built-in shell commands and functions over external commands. Built-ins execute faster as they do not require launching a separate process. For example, using shell arithmetic or string manipulation facilities like $VAR%%pattern for trimming can be more efficient than external tools like expr or sed.

```
# Using built-in string manipulation
filename="example.txt"
basename="${filename%.txt}"

# Instead of
basename=$(echo "$filename" | sed 's/\.txt$//')
```

Loop constructs also play a vital role in performance. Avoid for loops iterating over command substitutions that generate large lists. Execute while loops with piped input, which is generally more efficient.

```
# Inefficient for loop
for file in $(ls *.txt); do
  echo "$file"
done

# Efficient while loop
ls *.txt | while read -r file; do
  echo "$file"
done
```

When processing large text data, tools like awk and sed are preferable over the native bash for complex text manipulation due to their optimized execution speed. Combine commands in a single awk or sed script when possible, to reduce overhead from multiple tool invocations.

```
# Using multiple tools
grep "pattern" file | cut -d \t -f 1 | sort | uniq

# Combining into one awk
awk '/pattern/ {print $1}' file | sort | uniq
```

Reading files in a script should be accomplished through efficient constructs like mapfile (also known as readarray) for reading into an array, or direct redirection into a while loop.

```
# Using mapfile
mapfile -t lines < file

# Redirect into while loop
while IFS= read -r line; do
  echo "$line"
done < file
```

Minimizing process forks and subshells is another crucial optimization. Each fork or execution of a subshell ((command)) adds overhead. Where possible, use shell constructs that avoid these.

```
# Forking with subshell
result=$(command)

# Using parameter expansion
if [[ "$variable" == *"pattern"* ]]; then
  result="matched"
```

```
fi
```

The efficiency of mathematical operations is significantly enhanced by using shell arithmetic and avoiding external utilities like bc or expr.

```
# Using shell arithmetic
result=$(( a + b ))

# Instead of external tools
result=$(expr $a + $b)
```

Furthermore, for lengthy scripts, especially those intended for repetitive execution, consider compiling frequently used portions with a Just-In-Time (JIT) compiler using tools like shc which can convert shell scripts into binaries.

```
# Compiling script with shc
shc -f script.sh -o script
```

Additionally, profile and benchmark scripts to identify performance bottlenecks. Tools such as time, bash -x, and dedicated profilers like perf can provide valuable insights.

```
# Simple profiling with time
time ./script.sh

# Using bash debugging
bash -x script.sh > debug.log 2>&1
```

Parallel execution of independent tasks can significantly cut down runtime. Utilize background jobs and tools like GNU Parallel to achieve concurrent execution across multiple cores.

```
# Using background jobs
command1 &
command2 &
wait

# Using GNU Parallel
parallel ::: command1 command2 command3
```

Appending these optimization techniques to your scripting practice not only improves performance but also ensures scripts are robust and scalable, capable of handling more extensive datasets and more complex operations effectively.

9.13 Practical Examples of Advanced Shell Scripting

To effectively harness the capabilities discussed throughout this chapter, we will explore practical examples that consolidate various advanced shell scripting techniques. These examples will illustrate the practical application of advanced concepts such as arrays, getopts for command-line argument processing, file descriptors, named pipes, and more.

Example 1: Batch Renaming Files Using Arrays and Regular Expressions

This example demonstrates how to batch rename files in a directory using arrays and regular expressions. We will rename all .txt files by appending the current date to their filenames.

```
#!/bin/bash

# Define an array to store .txt files
files=( *.txt )
current_date=$(date +%Y-%m-%d)

for file in "${files[@]}"
do
    # Using regular expression to extract base file name
    if [[ $file =~ (.*)\.txt$ ]]; then
        base_name="${BASH_REMATCH[1]}"
        new_name="${base_name}_${current_date}.txt"
        mv "$file" "$new_name"
        echo "Renamed $file to $new_name"
    fi
done
```

The script begins by defining an array, files, containing all .txt files in the current directory. The date command captures the current date, used as a suffix for the new filenames. A for loop iterates over each file, employing a regular expression to extract the base name, which is then appended with the date before renaming occurs using the mv command.

Example 2: Command-Line Argument Processing with getopts

This script uses getopts to process command-line arguments for a hypothetical backup utility. It supports options for specifying a source directory, a destination directory, and verbosity.

```
#!/bin/bash

while getopts ":s:d:v" opt; do
  case $opt in
    s)
      source_dir=$OPTARG
      ;;
    d)
      dest_dir=$OPTARG
      ;;
    v)
      verbose=1
      ;;
    \?)
      echo "Invalid option: -$OPTARG" >&2
      exit 1
      ;;
    :)
      echo "Option -$OPTARG requires an argument." >&2
      exit 1
      ;;
  esac
done

# Check if source and destination directories are provided
if [[ -z $source_dir || -z $dest_dir ]]; then
  echo "Source and destination directories are required." >&2
  exit 1
fi

# Perform backup
if [[ $verbose -eq 1 ]]; then
  echo "Backing up from $source_dir to $dest_dir"
fi

cp -r "$source_dir"/* "$dest_dir"/

if [[ $? -eq 0 ]]; then
  if [[ $verbose -eq 1 ]]; then
    echo "Backup completed successfully."
  fi
else
  echo "An error occurred during backup." >&2
  exit 1
fi
```

The script processes three possible options: -s (source directory), -d (destination directory), and -v (verbose mode). The getopts command parses these options and sets respective variables. After validation, it performs a directory backup using cp -r, displaying messages based on verbosity.

Example 3: Parallel Execution with Background Processes

This script demonstrates running multiple tasks in parallel to reduce execution time. It will compress several log files concurrently.

```
#!/bin/bash

# Array to store log files
log_files=( *.log )

# Function to compress a log file
compress_log() {
    gz_file="$1.gz"
    gzip -c "$1" > "$gz_file" && echo "Compressed $1 to $gz_file"
}

# Compress each log file in the background
for log_file in "${log_files[@]}"
do
    compress_log "$log_file" &
done

# Wait for all background processes to complete
wait
echo "All files have been compressed."
```

The script defines a function compress_log to handle the compression of individual log files. The for loop iterates over each log file in the log_files array and executes compress_log in the background using the & operator. The wait command ensures the script waits for all background processes to finish before proceeding.

Example 4: Inter-Process Communication Using Named Pipes

This script uses named pipes (FIFOs) to enable communication between a producer and a consumer process. The producer generates numbers and the consumer sums these numbers.

```
#!/bin/bash

pipe="/tmp/numbers_pipe"

# Create the named pipe
if [[ ! -p $pipe ]]; then
    mkfifo $pipe
fi
```

```
# Producer process
producer() {
    for i in {1..10}; do
        echo $i > $pipe
        sleep 1
    done
    echo "STOP" > $pipe
}

# Consumer process
consumer() {
    sum=0
    while true; do
        number=$(cat $pipe)
        if [[ $number == "STOP" ]]; then
            break
        fi
        sum=$((sum + number))
    done
    echo "Total sum: $sum"
}

# Run producer and consumer in the background
producer &
consumer &

# Wait for both processes to complete
wait

# Clean up
rm -f $pipe
```

A named pipe $pipe is created to facilitate data transfer between the producer and consumer. The producer sends a series of numbers to the pipe, culminating with a STOP signal. The consumer reads these numbers, calculates their total sum, and displays it. Both producer and consumer run concurrently in the background, employing wait to synchronize completion before cleanup.

These examples encompass crucial advanced techniques, enhancing functional and efficient shell scripting skills by integrating arrays, getopts, background processing, and inter-process communication.

Chapter 10

Debugging and Troubleshooting Shell Scripts

This chapter focuses on methods for debugging and troubleshooting shell scripts to ensure reliability and correctness. It explores common script errors, using the 'set' command for debugging, and employing 'trap' for error handling. Techniques like logging, trace debugging, interactive shell debugging, and using 'bash -x' and 'bash -v' are explained. The chapter also covers utilizing 'shellcheck' for static analysis, handling exit codes and error messages, and best practices for writing robust scripts. Practical troubleshooting examples are provided to reinforce these concepts.

10.1 Introduction to Debugging

Shell scripting, while a powerful and versatile tool in Unix-like systems, is not immune to errors and bugs. Debugging is the process of identifying, isolating, and fixing these errors to ensure that scripts behave as expected. This section will provide foundational knowledge on debugging techniques, equipping readers with the essential skills to troubleshoot and rectify issues in their scripts.

When a shell script behaves unexpectedly, the first step is to determine the type of error. These could be syntax errors, logical errors, or runtime errors. Syntax errors occur when the script violates the grammar rules of the shell language. Logical errors are mistakes in the algorithm or logic that lead to incorrect results, even though the script runs without crashing. Runtime errors are those that occur when the script encounters an unexpected condition during execution, such as trying to read a non-existent file or divide by zero.

Identifying the nature of the error is crucial. For syntax errors, the shell often provides messages that indicate the line number and a brief description of the problem. Consider the following script:

```
#!/bin/bash
for i in {1..10}
do
  echo "Number $i"
done
```

Executing this script will produce a syntax error:

```
/tmp/test.sh: line 2: syntax error: unexpected end of file
```

The error message indicates that there is an unexpected end of file, prompting the developer to check for unclosed braces or missing elements in the for loop syntax.

Logical errors require a more nuanced approach. They often necessitate a thorough review of the script's logic to ensure every step produces the intended result. For example, consider a script designed to calculate the factorial of a number:

```
#!/bin/bash
factorial() {
  n=$1
  result=1
  while [ $n -gt 1 ]; do
    result=$((result * n))
    n=$((n - 1))
  done
  echo $result
}

result=$(factorial 5)
echo "Factorial of 5 is $result"
```

If the script returns an incorrect value, it suggests a logical error. A careful walkthrough or insertion of debugging statements such as echo can help trace the values of variables at each step to identify where the logic goes awry.

Runtime errors can result from various unforeseen conditions, such as missing files, absent permissions, or incorrect user inputs. It is essential to handle these gracefully, which is where robust error-checking mechanisms come into play. For instance, adding checks for file existence before attempting to read it can prevent such errors:

```
#!/bin/bash
file="example.txt"

if [ -f "$file" ]; then
  while read -r line; do
    echo "$line"
  done < "$file"
else
  echo "File not found."
fi
```

Understanding these types of errors sets the stage for effective debugging. The subsequent techniques covered in this chapter form a toolkit for diagnosing problems at various levels, enabling the determination of error sources and their rectification.

10.2 Common Shell Script Errors

In shell scripting, errors are practically unavoidable, especially for beginners. However, even experienced scriptwriters may encounter common pitfalls that can disrupt the expected behavior of a script. Understanding these typical errors is the first step towards proficient debugging and ensures your scripts run as intended.

One common source of errors in shell scripts is *syntax mistakes*. These errors arise from incorrect use of shell language constructs and can quickly cause a script to fail. Examples include missing semicolons, unmatched parentheses, forgetting to close quotation marks, or incorrect indentation. Consider the following erroneous segment of a script:

```
#!/bin/bash
echo "Starting the process
if [ $VAR -gt 0 ]; then
echo "VAR is greater than 0"
# Missing fi to close the if statement
```

Running this script will emit a syntax error specifying unexpected 'end of file', indicating the absence of the necessary closing statement 'fi'.

Another prevalent category of errors is *variable mismanagement*. Often, scripts either misuse variables or overlook scope rules, leading to unexpected results or script failures. Inadequate quoting of variables can yield unintended word splitting. For example:

```
#!/bin/bash
FILES=*.txt
for file in $FILES; do
    echo File is $file
done
```

If the directory contains file names with spaces, the 'for' loop will fail to handle them correctly. Enclosing variable expansions in double quotes:

```
for file in "$FILES"; do
```

ensures proper handling of file names with spaces.

Another issue related to variables is uninitialized variables. The script:

```
#!/bin/bash
echo "User name is $USER_NAME"
```

will produce no output for '$USER_NAME' if it hasn't been previously set. Including a default value or ensuring the variable is initialized can prevent such issues:

```
: "${USER_NAME:="default_user"}"
echo "User name is $USER_NAME"
```

Incorrect command usage or command not found errors also frequently disrupt scripts. These inaccuracies often stem from typos, misunderstandings of a command's functionality, or omitting required command options. Consider a script trying to list files using 'ls' with an unknown option:

```
#!/bin/bash
ls -r --random-option
```

The above command will fail because '–random-option' is not a valid option for 'ls'. Consulting the command's manual ('man' pages) prevents such errors.

Errors involving loop constructs are another pitfall in shell scripting. Off-by-one errors, incorrectly defined termination conditions, or faulty break/continue statements lead to infinite loops or premature termination. For instance, an incorrect loop decrementing a variable might be formatted as follows:

```
#!/bin/bash
COUNT=5
while [ $COUNT -ge 0 ]; do
    echo "Count is $COUNT"
    COUNT=$((COUNT + 1)) # Should be COUNT - 1
done
```

This will create an infinite loop unless corrected by decrementing 'COUNT' properly.

Additionally, file handling mistakes are rampant. Scripts may attempt operations on non-existent files or improperly handle file paths. The below example tries to read a file without verifying its existence:

```
#!/bin/bash
while read line; do
    echo "$line"
done < missingfile.txt
```

To safeguard against such errors, it's prudent to check if a file exists before processing it:

```
#!/bin/bash
if [ -f "missingfile.txt" ]; then
    while read line; do
        echo "$line"
    done < missingfile.txt
else
    echo "File missingfile.txt does not exist"
fi
```

Permission issues also frequently trouble scripts. Scripts aimed to read, write, or execute files must have appropriate permissions. If a script tries to execute a file lacking execution permission:

```
#!/bin/bash
./script.sh
```

It's crucial to ensure the file has the execute bit set:

```
$ chmod +x script.sh
```

Finally, *exit status mishandling* poses significant issues in robust scripting. Neglecting to check or correctly handle exit statuses of commands can lead to silent failures that cascade into larger problems:

```
#!/bin/bash
mkdir /some/protected/directory
echo "Directory created"
```

Since 'mkdir' will fail without the necessary permissions, it's vital to verify its success:

```
#!/bin/bash
if mkdir /some/protected/directory; then
    echo "Directory created"
else
    echo "Failed to create directory"
    exit 1
fi
```

By acknowledging these common shell script errors and understanding their root causes, one equips themselves with the knowledge to mitigate such issues preemptively.

10.3 Using set for Debugging

The set command in bash is a powerful tool, offering numerous options that can greatly assist in debugging shell scripts. By manipulating the shell environment and settings, it allows for better control and visibility of the script's behavior.

One of the commonly used options for debugging is set -x, which enables a mode of the shell where all executed commands are printed to the terminal. This is particularly useful for tracing the flow of execution and identifying where the script is deviating from its intended behavior. The set -x can be placed at any point in the script to start the trace, and set +x can be used to stop it.

```
#!/bin/bash
echo "Starting script"
set -x
var1="Hello"
var2="World"
echo "$var1 $var2"
set +x
echo "Script terminated"
```

When executed, the script will output:

```
Starting script
+ var1=Hello
+ var2=World
+ echo Hello World
Hello World
Script terminated
```

In the output, the + indicates lines generated by the set -x option, showing the exact commands as they are executed. This can help identify if variable values are being correctly assigned and if commands are executed in the intended order.

Another helpful option is set -e, which causes the script to exit immediately if any command returns a non-zero status. This can be especially valuable for scripts that rely on the success of sequential commands. By ensuring the script halts on encountering an error, it prevents subsequent commands from executing under potentially invalid conditions.

```
#!/bin/bash
set -e
```

```
echo "Starting script"
cp file1 /nonexistent_directory/
echo "This line will not execute if cp fails"
```

In this example, if cp file1 /nonexistent_directory/ fails because the directory doesn't exist, the script will terminate immediately, and the echo statement following it will not be executed.

Additionally, the set -u option can be used to treat unset variables as an error. This is particularly useful in catching typographical errors and ensuring all variables are deliberately initialized before use.

```
#!/bin/bash
set -u
echo "Starting script"
echo "Value of undefined_var: \$undefined_var"
echo "This line will not execute if undefined_var is not set"
```

Executing this will result in an error:

```
Starting script
./script.sh: line 4: undefined_var: unbound variable
```

The set -o pipefail option ensures that the return value of a pipeline is the status of the last command to exit with a non-zero status. This is crucial for detecting errors in pipelines, which normally return the exit status of the last command in the series, potentially overlooking earlier failures.

```
#!/bin/bash
set -o pipefail
echo "Starting script"
cat nonexistentfile.txt | grep "somecontent"
echo "This line will not execute if cat fails"
```

If cat nonexistentfile.txt fails, the script will terminate due to the set -o pipefail, preventing the misleading impression that the pipeline succeeded simply because grep executed (though it processed no input).

For comprehensive debugging, these set options can be combined. For instance:

```
#!/bin/bash
set -euxo pipefail
echo "Starting script"
var1="Hello"
var2="World"
echo "$var1 $var2"
cp file1 /nonexistent_directory/
cat nonexistentfile.txt | grep "somecontent"
```

This script enables command echoing, treats unset variables as errors, exits on any command failure, and ensures entire pipelines are checked for errors. Such settings provide robust error detection and command tracing, significantly aiding in debugging and troubleshooting complex scripts. Usage of set for debugging is thus instrumental in developing reliable and maintainable shell scripts.

10.4 Using trap for Error Handling

The trap command in shell scripting is a powerful tool designed to catch and respond to signals and system events. This command enhances script reliability by allowing the developer to define custom behavior in the presence of errors or other specified conditions. Utilizing trap can be instrumental in managing cleanups, logging errors, and maintaining state integrity when abnormal terminations occur.

The syntax of the trap command is as follows:

```
trap 'handler' signals
```

Here, handler is a command or a set of commands enclosed in quotes, and signals are either signal names or signal numbers. Multiple signals can be specified, separated by spaces.

Some common signals used with trap include:

- EXIT: This signal is triggered when a script exits, regardless of the exit status.
- ERR: This signal is triggered when a command within the script fails (non-zero exit status).
- SIGINT: This signal corresponds to an interrupt signal, commonly invoked by Ctrl+C.
- SIGTERM: This signal is used to request the termination of a process and can be sent by commands like kill.

To illustrate the usage of trap, consider the following example. This script creates a temporary file and ensures its removal upon script termination, whether due to an error or an interrupt signal.

```
#!/bin/bash

tempfile=$(mktemp)

trap 'rm -f "$tempfile"; echo "Temporary file removed"' EXIT
```

```
echo "This script is running"
# simulate some operations that might fail
sleep 10

trap 'echo "Interrupt signal received"; rm -f "$tempfile"; exit 1' SIGINT

# simulate operations
sleep 10

echo "Script completed successfully"
```

In this example:

- A temporary file is created using the mktemp command and its name is stored in the tempfile variable.
- A trap command sets up an action to remove the temporary file upon the script's exit. The EXIT signal ensures that the file is deleted regardless of how the script terminates.
- The script proceeds to a sleep command, mimicking operations that might fail or be interrupted.
- Another trap command is configured to handle SIGINT. If Ctrl+C is pressed, a custom message is printed, the temporary file is removed, and the script exits with status 1.
- If the script completes without interruption, a success message is displayed.

By employing trap, we ensure that resources like temporary files are properly cleaned up even when unexpected events occur.

Another useful scenario for trap is managing complex cleanup operations involving multiple steps. Consider the following case where a script creates multiple temporary resources that need to be cleaned up in a specific order:

```
#!/bin/bash

tempfile1=$(mktemp)
tempfile2=$(mktemp)

handle_exit() {
    rm -f "$tempfile2"
    echo "Temporary file 2 removed"
    rm -f "$tempfile1"
    echo "Temporary file 1 removed"
}

trap 'handle_exit' EXIT
```

```
# Simulate operations that might fail
touch "$tempfile1" "$tempfile2"
echo "Temporary files created"
sleep 10

trap 'echo "Termination signal received"; handle_exit; exit 1' SIGTERM

# Simulate operations
sleep 10

echo "Script completed successfully"
```

This script demonstrates:

- Creation of two temporary files.
- A function handle_exit is defined to clean these files up in the reverse order of their creation.
- The trap command uses this function to handle the EXIT signal, ensuring the resources are cleaned up correctly.
- An additional trap handles the SIGTERM signal to respond to termination requests gracefully.

For robust error handling, it is also practical to use the ERR signal to catch and handle errors at the command level:

```
#!/bin/bash

trap 'echo "An error occurred. Exiting..."; exit 1' ERR

# Simulate a failing command
false
echo "This will not be printed"
```

In this example:

- The trap command sets up a handler for the ERR signal, echoing an error message and exiting the script with status 1.
- The subsequent command false simulates a command failure.
- Because the ERR trap is set, the script halts immediately and the final echo statement is never executed.

Leveraging trap effectively can significantly enhance the robustness and maintainability of shell scripts, enabling developers to handle errors gracefully and ensure proper cleanup in various scenarios. Proper usage ensures that scripts behave predictably and are easier to debug and maintain, particularly in complex automation and system administration tasks.

10.5 Logging and Trace Debugging

In shell scripting, pinpointing the exact location and time at which a script encounters issues is paramount. Two essential techniques that can significantly aid in achieving this goal are logging and trace debugging. Proper implementation of these techniques will enable both real-time monitoring and post-execution analysis.

Logging is the process of recording events, messages, or outputs generated by a script. This can help in understanding the script's flow and in documenting any anomalies or errors encountered during its execution.

Trace debugging involves monitoring the script as it executes, presenting a detailed account of the operations performed. This can be particularly useful for identifying logic errors and understanding variable transformations.

Implementing Basic Logging

One of the simplest methods to implement logging within a shell script is to use the echo command in combination with file redirection. By redirecting the output of echo to a log file, you can maintain a record of the script's execution:

```
echo "Starting the script..." >> /path/to/logfile.log
```

More sophisticated logging mechanisms involve capturing the exact time of each log entry. Using the date command, you can prepend timestamps to each log entry:

```
echo "$(date '+%Y-%m-%d %H:%M:%S') - Starting the script..." >> /path/to/logfile.
    log
```

This approach provides temporal context to each log message, which is crucial for debugging temporal issues.

Redirecting Standard and Error Output

To capture both standard output and error messages, you can redirect stdout and stderr:

```
exec > $(tee -a /path/to/logfile.log) 2>&1
```

The exec command replaces the shell's standard output and standard error file descriptors, while tee writes the output to both the terminal and the log file.

Trace Debugging with set -x

The set command can be used to enable trace debugging by activating the -x option in a shell script. When enabled, the shell prints each command along with its arguments as they are executed:

```
set -x
# Script contents go here
set +x
```

Placing set -x at the start of a script and set +x at the end of specific sections can selectively enable tracing. This selective tracing reduces log verbosity and focuses on critical script segments.

Combined Logging and Trace Debugging Example

Consider an example script that processes user files. By integrating logging and trace debugging, you can gain comprehensive insights into its execution:

```
#!/bin/bash

# Enable trace debugging
set -x

# Redirect stdout and stderr to log file
exec > $(tee -a /var/log/userfile_processing.log) 2>&1

echo "$(date '+%Y-%m-%d %H:%M:%S') - Script start."

# Example of processing user files
for userfile in /home/*; do
  if [ -f "$userfile" ]; then
    echo "$(date '+%Y-%m-%d %H:%M:%S') - Processing $userfile"
    # Simulate some processing
    sleep 1
  else
    echo "$(date '+%Y-%m-%d %H:%M:%S') - Skipping $userfile as it is not a file."
  fi
done

echo "$(date '+%Y-%m-%d %H:%M:%S') - Script end."

# Disable trace debugging
set +x
```

This script combines logging timestamps with the trace output, providing a granular view of each step. The log output will resemble the following:

```
+ date '+%Y-%m-%d %H:%M:%S'
+ echo '2023-04-05 13:14:15 - Script start.'
2023-04-05 13:14:15 - Script start.
+ for userfile in /home/*
+ '[' -f /home/userfile ']'
+ echo '2023-04-05 13:14:16 - Processing /home/userfile'
2023-04-05 13:14:16 - Processing /home/userfile
+ sleep 1
...
+ date '+%Y-%m-%d %H:%M:%S'
+ echo '2023-04-05 13:14:30 - Script end.'
2023-04-05 13:14:30 - Script end.
```

This output illustrates each executed command and its outcome, interspersed with custom log messages providing context.

Conditional Logging Levels

To manage the verbosity of logs, conditional logging levels can be implemented. For instance, using variables to represent logging levels (e.g., INFO, DEBUG, ERROR) allows flexible control over what gets logged:

```
LOG_LEVEL="DEBUG"

log() {
  local LEVEL="$1"
  shift
  if [ "$LEVEL" == "$LOG_LEVEL" ] || [ "$LEVEL" == "ERROR" ]; then
    echo "$(date '+%Y-%m-%d %H:%M:%S') - $LEVEL - $*"
  fi
}

log "DEBUG" "This is a debug message"
log "INFO" "This is an informational message"
log "ERROR" "This is an error message"
```

This function filters log messages based on the set LOG_LEVEL, recording only messages of equal or higher severity.

Effective logging and trace debugging practices are crucial for identifying and rectifying issues in shell scripts. Through methodical implementation, logging captures the history of operations performed by the script, while trace debugging elucidates the internal execution flow.

10.6 Interactive Shell Debugging

Interactive shell debugging is an essential technique for identifying and correcting errors in shell scripts. By allowing you to pause execution and inspect the state of the script interactively, it provides a powerful and flexible approach to troubleshooting. In this section, we will delve into the mechanics of interactive shell debugging using bash, detailing commands and concepts useful for effective debugging.

Interactive debugging can be initiated using the built-in command set -e in combination with trap or by invoking the debugger bashdb. The bashdb tool is designed explicitly for debugging bash scripts and provides a range of features for interactive inspection.

Using set -e and trap for Manual Interaction

The command set -e makes your script exit immediately if a command exits with a non-zero status. This approach is useful for catching errors as they occur, but it does not provide an interface for interactive debugging. Instead, combining set -e with trap allows you to drop into a debugging shell when the script encounters an error.

Consider the following example script:

```
#!/bin/bash
set -e
trap 'echo "Error occurred at line $LINENO"; /bin/bash' ERR

echo "Executing step 1"
false

echo "Executing step 2"
```

In this script, we use set -e to ensure execution stops when an error occurs. The trap command is configured to print an error message and then open an interactive shell when an error (denoted by ERR) is trapped. The message includes the line number where the error occurred, which helps in pinpointing the issue.

When running this script, the output will be:

```
Executing step 1
Error occurred at line 5
```

After the error message, the script opens an interactive shell at the error location, allowing you to inspect and debug interactively.

Using bashdb for Enhanced Debugging

bashdb is a full-fledged debugger for bash scripts and provides features akin to those found in debuggers for other programming languages. To utilize bashdb, ensure it is installed on your system. You can install it via package managers like apt, yum, or by compiling from source.

To start an interactive session with bashdb, use the following command:

```
bashdb example.sh
```

This command starts the debugger and loads the script example.sh. In the interactive debugger, you have several commands at your disposal:

- step or s: Executes the script one line at a time, stepping into any functions.
- next or n: Executes the next line of the script, but skips function calls.
- continue or c: Resumes execution until the next breakpoint or the end of the script.
- break <line_number>: Sets a breakpoint at a specified line number.
- print <variable>: Prints the value of a variable.
- list or l: Lists the lines around the current line being executed.

For example, setting a breakpoint at line 5 and stepping through the script might look like this:

```
(bashdb) break 5
Breakpoint 1 at line 5
(bashdb) run
Running: example.sh
source_file=$(/example.sh)
PREFIX=/usr
Executing step 1
Breakpoint 1, example.sh at line 5
  5 false
(bashdb) print LINENO
5
(bashdb) step
  5: false
```

With this setup, you interactively debug the script using breakpoints and command inspection, similar to other popular debuggers.

Interactive shell debugging, by facilitating real-time inspection and modification, helps uncover subtle scripting errors which might be tricky to identify through static analysis or logging alone.

10.7 Debugging with bash -x and bash -v

Debugging shell scripts efficiently requires understanding the tools and techniques that provide insights into script behavior. The bash -x and bash -v options serve as powerful mechanisms for tracing and visually inspecting the execution of scripts.

The bash -x option enables execution tracing, wherein each command and its arguments are displayed as they are executed. This feature is particularly useful for identifying the exact sequence of operations, ensuring that the script follows the expected flow, and isolating errors in the execution path.

To illustrate the usage of bash -x, consider the following shell script example:

```
#!/bin/bash

greet_user() {
    local user_name=$1
    echo "Hello, $user_name!"
}

user="Alice"
greet_user $user
```

To execute this script with the -x option, use the following command:

```
bash -x script.sh
```

The output will be similar to:

```
+ greet_user Alice
+ local user_name=Alice
+ echo 'Hello, Alice!'
Hello, Alice!
```

In the above output, each command prefixed with a '+' signifies the command being executed along with its evaluated arguments. This trace provides clarity on variable assignments, function calls, and the overall script flow, enabling identification of discrepancies with expected behavior.

The bash -v option, on the other hand, displays each command before executing it, offering visibility into the script's commands without necessarily showing their results. This option is beneficial for verifying the script's content, ensuring that intended commands are being executed as authored.

Consider the same shell script example mentioned earlier. Executing it with the -v option results in:

```
bash -v script.sh
```

The output will be similar to:

```
#!/bin/bash

greet_user() {
    local user_name=$1
    echo "Hello, $user_name!"
}

user="Alice"
greet_user $user
#!/bin/bash
greet_user ()
{
    local user_name=$1;
    echo "Hello, $user_name!";
}
user="Alice"
greet_user $user
Hello, Alice!
```

Here, the entire script content is echoed before execution, which assists in verifying the script's commands and structure. This is particularly useful for longer scripts where visual inspection of the entire command sequence ensures accuracy.

Combining -x and -v options provides a comprehensive debugging approach, tracing both the command sequences and their evaluations. This can be executed using the following command:

```
bash -x -v script.sh
```

The resultant output will merge the benefits of both options, offering a verbose trace of each command before and during execution, making it apparent where the script's logic may diverge from expected behavior.

Utilizing these options effectively entails recognizing the context where each is most beneficial. bash -x offers fine-grained insight into command evaluation and execution sequence, suitable for detecting logical errors within complex scripts or functions. bash -v emphasizes script content, ensuring that each command intended by the developer is being processed as written.

In practice, judicious use of -x and -v can significantly expedite the debugging process, transforming opaque errors and logical pitfalls into transparent, actionable insights. Integrating these options into regular development and debugging workflows fosters a robust, reliable scripting practice, aligned with systematic error identification and correction.

When debugging scripts interacting with external inputs or system commands, the verbosity these options provide aids in logging detailed operations, capturing not only the shell's interpretation but also the interplay with external environments. This holistic observational capability serves as a cornerstone for advanced debugging and script optimization, ensuring scripts perform reliably under varied and unforeseen conditions.

10.8 Using shellcheck for Static Analysis

Static analysis is a method of debugging that examines the code without executing it. One of the most effective tools for static analysis in the context of shell scripting is shellcheck. shellcheck is a GPLv3 tool that provides static analysis for shell scripts, ensuring that potential errors are identified before runtime. It helps script authors to adhere to best practices, detect subtle bugs, and improve code readability.

shellcheck can be installed on various platforms, and instructions for installation are available on the official shellcheck website. For instance, on a Debian-based system, shellcheck can be installed using the following command:

```
sudo apt-get install shellcheck
```

To use shellcheck, simply invoke the command followed by the script file you wish to analyze. Below is an example of running shellcheck on a script file named example.sh:

```
shellcheck example.sh
```

After running the above command, shellcheck will output warnings and suggestions based on the script analysis. Consider the following simple script stored in example.sh:

```
#!/bin/bash
echo "Enter your name:"
read name
echo "Hello, \$name"
```

Running shellcheck on this script might provide the following output:

```
In example.sh line 4:
echo "Hello, \$name"
             ^-- SC2086: Double quote to prevent globbing and word splitting.
```

The warning indicates that the variable $name should be enclosed in double quotes to prevent potential issues with word splitting and globbing. The corrected line should therefore be:

```
echo "Hello, \$name"
```

This adjustment improves the script's robustness by ensuring that if

$name contains spaces or special characters, it will still be handled correctly. Another frequent issue detected by shellcheck is the usage of uninitialized variables. Consider the following script:

```
#!/bin/bash
if [ "\$var" -eq 0 ]; then
  echo "Variable is zero."
fi
```

Analyzing this script with shellcheck will result in a warning:

```
In example.sh line 2:
if [ "\$var" -eq 0 ]; then
     ^-- SC2154: var is referenced but not assigned.
```

This warning suggests that var is used before it has been assigned a value, which could lead to unpredictable behavior. Initializing the variable, as shown below, resolves the issue:

```
#!/bin/bash
var=0
if [ "\$var" -eq 0 ]; then
  echo "Variable is zero."
fi
```

The tool can also detect more complex issues, such as improper usage of shell built-ins, improper exit statuses, unnecessary use of external commands, and more. To illustrate, consider the following script:

```
#!/bin/bash
cat file.txt | grep "search"
```

shellcheck will point out that the use of cat here is unnecessary and can be optimized:

```
In example.sh line 2:
cat file.txt | grep "search"
^-- SC2002: Useless cat. Consider 'grep search file.txt' instead.
```

The optimized version reads:

```
#!/bin/bash
grep "search" file.txt
```

These examples illustrate how shellcheck can significantly improve script quality by highlighting potential issues and suggesting best practices. While shellcheck covers a wide range of common pitfalls, it should not be relied upon exclusively. It serves as an invaluable tool for catching errors early in the development process, complementing runtime debugging tools and practices discussed elsewhere in this chapter.

For comprehensive usage, users can leverage shellcheck's support for ignoring specific rules, customizing checks, and integrating with continuous integration (CI) systems to automate script verification. For instance, to ignore a specific shellcheck check, add a directive to your script:

```
#!/bin/bash
# shellcheck disable=SC2086
echo Hello, \$name
```

This directive tells shellcheck to ignore the specified warning, enabling focused and customized analysis. Such capabilities make shellcheck an adaptable and potent tool for producing high-quality, robust shell scripts.

10.9 Handling Exit Codes and Error Messages

In shell scripting, the management of exit codes and error messages is a critical aspect of ensuring script reliability and robustness. By meticulously handling these elements, script developers can create resilient scripts that behave predictably under varied conditions.

The exit code, or return status, of a command is crucial for understanding the success or failure of command execution. In Unix-based systems, every command returns an integer exit code between 0 and 255 upon completion. By convention, an exit code of 0 signifies success, whereas non-zero exit codes indicate specific errors.

To capture the exit code of the last executed command, use the special variable $?. This variable is immediately populated with the exit status of the recently completed command, as shown in the example below:

```
#!/bin/bash

ls /nonexistent_directory
echo "Exit code: $?"
```

```
# Output:
# ls: cannot access '/nonexistent_directory': No such file or directory
# Exit code: 2
```

The above script attempts to list a non-existent directory. The $? variable captures the exit code of the ls command, which is 2, indicating a failure.

Error handling can be improved by consistently checking exit codes and responding appropriately to failures. Consider the script below, which attempts to create a directory and handle potential errors:

```
#!/bin/bash

mkdir /existing_directory
if [ $? -ne 0 ]; then
    echo "Error: Directory creation failed." >&2
    exit 1
fi
echo "Directory created successfully."
```

Here, the mkdir command attempts to create a directory. If the directory already exists, the command exits with a non-zero code, prompting an error message and script termination using exit 1. The !!>!!2 syntax directs the error message to standard error (stderr), which is a best practice for clear separation of logs and regular output.

Advanced scripts might involve error handling encompassing multiple commands. The implementation of logical constructs like && (logical AND) and || (logical OR) help manage such scenarios efficiently:

```
#!/bin/bash

cp source_file.txt destination_directory/ && echo "Copy successful." || {
    echo "Copy failed." >&2
    exit 2
}
```

The double ampersand && ensures the success message is echoed only if the cp command executes without error. Conversely, the braces {} group the error-handling actions, executed if cp fails, as indicated by the double pipe ||.

Comprehensive error handling necessitates defining meaningful exit codes for different failure cases. By doing so, the script becomes more predictable and easier to debug. Below is an extended example with diversified exit codes:

```
#!/bin/bash

check_file_presence() {
    if [ ! -f "$1" ]; then
        echo "Error: File $1 not found." >&2
        return 10
    fi
}

check_write_permission() {
    if [ ! -w "$1" ]; then
        echo "Error: No write permission for $1." >&2
        return 20
    fi
}

file="example.txt"
```

```
check_file_presence "$file"
if [ $? -ne 0 ]; then
    exit 10
fi

check_write_permission "$file"
if [ $? -ne 0 ]; then
    exit 20
fi

echo "File checks passed."
```

In the script above, two functions (check_file_presence and check_write_permission) are defined to verify the existence of the file and the write permissions, respectively. Distinct exit codes (10 and 20) elucidate the nature of the failure, aiding debugging.

Integration of descriptive and informative error messages enhances script user-friendliness. Moreover, employing external logging mechanisms or redirecting verbose output to log files can be invaluable in production environments. Below is a variant incorporating logging:

```
#!/bin/bash

log_file="script.log"

exec 2>>"$log_file" # Redirect stderr to log file

echo "Script started."

cp source_file.txt destination_directory/
if [ $? -ne 0 ]; then
    echo "Error: Failed to copy source_file.txt." >&2
    exit 1
fi

echo "Copy successful."
```

In this script, exec 2»"$log_file" redirects standard error to the specified log file, preserving a log of errors without cluttering the standard output.

Handling exit codes and error messages meticulously not only ensures the reliability of shell scripts but also facilitates easier maintenance and debugging. By systematically employing exit codes, performing conditional checks, and providing informative error messages, developers can create robust and dependable shell scripts.

10.10 Best Practices for Writing Robust Scripts

Writing robust shell scripts is an essential skill for efficient and reliable automation. This section will discuss several key practices that can significantly enhance the stability and maintainability of your scripting projects. Adhering to these practices allows you to preemptively address potential issues, ensuring your scripts run smoothly under diverse conditions.

- **1. Use Consistent and Descriptive Naming Conventions**
  Variable and function names should be clear and descriptive, indicating their purpose. Employ camelCase or underscores to separate words. For instance:

```
# Descriptive variable name
backupDir="/var/backups"

# Consistent function name
calculateTotalSize() {
    # function implementation
}
```

- **2. Include Comments and Documentation**
  Comments are crucial for explaining the logic and purpose of your code blocks. This improves readability and helps other developers (or your future self) understand the script. Use comments to describe the function of complex sections:

```
# Calculate the total size of the backup directory
calculateTotalSize() {
    local totalSize=$(du -sh "$backupDir" | cut -f1)
    echo "$totalSize"
}
```

- **3. Validate Input Parameters and Arguments**
  Incorporate checks to validate inputs and arguments provided to the script. This ensures that the script does not proceed with invalid or unexpected input, reducing the risk of errors:

```
# Check if the required argument is supplied
if [ -z "$1" ]; then
    echo "Error: No directory specified."
    exit 1
fi
```

- **4. Use 'set' Options to Enhance Script Reliability**

The ‘set‘ command offers several options to improve script reliability. Commonly used options include ‘-e‘, which stops script execution upon encountering an error, and ‘-u‘, which treats unset variables as an error:

```
# Exit immediately if a command exits with a non-zero status
set -e
# Treat unset variables as an error
set -u
```

- **5. Handle Errors Gracefully**
  Implement error handling using conditional statements and the ‘trap‘ command to manage unexpected errors effectively:

```
# Function to handle errors
errorHandler() {
    echo "An error occurred. Exiting script."
    exit 1
}

# Trap errors and execute errorHandler function
trap 'errorHandler' ERR
```

- **6. Leverage Logging and Debugging Information**
  Incorporate logging to track script execution and facilitate debugging. Use ‘echo‘ or ‘logger‘ to record critical steps and error messages:

```
# Log a message
logMessage() {
    local message="$1"
    echo "$(date +'%Y-%m-%d %H:%M:%S') - $message"
}

# Use the log function
logMessage "Script started."
```

- **7. Optimize Script Performance**
  Optimize scripts for performance by avoiding unnecessary commands, using efficient looping constructs, and minimizing subshell usage. For instance, prefer using built-in shell constructs over external commands when possible:

```
# Inefficient use of external command
for file in $(ls); do
    echo "$file"
done

# Efficient use of shell built-in
for file in *; do
    echo "$file"
done
```

- **8. Use Functions to Organize Code**
  Break down complex tasks into smaller, reusable functions. This enhances readability and makes it easier to debug and maintain scripts:

```
# Function to perform a specific task
performTask() {
    # Task implementation
}

# Main script execution
performTask
```

- **9. Ensure Portability**
  Write scripts to be portable across different environments. Avoid using features or syntaxes that are shell-specific unless necessary. For example, prefer POSIX-compliant syntax:

```
#!/bin/sh
# POSIX-compliant shebang for portability
```

- **10. Test Scripts Thoroughly**
  Thoroughly test scripts in various scenarios to uncover potential issues. Automate test cases where feasible to ensure consistent and repeatable test coverage:

```
# Example test case
testBackupFunctionality() {
    # Test implementation
}

# Execute tests
testBackupFunctionality
```

Applying these best practices in your shell scripting endeavors will lead to more reliable, maintainable, and efficient scripts. This, in turn, minimizes the likelihood of unexpected behaviors and errors, ultimately contributing to smoother and more predictable automated workflows.

10.11 Practical Troubleshooting Examples

Troubleshooting shell scripts can often be challenging, especially when scripts become complex with multiple interacting components. This section includes practical examples to illustrate the application of various debugging and troubleshooting techniques discussed earlier.

Consider a simple script intended to back up a directory:

```
#!/bin/bash
SOURCE_DIR="/path/to/source"
DEST_DIR="/path/to/destination"
DATE=$(date +'%Y-%m-%d')
TAR_FILE="$DEST_DIR/backup-$DATE.tar.gz"

if [ -d "$SOURCE_DIR" ]; then
    tar -czf "$TAR_FILE" -C "$SOURCE_DIR" .
    echo "Backup completed successfully."
else
    echo "Source directory does not exist."
fi
```

To illustrate troubleshooting, assume this script fails to create the backup. The first step involves confirming the correct functioning of each component.

Step 1: Verify Variables

Start by checking the values of variables. You can do this by adding 'echo' statements before critical operations:

```
echo "SOURCE_DIR=$SOURCE_DIR"
echo "DEST_DIR=$DEST_DIR"
echo "DATE=$DATE"
echo "TAR_FILE=$TAR_FILE"
```

Step 2: Check Directory Existence

Ensure both the source and destination directories exist:

```
if [ ! -d "$SOURCE_DIR" ]; then
    echo "Error: Source directory $SOURCE_DIR does not exist."
fi

if [ ! -d "$DEST_DIR" ]; then
    echo "Error: Destination directory $DEST_DIR does not exist."
fi
```

Step 3: Analyze Commands

Run the 'tar' command manually to isolate the problem. Navigate to the destination directory and execute:

```
cd /path/to/source || exit
tar -czf /path/to/destination/backup-$(date +'%Y-%m-%d').tar.gz .
```

By executing commands step-by-step, you can verify each part's correctness.

Step 4: Using 'set' Command

Enable 'set -x' at the script's start to trace command execution:

```
#!/bin/bash
```

```
set -x
# rest of the script
```

Step 5: Using 'trap'

Catch and handle errors using 'trap':

```
#!/bin/bash
trap 'echo "An error occurred on line $LINENO"; exit 1' ERR
# rest of the script
```

Step 6: Script Execution Output

Run the script with added debugging statements. The output might reveal errors directly:

```
SOURCE_DIR=/path/to/source
DEST_DIR=/path/to/destination
DATE=2023-10-10
TAR_FILE=/path/to/destination/backup-2023-10-10.tar.gz
Error: Source directory /path/to/source does not exist.
An error occurred on line 7
```

This output indicates the source directory does not exist.

Step 7: Corrective Actions

After isolating the problem (missing directory), correct the path or create the required directory:

```
SOURCE_DIR="/correct/path/to/source"
```

Ensure the directory's existence with:

```
mkdir -p "$SOURCE_DIR"
```

Step 8: Ensuring Permissions

Verify necessary permissions. If the script lacks adequate permissions, address this issue:

```
chmod +x backup_script.sh
chmod -R 755 /path/to/source
chmod -R 755 /path/to/destination
```

Final Validation

After making corrections, run the script again and verify the successful creation of the backup file. Trace outputs, confirm error-free execution, and check the presence of the backup file in the destination directory.

Through these incremental steps, the debugging and troubleshooting of the script proceed methodically, ensuring each potential issue is addressed and resolved.

Chapter 11

Security and Best Practices

This chapter addresses the critical aspects of security and best practices in shell scripting. It begins with identifying potential security risks and emphasizes the importance of validating and sanitizing user input. The chapter provides guidance on handling sensitive data securely, setting appropriate file permissions, and avoiding common security mistakes. It covers using SSH for secure connections, implementing access controls, and monitoring and auditing scripts. Regular updates and security patches are also discussed, along with practical examples to illustrate secure scripting practices.

11.1 Introduction to Shell Script Security

Shell scripting in Linux offers powerful capabilities, but it also presents various security risks when not properly managed. Given the inherent flexibility and control that shell scripts provide, it is critical to understand the potential vulnerabilities and how to mitigate them. This section focuses on foundational principles and introduces key concepts for securing shell scripts.

Understanding shell script security begins by recognizing the context in which these scripts operate. Shell scripts often run with elevated privileges and can manipulate sensitive data or system configurations. Thus, an attacker who exploits a shell script can potentially gain unauthorized access to the system, causing significant damage.

One primary area of concern is the misuse or mishandling of user input. Scripts that do not adequately validate and sanitize their inputs are particularly susceptible to injection attacks. Injection attacks occur when an attacker provides malicious input that the script then inadvertently executes. For instance, consider a script that takes user input and passes it directly to a system command without appropriate checks. Such practices can lead to severe security breaches.

Ensure proper input handling by implementing robust validation and verification mechanisms. Input validation involves checking whether the provided data meets the expected format and constraints before processing it. Sanitization means cleaning the input data to remove or escape any potentially harmful characters or sequences.

Example of dangerous user input handling:

```
#!/bin/bash
echo "Enter the filename to delete:"
read filename
rm $filename
```

This script is perilous as an attacker could input a filename with malicious characters, such as ; rm -rf /, causing catastrophic data loss. To safeguard against such threats, always quote variable expansions and employ explicit whitelisting.

Secure input handling example:

```
#!/bin/bash
echo "Enter the filename to delete:"
read filename
if [[ -n $filename && $filename =~ ^[A-Za-z0-9._-]+$ ]]; then
    rm "$filename"
else
    echo "Invalid filename."
fi
```

In this example, the script checks if the input is non-empty and contains only valid characters (alphanumeric characters, underscores, hyphens, and dots). Quoting the variable expansion ensures that special characters do not break out of the intended context.

Another key aspect of shell script security involves managing sensitive data, such as passwords, API keys, and personal information. Embedded credentials within scripts pose significant risks if the scripts are exposed. Employ environment variables or dedicated secret management tools to handle such critical information securely.

Access control is another fundamental principle. Always adhere to the principle of least privilege, granting the minimum required access permissions to users, files, and scripts. By reducing the attack surface, you minimize the potential impact of any compromised component.

Example of setting restrictive file permissions:

```
chmod 700 script.sh
```

Above, the script script.sh is made readable, writable, and executable only by its owner. This practice restricts unauthorized access and alteration.

The use of Secure Shell (SSH) for remote access and script execution necessitates strong security measures. Always use encryption protocols and disable root login to mitigate potential attack vectors. Key-based authentication is preferable over password-based methods for enhanced security.

Monitoring and auditing scripts is crucial for maintaining security. Implement logging mechanisms to capture script activities and establish audit trails. Regularly review logs for any suspicious behavior and adapt scripts as necessary to address newly identified vulnerabilities.

Lastly, maintaining an up-to-date system is vital. Ensuring that your scripts and the underlying system libraries are current helps protect against known vulnerabilities. Regularly applying security patches and updates is a best practice to safeguard the environment in which your scripts operate.

Throughout the subsequent sections, we will delve more deeply into each of these principles, providing concrete examples and best practices to enhance the security of your shell scripts. With a comprehensive understanding of these foundational concepts, you'll be better equipped to write secure, robust, and reliable scripts.

11.2 Understanding Security Risks

Understanding the security risks associated with shell scripting is essential for writing robust and secure scripts. This section delves into various security vulnerabilities and demonstrates how they can compromise system integrity and confidentiality. The goal is to equip the reader with the knowledge needed to identify and mitigate these risks effectively.

- **Command Injection Attacks**

  One of the primary security risks in shell scripting is command injection attacks. This occurs when an attacker can manipulate the input to a script to execute arbitrary commands. If user inputs are not validated and sanitized appropriately, an attacker can inject malicious commands, potentially gaining unauthorized access to the system or executing harmful operations.

  Consider the following vulnerable script that takes a filename as input and displays its contents:

```
#!/bin/bash
echo "Enter filename:"
read filename
cat $filename
```

  An attacker could exploit this script by providing a filename that includes additional shell commands. For example, entering '/etc/-passwd; rm -rf /' would result in the following execution:

```
cat /etc/passwd; rm -rf /
```

  To mitigate this risk, user input must be sanitized. A safer version of the script might use built-in commands to validate the input:

```
#!/bin/bash
echo "Enter filename:"
read filename
if [[ -f "$filename" ]]; then
  cat "$filename"
else
  echo "File does not exist."
fi
```

  In this revised script, the -f test ensures the input is a valid file.

- **Script Injection**

  Script injection vulnerabilities arise when user input is incorporated directly into script execution without proper sanitization. This can occur in environments where scripts generate and execute other scripts dynamically.

  Suppose we have a script that constructs another script based on user input:

```
#!/bin/bash
echo "Enter command:"
read user_command
echo "$user_command" > temp_script.sh
bash temp_script.sh
```

In this scenario, an attacker can supply a harmful command. To prevent script injection, user inputs should be strictly validated. One approach is to use a whitelist of allowed commands:

```
#!/bin/bash
allowed_commands=("ls" "pwd" "date")
echo "Enter command:"
read user_command
if [[ " ${allowed_commands[@]} " =~ " ${user_command} " ]]; then
  "$user_command"
else
  echo "Command not allowed."
fi
```

- **Environment Variable Poisoning**

  Shell scripts often rely on environment variables, which can be manipulated by an attacker if not properly controlled. Environment variable poisoning occurs when an attacker alters environment variables to influence script behavior.

  Consider a script that uses the $PATH environment variable to locate executables:

```
#!/bin/bash
echo "Running backup..."
backup_script
```

  If an attacker can modify the $PATH variable to include a directory with a malicious backup_script, this script may execute unintended commands. Mitigating this risk involves avoiding reliance on environment variables that can be altered by untrusted users.

  A safer approach is to use absolute paths for critical commands:

```
#!/bin/bash
echo "Running backup..."
/usr/local/bin/backup_script
```

- **Race Conditions**

  Race conditions occur when the timing of events affects the system state, potentially leading to security vulnerabilities. They are particularly problematic in scripts that involve file creation, deletion, or modification.

  Consider the case where a script checks for the existence of a file before creating it:

```
#!/bin/bash
if [[ ! -e /tmp/myfile ]]; then
  touch /tmp/myfile
fi
```

An attacker could exploit the timing between the check and the creation of the file, creating a symbolic link to a sensitive file. This may cause the script to overwrite critical system files. To prevent race conditions, use mechanisms like file locks or atomic operations.

```
#!/bin/bash
(
  flock -n 200 || exit 1
  if [[ ! -e /tmp/myfile ]]; then
    touch /tmp/myfile
  fi
) 200>/tmp/myfile.lock
```

In this script, flock ensures that the operations on /tmp/myfile are atomic, preventing race conditions.

- **Permissions and Privilege Escalation**

  Improper management of file permissions and execution contexts in scripts can lead to privilege escalation, where an attacker gains higher system privileges. Scripts running with elevated privileges (e.g., root) should be handled with utmost caution to prevent exploitation.

  For example, consider a script that modifies a system configuration file:

```
#!/bin/bash
sudo cp /etc/config /etc/config.bak
sudo echo "New configuration" > /etc/config
```

  To mitigate this risk, scripts should minimize the use of privileged commands, instead using privileged roles only when necessary. Furthermore, the principle of least privilege should be followed, ensuring scripts and files have the minimal permissions required for their function.

The implementation of these practices and understanding these security risks can vastly improve the robustness and security of shell scripts, making them less vulnerable to exploitation by malicious entities.

11.3 Validating and Sanitizing User Input

When developing shell scripts, one of the primary security concerns is handling user input. Unvalidated and unsanitized inputs can lead to severe security vulnerabilities, including command injection, unintended file modifications, and other malicious activities. Ensuring that all user inputs are validated and sanitized is critical to enhance the integrity and security of your scripts.

Input Validation is the process of ensuring that the user inputs conform to the expected format, type, and range. This process typically involves checking that the input values fall within predefined constraints before they are processed further.

Input Sanitization refers to cleaning or filtering the input to remove any potentially harmful data. This entails escaping special characters, removing or altering invalid characters, and ensuring that the input does not contain any executable code or other dangerous elements.

Essential Steps in Input Validation and Sanitization:

- **1. Define Valid Input Criteria:** Before you can validate or sanitize input, it is critical to define what constitutes valid input. For example, if a script expects a username, the valid input could be defined as an alphanumeric string between 1 and 32 characters long, without spaces or special characters.

```
# Example: Validating a Username
valid_username_regex="^[a-zA-Z0-9]{1,32}$"
```

- **2. Input Validation:** Validation checks confirm that the input data meets the criteria defined. It can be implemented by using conditional statements to compare input against the validation regex or other rules.

```
#!/bin/bash

read -p "Enter username: " username

if [[ $username =~ $valid_username_regex ]]; then
    echo "Username is valid."
else
    echo "Invalid username. Please enter a valid alphanumeric username."
    exit 1
fi
```

  In the above script, the username is validated against the predefined regular expression. If it does not match, the script terminates with an error message.

- **3. Input Sanitization:** Sanitization ensures that even if the input is syntactically correct, it is free from malicious content. For instance, filenames or paths entered by the user should not contain dangerous characters.

Sanitization can involve:

- Removing unsafe characters
- Escaping special characters
- Trimming excess whitespace

```
#!/bin/bash

read -p "Enter the filename: " filename

# Remove potentially dangerous characters
safe_filename=$(echo "$filename" | tr -cd '[:alnum:]._-')

echo "Sanitized filename: $safe_filename"
```

In this script, the 'tr' command is used to remove any characters from the input filename that are not alphanumeric, dots, underscores, or hyphens, ensuring the filename is safe to use.

- **4. Combining Validation and Sanitization:** It is beneficial to combine both validation and sanitization to enhance script security.

```
#!/bin/bash

read -p "Enter username: " username
read -p "Enter filename: " filename

# Check if username is valid
if [[ $username =~ $valid_username_regex ]]; then
    echo "Username is valid."
else
    echo "Invalid username. Please enter a valid alphanumeric username."
    exit 1
fi

# Sanitize filename input
safe_filename=$(echo "$filename" | tr -cd '[:alnum:]._-')

echo "Sanitized filename: $safe_filename"
```

- **5. Avoiding Command Injection:** A common vulnerability introduced by unsanitized user inputs is command injection. This occurs when an attacker can inject and execute arbitrary commands within your script.

  To prevent command injection:

  - Avoid using user input directly within commands.
  - Use safer alternatives like arrays or built-in methods.

```
#!/bin/bash

# Read user input
read -p "Enter directory name: " dir

# Validate directory name
if [[ $dir =~ ^[a-zA-Z0-9_-]+$ ]]; then
    echo "Valid directory name."
else
    echo "Invalid directory name."
    exit 1
fi

# Safely create a directory
mkdir -- "$dir"
```

The '–' in the 'mkdir' command ensures that arguments following it are treated as operands even if they begin with a '-'. This guards against filenames that might appear as options.

Overall, validating and sanitizing user input are fundamental practices to secure shell scripting. By rigorously checking and cleaning input data, we can mitigate risks associated with unauthorized access, data tampering, and other security threats.

11.4 Handling Sensitive Data Securely

Handling sensitive data securely in shell scripting is paramount to ensuring the confidentiality, integrity, and availability of critical information. Sensitive data includes passwords, API keys, encryption keys, and personal identifiable information (PII). Mishandling such data can lead to severe security breaches, data leaks, and unauthorized access. This section explores methodologies and tools to manage sensitive information securely within shell scripts.

Storing sensitive information directly within scripts or configuration files is a common, yet risky, practice. Consider the following example:

```
#!/bin/bash
DB_PASSWORD="my_secure_password"
echo "Connecting to database with password ${DB_PASSWORD}"
```

In this example, if the script is accidentally shared or accessed by unauthorized individuals, the database password is compromised. To mitigate such risks, avoid hardcoding sensitive information. Instead, leverage environment variables, secure storage mechanisms, and access controls.

Environment Variables

Using environment variables is a preferable approach to handle sensitive data. They allow separation of data from script logic, reducing the risk of exposure. Securely setting environment variables can be achieved as follows:

```
export DB_PASSWORD="my_secure_password"
```

Shell scripts can then access this variable without directly exposing the sensitive information within the script:

```
#!/bin/bash
echo "Connecting to database with password ${DB_PASSWORD}"
```

While environment variables improve security, they are not foolproof. Any user or process with appropriate permissions can read environment variables. Ensure minimal access by restricting user permissions and avoiding insecure practices such as placing environment variables in publicly accessible files (.bashrc, .profile).

Using Configuration Files with Restricted Access

Storing sensitive information in configuration files with restricted permissions is another approach. Place such files outside version-controlled directories and configure file permissions to limit access:

```
touch /etc/my_sensitive_config.conf
chmod 600 /etc/my_sensitive_config.conf
echo "DB_PASSWORD=my_secure_password" > /etc/my_sensitive_config.conf
```

Scripts can source the configuration file to read sensitive data:

```
#!/bin/bash
source /etc/my_sensitive_config.conf
echo "Connecting to database with password ${DB_PASSWORD}"
```

Restricting file access using the ‘chmod 600‘ command ensures only the owner (root, in this case) can read or write the configuration file. Regularly audit file permissions and contents to prevent unauthorized access.

Secure Password Storage with ‘GPG‘

GNU Privacy Guard (GPG) allows encryption and decryption of files on Linux systems, providing a robust method to secure sensitive information. The procedure involves generating a key pair and encrypting the data file with the public key:

```
# Generate a key pair
```

```
gpg --gen-key

# Encrypt the file with sensitive data
echo "DB_PASSWORD=my_secure_password" > db_password.txt
gpg --output db_password.gpg --encrypt --recipient "Your Name" db_password.txt
rm db_password.txt
```

To use the encrypted file in a script, decrypt it at runtime:

```
#!/bin/bash
gpg --output db_password.txt --decrypt db_password.gpg
source db_password.txt
echo "Connecting to database with password ${DB_PASSWORD}"
rm db_password.txt
```

This process ensures the plaintext password is only available in memory temporarily during script execution.

Using Secret Management Tools

Modern systems offer dedicated secret management solutions, such as HashiCorp Vault or AWS Secrets Manager, designed to store and access sensitive information securely. These tools provide advanced features like dynamic secrets, access logging, and fine-grained access controls.

Integrating HashiCorp Vault with shell scripts involves:

- Setting up Vault Server:

  ```
  vault server -config=/path/to/config.hcl
  ```

- Storing Secrets:

  ```
  vault kv put secret/db_password value="my_secure_password"
  ```

- Accessing Secrets in Scripts:

  ```
  #!/bin/bash
  export VAULT_ADDR='http://127.0.0.1:8200'
  vault kv get -format=json secret/db_password | jq -r '.data.data.value'
  ```

By using such tools, sensitive data management is centralized, reducing the risk of accidental exposure.

Securely handling sensitive data necessitates employing multiple strategies and best practices. Adopting environment variables, restricting file access, using encryption tools like GPG, and leveraging secret management solutions collectively fortify the security posture of shell scripts. Consistent audit and review processes will ensure continued adherence to security standards.

11.5 Using Secure File Permissions

File permissions in a Linux environment are integral to maintaining the security of a system. They control the levels of interaction that users and processes may have with the filesystem, ensuring that only authorized entities may read, modify, or execute specified files. Understanding and correctly implementing file permissions is a critical step in shell script security.

Basic File Permissions Structure

Each file and directory in Linux has an associated set of permissions that can be viewed using the ls -l command. The output is formatted to display the permissions, number of links, owner, group, size, modification date, and file name. For example:

```
-rw-r--r-- 1 user user 1048 Jan 1 12:34 example.txt
```

In this output, the first column -rw-r–r– represents the file permissions. These permissions are divided into three sets of three characters each: rw-, r–, and r–.

- rw- – Owner permissions: The owner has read and write permissions.
- r– – Group permissions: The group has read-only permissions.
- r– – Others permissions: Others have read-only permissions.

The first character indicates the type of file. For example, - represents a regular file, while d would represent a directory.

Changing File Permissions

The chmod command is used to change the permissions of files and directories. Permissions can be modified using symbolic mode or numeric (octal) mode.

Symbolic mode uses characters to add (+), remove (-), or set (=) permissions. For example:

```
chmod u+rwx,g-w,o=r example.txt
```

This command sets the owner (u) permissions to read, write, and execute; removes write permissions for the group (g); and sets others (o) permissions to read-only.

Numeric mode uses three octal digits to represent the permissions, with each digit ranging from 0 to 7. Each place represents the owner, group, and others respectively. For example:

```
chmod 754 example.txt
```

This command sets the owner permissions to read, write, and execute (7), group permissions to read and execute (5), and others permissions to read-only (4).

Understanding Special Permissions

In addition to basic permissions, there are three special permissions: SUID, SGID, and Sticky bit. Each modifies how permissions are handled for executable files and directories.

Set User ID (SUID): When set on an executable file, this allows the file to execute with the permissions of the file owner, rather than the user who executes it. This is indicated by an s in the user execute position (-rwsr-xr-x). It is set using:

```
chmod u+s /path/to/executable
```

Set Group ID (SGID): When set on an executable, this allows the file to execute with the permissions of the file's group. When set on a directory, new files within the directory inherit the group ID of that directory. This is indicated by an s in the group execute position (-rwxr-sr-x). It is set using:

```
chmod g+s /path/to/file_or_directory
```

Sticky Bit: When set on a directory, it allows only the file owner, directory owner, or root to delete or rename files within that directory. This is indicated by a t in the others execute position (drwxrwxrwt). It is set using:

```
chmod +t /path/to/directory
```

Setting Default Permissions with umask

The umask command determines the default permissions for newly created files and directories. It essentially modifies the default permissions by "masking" certain permission bits. For example, a umask of 022 ensures that new files are created with permissions 644 and new directories with permissions 755.

The umask value can be set in the shell configuration files (.bashrc, .profile, etc.):

```
umask 022
```

This ensures that all new files and directories adhere to this permission scheme unless explicitly modified.

Understanding and applying secure file permissions and special permissions safeguards critical data from unauthorized access and modification. Proper utilization of chmod and umask fortifies the defensive measures against potential security breaches.

11.6 Avoiding Common Security Mistakes

When developing shell scripts, it is paramount to avoid common security mistakes that can introduce vulnerabilities. In this section, we will examine prevalent errors and best practices to mitigate these risks. Each sub-topic will focus on a specific mistake, illustrated with both problematic and corrected code examples.

Improper Handling of User Input: One of the most frequent mistakes is inadequate handling of user input, which may lead to injection attacks. Scripts should always validate and sanitize user input.

```
read -p "Enter a filename to delete: " filename
rm $filename
```

In the above code, if the user inputs '; rm -rf /', it could lead to catastrophic data loss. To safeguard against this, always quote variables and use safer alternatives.

```
read -p "Enter a filename to delete: " filename
# Validate the filename (basic example: check if it contains only valid characters)
if [[ "$filename" =~ ^[a-zA-Z0-9._-]+$ ]]; then
    rm -- "$filename"
else
    echo "Invalid filename."
fi
```

Environment Variable Manipulation: Another common mistake is relying on or modifying environment variables without caution. Attackers can exploit environment variables to alter a script's behavior.

```
PATH=$PATH:/custom/bin
```

If an attacker places a malicious script named 'ls' in '/custom/bin', it could be executed instead of the legitimate 'ls' command. To prevent this, the script should reference executables with absolute paths.

```
/bin/ls -l
```

Insecure File Handling: Handling files insecurely, such as temporary files, can expose scripts to race conditions and unauthorized access. It is crucial to create files securely and set appropriate permissions.

```
tmpfile="/tmp/mytempfile"
echo "Temporary data" > $tmpfile
```

A secure approach involves using 'mktemp' which creates a unique and secure temporary file.

```
tmpfile=$(mktemp /tmp/mytempfile.XXXXXX)
echo "Temporary data" > "$tmpfile"
trap 'rm -f "$tmpfile"' EXIT
```

Not Checking Command Success: Ignoring the exit status of commands can lead to unintended behavior and errors going unnoticed.

```
mkdir /some/directory
cp file1 /some/directory/
```

Always check the exit status and handle errors appropriately.

```
mkdir /some/directory
if [ $? -ne 0 ]; then
    echo "Failed to create directory."
    exit 1
fi
cp file1 /some/directory/
if [ $? -ne 0 ]; then
    echo "Failed to copy file."
    exit 1
fi
```

Hardcoding Sensitive Information: Hardcoding sensitive information such as passwords or tokens in scripts is a significant security risk as it can be easily exposed.

```
PASSWORD="supersecretpassword"
some_command --password=$PASSWORD
```

Instead, use environment variables or secure vault services to manage sensitive data.

```
some_command --password=$PASSWORD
```

Improper Use of eval: The 'eval' command can execute arbitrary code and is susceptible to injection attacks. Avoid using ‘eval‘ unless absolutely necessary.

```
eval $user_input
```

Instead, find safer alternatives to achieve the desired functionality.

```
case $user_input in
    "option1") some_command ;;
    "option2") another_command ;;
    *) echo "Invalid option" ;;
esac
```

Inadequate Logging and Monitoring: Without proper logging and monitoring, detecting security incidents can be challenging. Ensure scripts log important activities and errors.

```
command
```

Implement logging to track script activity and errors.

```
command >> /var/log/script.log 2>&1
if [ $? -ne 0 ]; then
    echo "Command failed, check /var/log/script.log for details."
fi
```

Adhering to these practices helps secure shell scripts against a range of common vulnerabilities. Always validate user input, use secure methods for file handling, check command success, avoid hardcoding sensitive information, cautiously use ‘eval‘, and ensure adequate logging and monitoring. Proper attention to these areas significantly enhances the robustness and security of your scripts.

11.7 Using SSH for Secure Connections

Secure Shell (SSH) is a protocol used to securely connect to remote machines over a network. The secure channel it provides ensures encryption of data, preventing interception and tampering. Implementing SSH effectively is pivotal for maintaining the security integrity of operations involving remote script execution, file transfers, and system administrative tasks.

SSH uses public-key cryptography to authenticate the remote computer and allow it to authenticate the user if necessary. Before delving into the details of using SSH for secure connections, let’s look at generating and configuring SSH keys.

Generating SSH Keys

To generate a new SSH key pair, the following command is used:

```
ssh-keygen -t rsa -b 4096 -C "your_email@example.com"
```

This command initiates the generation of a new RSA key pair with a key size of 4096 bits. The comment your_email@example.com helps in identifying the key. Upon execution, the prompt will ask where to save the new key, offering a default location. Accept the default location by pressing Enter or specify a different path.

The system will thereafter prompt for a passphrase—a security measure to further protect the private key. Adding a passphrase will require unlocking the private key upon use:

```
Enter passphrase (empty for no passphrase):
Enter same passphrase again:
```

Upon completion, two files are generated: the private key (id_rsa) and the public key (id_rsa.pub). The private key should be kept secure and not shared, while the public key will be placed on remote machines to facilitate secure connections.

Copying Public Key to Remote Host

To copy the public key to a remote host, the utility ssh-copy-id can be employed, streamlining the process:

```
ssh-copy-id user@remote_host
```

The above command copies the public key to the ~/.ssh/authorized_keys file on the remote host under the specified user account. If ssh-copy-id is not available, manual copying can be achieved through the following:

```
cat ~/.ssh/id_rsa.pub | ssh user@remote_host "mkdir -p ~/.ssh && cat >> ~/.ssh/
    authorized_keys"
```

This command concatenates the local public key and appends it to the authorized_keys file on the remote host, creating the .ssh directory if it doesn't exist.

Configuring SSH for Enhanced Security

Modifying the SSH daemon configuration further enhances security. The configuration file /etc/ssh/sshd_config on the remote host provides a range of settings. Key considerations include:

- **Disabling SSH Protocol 1**: Ensure that only SSH Protocol 2 is enabled as it is more secure:

```
Protocol 2
```

- **Restricting Root Login**: Disabling root login over SSH prevents potential misuse:

```
PermitRootLogin no
```

- **Allowing Specific Users**: Limiting SSH access to certain users:

```
AllowUsers alice bob
```

- **Disabling Password Authentication**: Utilizing key-based authentication exclusively enhances security:

```
PasswordAuthentication no
```

After making necessary changes, reload the SSH service for the changes to take effect:

```
sudo systemctl reload sshd
```

Using SSH for Script Execution and File Transfer

SSH facilitates secure execution of scripts on remote machines. By utilizing the ssh command in conjunction with a script, one can execute scripts remotely:

```
ssh user@remote_host 'bash -s' < local_script.sh
```

This command streams and executes local_script.sh on the specified remote host.

For secure file transfers, scp and rsync are employed:

- **Using scp**:

```
scp local_file user@remote_host:/remote/directory
```

- **Using rsync**: Synchronize files/directories efficiently:

```
rsync -avz local_directory user@remote_host:/remote/directory
```

Both commands ensure encrypted transfer of data, preserving integrity and confidentiality.

Tunneling and Port Forwarding

SSH supports tunneling and port forwarding, enabling secure forwarding of network traffic. Port forwarding enables clients to securely access remote services. For instance, to forward a local port to a remote service:

```
ssh -L local_port:localhost:remote_port user@remote_host
```

This command forwards local_port on the local machine to remote_port on the remote machine through the SSH connection. For reverse port forwarding:

```
ssh -R remote_port:localhost:local_port user@remote_host
```

This setup forwards remote_port on the remote host to local_port on the local machine, useful for exposing local services to remote hosts securely.

SSH remains an indispensable tool for secure operations in shell scripting, offering robust authentication and encryption mechanisms. Proper generation, deployment, and configuration of keys, alongside the diligent use of SSH features, can significantly bolster the security posture of remote scripting activities.

11.8 Best Practices for Writing Secure Scripts

In developing secure shell scripts, adhering to best practices is essential in mitigating risks and ensuring script integrity. This section provides comprehensive guidelines for writing secure scripts, emphasizing key principles applicable to various stages of script development.

First and foremost, always define a clear, constrained execution environment for your script. Begin by explicitly setting the $PATH variable to eliminate ambiguity in command execution paths. This practice mitigates the risk of command injection by ensuring commands are executed from trusted directories only.

```
export PATH='/bin:/usr/bin:/usr/local/bin'
```

Handling user inputs securely is pivotal. Always validate and sanitize inputs to prevent malicious data from being processed. Utilize regular expressions to ensure inputs match expected patterns. Consider the following example where a username input is validated:

```
read -p "Enter your username: " username
if [[ ! "$username" =~ ^[a-zA-Z0-9_]+$ ]]; then
    echo "Invalid username. Only alphanumeric characters and underscores are allowed."
    exit 1
fi
```

Another key practice is the principle of least privilege. Run your scripts with the minimum required privileges to reduce the impact of potential vulnerabilities. Avoid using the root account unless absolutely necessary.

- **File permissions** should be managed carefully to prevent unauthorized access. Use the most restrictive permissions that still allow the necessary operations. For instance, a script that requires read and write access by the owner but should not be executed by others might be set as follows:

```
chmod 600 myscript.sh
```

- **Input validation** is further critical when handling files. Use absolute paths and validate file names to avoid directory traversal attacks.

```
filename="/var/log/mylogfile"
if [[ ! -f "$filename" ]]; then
    echo "Log file does not exist."
    exit 1
fi
```

- **Error handling** is another essential habit. Always check the exit status of commands and handle errors appropriately to avoid script failures that could lead to insecure states. For example:

```
mkdir /secure/dir
if [[ $? -ne 0 ]]; then
    echo "Failed to create directory."
    exit 1
fi
```

- **Avoid using hardcoded sensitive data** such as passwords within your scripts. Instead, read sensitive data from secure locations, such as environment variables or secure storage solutions. Here's an example involving environmental variables:

```
db_pass="$DB_PASS"
if [[ -z "$db_pass" ]]; then
    echo "Database password not set."
    exit 1
fi
```

- Implement mechanisms to **log relevant activities**, ensuring that the logs themselves are protected from unauthorized access.

```
log_file="/var/log/myscript.log"
exec > >(tee -a $log_file) 2>&1
```

- In addition, the use of trap statements ensures that scripts handle interrupts and other termination signals gracefully, thus preventing the script from leaving the system in an insecure state.

```
trap 'echo "Script interrupted"; exit' INT TERM
```

- Utilize **secure temporary file handling** by leveraging tools like mktemp to create temporary files safely.

```
tempfile=$(mktemp)
echo "Temporary file created at $tempfile"
```

- Maintain **script readability and simplicity**. Complex scripts are harder to audit and more prone to bugs. Clearly comment on each section of the script to explain its purpose and any security considerations being implemented.

Lastly,

- **keep your scripts and dependencies up to date**. Regularly updating your environment and scripts ensures that you benefit from the latest security patches and improvements. Integrate a routine check for updates as a part of your maintenance process.

By meticulously applying these best practices, you significantly enhance the security of your shell scripts, creating a robust defense against potential threats and vulnerabilities.

11.9 Implementing Access Controls

Access control in shell scripting is essential to ensure that only authorized users can execute, modify, or read particular scripts and files. This section will delve into the mechanisms of implementing access control, emphasizing the use of Unix file permissions, Access Control Lists (ACLs), and sudoers configuration for restricting elevated permissions.

File permissions in Unix-like systems are foundational to access control. Each file and directory is associated with three types of permissions: read (r), write (w), and execute (x). These permissions are further categorized into three classes: user (u), group (g), and others (o). To view or modify file permissions, the ls and chmod commands are widely used.

```
ls -l /path/to/file
```

The above command outputs the permissions of a file or directory in a long listing format.

```
-rwxr-xr-- 1 user group 1024 Mar 10 12:34 example.sh
```

Here, -rwxr-xr– denotes the permission string. The first character indicates the type (d for directory, - for regular file), followed by three sets of permissions for user, group, and others. In this example:

- rwx means the user can read, write, and execute the file.
- r-x signifies that the group can read and execute but not write.
- r– signifies that others can only read the file.

To modify these permissions, the chmod command is used. For instance, to make the example.sh script executable only by the user, the command would be:

```
chmod u+x,g-x,o-x example.sh
```

In addition to basic file permissions, Access Control Lists (ACLs) provide a more flexible permission model. ACLs allow specifying permissions for individual users and groups beyond the traditional owner/-group/others model. The setfacl and getfacl commands are utilized to set and view ACLs, respectively.

For example, to allow a specific user read access to a file without changing existing permissions, use:

```
setfacl -m u:username:r /path/to/file
```

To view the ACL for a file, the following command is used:

```
getfacl /path/to/file
```

For more restrictive environments where access control needs to be managed for commands requiring elevated permissions, configuring the sudoers file is essential. The sudoers file, typically located at /etc/sudoers, dictates which users can execute commands as the superuser or other users.

Modifications to the sudoers file should always be done using the visudo command to avoid syntax errors. A typical entry to allow a user to run specific commands as root would look like:

```
username ALL=(ALL) /bin/systemctl restart httpd
```

This configuration allows username to run the systemctl restart httpd command as root on any host.

Implementing robust access controls is a layered approach in shell scripting. Beyond permissions and ACLs, monitoring and auditing script usage is crucial. Using audit tools such as auditd ensures that any attempts to access or modify critical scripts are logged and reviewed.

Setting up an audit rule for a shell script might involve the following:

```
auditctl -w /path/to/script.sh -p rwxa -k script-audit
```

In this command:

- -w specifies the path to the file.
- -p specifies the permissions to monitor (read, write, execute, append).
- -k assigns an identifier to the audit rule.

Auditing logs can be reviewed using the ausearch command:

```
ausearch -k script-audit
```

Access control mechanisms in Linux shell scripting are critical for maintaining security and operational integrity. By utilizing Unix file permissions, ACLs, the sudoers file, and auditing, one can effectively control and monitor script access, ensuring only authorized actions are permitted.

11.10 Monitoring and Auditing Scripts

Effective monitoring and auditing are integral components in maintaining the security integrity of shell scripts. By establishing robust mechanisms for observing script behavior and meticulously examining logs, potential security breaches can be promptly identified and mitigated. This section delves into various tools and techniques available for monitoring and auditing shell scripts, emphasizing the creation of reliable and secure environments.

1. System Log Analysis

System logs are the primary source of information when monitoring script activities. Log files, found typically under the /var/log directory in Linux systems, contain detailed records of system events, application activities, and script executions. To facilitate effective log analysis, it is essential to:

- syslog: Utilize the syslog service to manage and organize log messages.
- journalctl: Leverage the journalctl command to query and display messages from the systemd journal. This can be particularly useful given its additional features over traditional logging mechanisms.

For instance, to view log messages from the last 24 hours:

```
$ sudo journalctl --since "24 hours ago"
```

2. Script Logging Techniques

Implementing logging within shell scripts is crucial for tracking operations and debugging. Usage of the logger command sends messages to the syslog system within the script execution. Example of a script that handles logging:

```
#!/bin/bash

LOG_TAG="MyScript"
LOG_FILE="/var/log/myscript.log"
```

```
log_message() {
    local message="$1"
    echo "$(date +"%Y-%m-%d %H:%M:%S") $message" | tee -a "$LOG_FILE" |
        logger -t "$LOG_TAG"
}

log_message "Script execution started."
# Script operations...
log_message "Script execution completed."
```

3. Real-Time Monitoring

Real-time monitoring tools, such as tail and htop, allow administrators to observe script executions dynamically. The tail command with the -f option can be used to follow log files in real-time:

```
$ tail -f /var/log/myscript.log
```

htop provides a detailed interactive process viewer that can help in monitoring processes spawned by scripts:

```
$ htop
```

4. Auditing with auditd

The Linux auditd framework offers comprehensive auditing capabilities for tracking system calls made by scripts. By configuring rules in auditd (stored in /etc/audit/audit.rules), you can monitor specific files and commands. Example rule to audit executions of a script:

```
$ sudo auditctl -w /path/to/myscript.sh -p x -k myscript_audit
```

To review audit logs generated by this rule, use:

```
$ sudo ausearch -k myscript_audit
```

5. Notifications and Alerts

Configuring notifications and alerts ensures prompt response to anomalies. This can be achieved via email or integration with monitoring tools like Nagios, Prometheus, or Grafana.

Example of sending email notifications from a script:

```
#!/bin/bash

RECIPIENT="admin@example.com"
log_and_notify() {
    local message="$1"
    echo "$(date +"%Y-%m-%d %H:%M:%S") $message" | mail -s "Script Alert" "
        $RECIPIENT"
}
```

```
log_and_notify "Anomaly detected in script execution."
```

6. Using Version Control Systems

In addition to runtime monitoring, employing version control systems (VCS) like Git can streamline auditing changes made to scripts. Every alteration is tracked with a unique commit ID, allowing for traceability and accountability.

Initializing a Git repository for scripts:

```
$ cd /path/to/scripts
$ git init
$ git add .
$ git commit -m "Initial commit"
```

To review changes over time:

```
$ git log
$ git diff commit_id1 commit_id2
```

7. Ensuring Compliance with Security Policies

Consistently reviewing scripts against organizational security policies and industry standards guarantees compliance and best practices. Conducting regular security audits and peer code reviews can identify and rectify issues early.

8. Automating Monitoring and Auditing

Automation tools such as cron jobs and CI/CD pipelines ensure continuous monitoring and auditing of scripts without manual intervention. Example of a cron job to regularly verify script integrity:

```
# Edit the crontab file
$ crontab -e

# Add the following line to run a script integrity check every day at 1 AM
0 1 * * * /path/to/integrity_check.sh
```

The described practices provide a comprehensive framework for monitoring and auditing scripts, aimed at enhancing security and facilitating the early detection of irregularities.

11.11 Regular Updates and Security Patches

Maintaining the security of your shell scripts often requires addressing vulnerabilities through regular updates and the application of security patches. These tasks are essential to protect your system and data from exploits, malware, and other threats. The software lifecycle keeps evolving, often delivering security patches to fix newly discovered vulnerabilities. Ignoring these updates can leave your system exposed to known threats.

Administrators must stay informed about the latest updates for the software and dependencies they manage. Most distributions and software repositories maintain a changelog that outlines changes, fixes, and new features. It is advisable to monitor these logs regularly to identify relevant updates.

- **Updating System Packages:**

  Updating system packages is a common task. Most Linux distributions provide package management tools to simplify the process. For example, on Debian-based systems, the apt tool is widely used:

  ```
  sudo apt update
  sudo apt upgrade
  ```

  The command apt update refreshes the local package index, while apt upgrade installs the latest versions of all packages currently installed on the system. For Red Hat-based systems, the yum or dnf package managers are commonly used:

  ```
  sudo dnf check-update
  sudo dnf update
  ```

- **Applying Security Patches:**

  Security patches specifically address vulnerabilities and are essential for maintaining the integrity of your system. These patches might be included in regular updates or released separately. It is crucial to prioritize these patches to mitigate potential risk as soon as possible.

  To check for and apply security patches on a Debian-based system, you can utilize the 'unattended-upgrades' package. It automates the installation of security updates:

```
sudo apt install unattended-upgrades
sudo dpkg-reconfigure --priority=low unattended-upgrades
```

The reconfiguration process will guide you through the setup, ensuring that security updates are applied automatically.

- **Kernel Updates:**

  Kernel updates are critical, as they often include patches for serious vulnerabilities. Some kernel updates may require a system reboot to take effect. To check for and install kernel updates:

  ```
  sudo apt update
  sudo apt install linux-image-$(uname -r)
  ```

  After installing a new kernel, you typically need to restart your system to boot into the updated kernel version. Monitoring the kernel version can ensure that the new version has been correctly applied:

  ```
  uname -r
  ```

- **Scripting for Regular Updates:**

  Automating the update process can help ensure that your systems remain up-to-date without manual intervention. Below is an example of a shell script that automates the update of Debian-based systems, including the application of security patches:

  ```
  #!/bin/bash

  # Update the package index
  apt update

  # Upgrade all installed packages
  apt upgrade -y

  # Distribute the unattended-upgrades configuration
  dpkg-reconfigure --priority=low unattended-upgrades

  # Install and configure the latest security updates
  unattended-upgrades

  # Cleanup
  apt autoremove -y
  apt clean

  # Logging
  echo "System updated on $(date)" >> /var/log/auto-update.log
  ```

  This script updates the package index, upgrades installed packages, configures unattended-upgrades, installs security updates, and performs cleanup. It logs the update process to /var/log/auto-update.log.

- **Monitoring and Notification:**

  Regular monitoring and receiving notifications about available updates is essential for timely action. Tools such as apticron or yum-cron can send email notifications when updates or security patches are available. Configuring apticron on Debian-based systems is straightforward:

  ```
  sudo apt install apticron
  ```

  Edit the configuration file to set the recipient email address:

  ```
  sudo nano /etc/apticron/apticron.conf
  # Set EMAIL="your-email@example.com"
  ```

  Notifications about package updates and security patches will be sent to the configured email address, allowing prompt actions to be taken.

Staying proactive with regular updates and applying security patches is fundamental to maintaining the security and performance of your Linux systems.

11.12 Practical Security Implementation Examples

To concretize the theoretical principles discussed throughout this chapter, practical examples demonstrate how to implement robust security measures in shell scripting. These examples cover validating user input, handling sensitive data, implementing secure file permissions, and more.

Example 1: Validating and Sanitizing User Input

Ensuring that user input is both valid and sanitized is crucial to prevent various attacks, such as injection attacks. The following shell script checks whether the user-provided input is a valid integer.

```
#!/bin/bash

read -p "Enter a number: " userInput

if [[ "$userInput" =~ ^[0-9]+$ ]]; then
```

```
    echo "Valid number: $userInput"
else
    echo "Invalid input. Please enter a valid number."
    exit 1
fi
```

This script reads an input from the user and uses a regular expression to validate that it contains only digits. If the input is not a valid number, the script exits with a status of 1, indicating an error.

Example 2: Handling Sensitive Data Securely

Sensitive data such as passwords should never be stored in plain text in scripts. Below is an example demonstrating the use of environment variables to handle sensitive data securely.

```
#!/bin/bash

# Securely read password input
read -s -p "Enter your password: " password
echo

# Use the password securely in your command
ssh user@server -p 22
```

This script uses the ‘read‘ command with the ‘-s‘ flag to securely read the password input without displaying it on the screen.

Example 3: Using Secure File Permissions

Secure file permissions ensure that only authorized users can access or modify files. In the following example, a script creates a file and sets secure permissions.

```
#!/bin/bash

# Create a file
touch securefile.txt

# Set file permissions
chmod 600 securefile.txt

echo "File created with secure permissions."
```

This script creates a file named ‘securefile.txt‘ and sets its permissions to ‘600‘, meaning only the owner can read and write it. This practice is critical when dealing with sensitive data.

Example 4: Avoiding Common Security Mistakes

One common security mistake is the inclusion of sensitive information within the script itself. The following example demonstrates an incorrect and a corrected approach to handle database credentials.

Incorrect Approach:

```
#!/bin/bash

DB_USER="admin"
DB_PASS="password" # Sensitive data should not be hardcoded in scripts

mysql -u $DB_USER -p$DB_PASS -e "SHOW DATABASES;"
```

Correct Approach:

```
#!/bin/bash

# Prompt user for database credentials
read -p "Enter DB Username: " DB_USER
read -s -p "Enter DB Password: " DB_PASS
echo

mysql -u $DB_USER -p$DB_PASS -e "SHOW DATABASES;"
```

In the corrected approach, the script prompts the user for the database credentials at runtime, avoiding the inclusion of sensitive information in the script.

Example 5: Using SSH for Secure Connections

Secure connections are a fundamental aspect of script security, particularly when interacting with remote servers. Below is an example of setting up an SSH connection using a key pair.

```
#!/bin/bash

REMOTE_USER="username"
REMOTE_HOST="remote.example.com"
REMOTE_PORT=22

# Ensure the private key is readable only by the owner
chmod 600 ~/.ssh/id_rsa

# Connect to the remote server securely
ssh -p $REMOTE_PORT $REMOTE_USER@$REMOTE_HOST
```

This script configures an SSH connection using a predefined username, host, and port while ensuring that the private SSH key's permissions are securely set to be readable only by the file owner.

Example 6: Monitoring and Auditing Scripts

Implementing logging within your scripts helps monitor and audit activities, which is crucial for security. The following example demonstrates adding basic logging to a script.

```
#!/bin/bash

LOGFILE="/var/log/myscript.log"
```

```
# Log a message with a timestamp
log_message() {
    local MESSAGE=$1
    echo "$(date +'%Y-%m-%d %T') - $MESSAGE" >> $LOGFILE
}

log_message "Script started."

# Simulate a protected operation
sleep 2
log_message "Completed operation 1."

# Simulate another protected operation
sleep 2
log_message "Completed operation 2."

log_message "Script ended."
```

```
2023-10-07 14:20:01 - Script started.
2023-10-07 14:20:03 - Completed operation 1.
2023-10-07 14:20:05 - Completed operation 2.
2023-10-07 14:20:05 - Script ended.
```

This script includes a log_message function that appends messages with timestamps to a specified log file, enabling the tracking of script activities for audit purposes.

These practical examples illustrate the application of secure scripting practices in various essential areas, providing a solid foundation for implementing stringent security measures in your scripts.

Chapter 12

Practical Shell Script Examples

This chapter presents a collection of practical shell script examples to demonstrate real-world applications of shell scripting concepts. It covers automating system maintenance tasks, file backup and restoration, log file analysis, network monitoring, disk usage management, and process management. Additional topics include user account management, automated report generation, data extraction and transformation, and integration with other tools. The chapter concludes by discussing script scheduling with cron and providing case studies to illustrate the implementation of these scripts in various scenarios.

12.1 Introduction to Practical Shell Scripts

In this section, we explore the essentials of practical shell scripting, emphasizing real-world applications. Shell scripting serves as a vital tool for automating and simplifying diverse system administration tasks. Proficient use of shell scripts can significantly enhance productivity, consistency, and reliability. This section sets the stage for comprehending the full potential of shell scripting through various examples detailed in subsequent sections.

Shell scripts are text files containing a sequence of commands that the shell interprets and executes. They are written using shell scripting languages such as Bash, which is commonly used on Unix-like systems. The fundamental construct of a shell script is a command or series of commands intended to achieve a specific outcome. Let's commence by examining the basic structure and components of a shell script.

A basic shell script typically begins with a shebang (#!/bin/bash) followed by the path to the shell interpreter, ensuring that the correct shell processes the script. Consider the following example:

```
#!/bin/bash
# This is a comment
echo "Hello, World!"
```

In the example above, #!/bin/bash specifies that the Bash interpreter executes the script. The comment line (# This is a comment) provides descriptions or annotations, aiding readability and maintenance. The echo command outputs the string "Hello, World!" to the terminal.

Variables in shell scripts store data that can be referenced and manipulated. They enhance the script's flexibility and reusability. Here's an example of defining and using variables:

```
#!/bin/bash
greeting="Hello"
name="Alice"
echo "$greeting, $name!"
```

In this script, the variables greeting and name are defined. The echo command prints their values combined, resulting in the output: Hello, Alice!. The dollar sign ($) is used to access the variable's value.

Control structures such as conditionals and loops enable the development of more complex and dynamic scripts. These constructs allow the script to perform different actions based on varying conditions or iterate through data sets. Consider a script using an if statement:

```
#!/bin/bash
read -p "Enter your age: " age
if [ "$age" -ge 18 ]; then
    echo "You are an adult."
else
    echo "You are a minor."
fi
```

In this script, the read command prompts the user to enter their age. The if statement checks if the entered age is greater than or equal to 18. Depending on the outcome, the script prints either "You are an adult." or "You are a minor."

Loops iterate over a set of data or repeat a block of commands until a specified condition is met. The for loop iterates over a list of items:

```
#!/bin/bash
for name in Alice Bob Charlie
do
    echo "Hello, $name!"
done
```

In this script, the for loop iterates over the names Alice, Bob, and Charlie, executing the echo command for each name, resulting in three greetings:

```
Hello, Alice!
Hello, Bob!
Hello, Charlie!
```

Functions in shell scripts compartmentalize code, promoting modularity and reusability. Functions are defined using the function keyword or simply the function name followed by parentheses:

```
#!/bin/bash
function greet {
    local name=$1
    echo "Hello, $name!"
}
greet "Alice"
greet "Bob"
```

In this script, the greet function takes a single argument (name). When invoked with "Alice" and "Bob" as arguments, the function prints personalized greetings.

Effective error handling in shell scripts ensures reliability and robustness. The exit command terminates a script, optionally returning a status code. The $? variable holds the exit status of the last executed command, enabling conditional execution based on command success or failure:

```
#!/bin/bash
cp source.txt destination.txt
if [ $? -ne 0 ]; then
    echo "Copy failed!"
    exit 1
else
    echo "Copy succeeded!"
fi
```

This script attempts to copy source.txt to destination.txt. If the cp command fails (denoted by a non-zero exit status), it prints an error message and exits with a status code of 1.

These foundational concepts form the bedrock upon which we'll build more sophisticated scripts to address various practical scenarios throughout this chapter. Each example script illustrates applying these principles to real-world tasks, enhancing your shell scripting proficiency and deploying robust solutions for system administration needs.

12.2 Automating System Maintenance Tasks

Automating system maintenance tasks is essential to ensure the smooth and efficient operation of Linux systems. These tasks can range from routine updates and cleaning of temporary files to the automation of security checks and resource monitoring. Automating these processes reduces the risk of human error and ensures that maintenance tasks are performed consistently and on schedule. This section explores various scripts that can automate common maintenance tasks, leveraging the power of shell scripting.

- **Example 1: Updating the System**

  Keeping the system updated is crucial for security and performance. The following script automates the process of updating package lists, upgrading installed packages, and cleaning up unnecessary files.

```
#!/bin/bash

# Update the package list
echo "Updating package list..."
sudo apt-get update

# Upgrade all installed packages
echo "Upgrading packages..."
sudo apt-get upgrade -y

# Remove unnecessary files
echo "Removing unnecessary files..."
sudo apt-get autoremove -y
sudo apt-get clean

echo "System update completed successfully."
```

  This script uses the apt-get command, which is common for Debian-based systems. The update command refreshes the package list, upgrade installs the newest versions of all packages installed on the system, and autoremove and clean commands remove unnecessary files and clean up partial package files, respectively. Running this script periodically ensures that the system remains up-to-date and free of clutter.

- **Example 2: Clearing Temporary Files**

  Temporary files can accumulate over time and consume valuable disk space. The following script automatically deletes temporary files older than a specified number of days.

```
#!/bin/bash

# Define the directory to clean and the age threshold
TEMP_DIR="/tmp"
DAYS_OLD=7

# Find and delete temporary files older than the specified number of days
echo "Cleaning temporary files older than $DAYS_OLD days..."
find $TEMP_DIR -type f -mtime +$DAYS_OLD -exec rm {} \;

echo "Temporary files cleanup completed."
```

  This script makes use of the find command to search for files in the /tmp directory that have not been modified in the last 7 days and deletes them. The -mtime option specifies the age threshold, and the -exec rm {} part executes the rm command to remove each file found.

- **Example 3: Disk Usage Monitoring**

  Monitoring disk usage is important to prevent disks from becoming full and causing system issues. The script below checks the disk usage and sends an alert if usage exceeds a specified threshold.

```
#!/bin/bash

# Define the threshold percentage
THRESHOLD=90

# Get the current disk usage percentage for the root filesystem
CURRENT_USAGE=$(df / | grep / | awk '{ print $5 }' | sed 's/%//g')

# Check if current usage exceeds the threshold
if [ $CURRENT_USAGE -gt $THRESHOLD ]; then
    echo "Warning: Disk usage has exceeded $THRESHOLD%. Current usage is
        $CURRENT_USAGE%."
    # Send an alert (this can be customized to send an email or other
        notification)
fi
```

  In this script, the df command displays the disk space usage, and awk is used to extract the percentage usage of the root filesystem. The script compares the current usage with the defined threshold and prints a warning message if the threshold is exceeded. This can be further extended to send email alerts using tools like mail or sendmail.

- **Example 4: Automating User Account Check**

  Regularly checking user accounts can help in identifying stale or unused accounts, which can be potential security risks. The following script lists user accounts that have not been active for a specified number of days.

```
#!/bin/bash

# Define the number of days of inactivity
DAYS_INACTIVE=30

# Find and list user accounts with last login older than the specified number of
    days
echo "Listing user accounts inactive for more than $DAYS_INACTIVE days..."
lastlog -b $DAYS_INACTIVE
```

  This script utilizes the lastlog command, which reports the most recent login of all users. The -b option is used to specify the days of inactivity. This helps in identifying user accounts that have not been accessed recently and could be candidates for review or deactivation.

The use of these scripts streamlines various system maintenance tasks, ensuring they are performed reliably and without manual intervention. Regularly updating and monitoring systems using automated scripts enhances both security and efficiency.

12.3 File Backup and Restoration Scripts

Creating reliable and efficient file backup and restoration scripts is crucial for maintaining data integrity and ensuring data availability in case of unforeseen events. This section delves into the essential aspects of writing shell scripts for automating file backup and restoration processes, illustrating various scenarios and techniques.

A standard approach to file backup involves copying files from specified directories to a backup location, often compressing the files to save space. Restoration scripts reverse this process, ensuring that files can be reliably retrieved to their original locations.

To illustrate, consider the following example of a script that performs a full backup of a directory /home/user/data to a backup directory /backups/. The script includes error handling to ensure reliable operation.

```
#!/bin/bash

# Define source and destination directories
SRC_DIR="/home/user/data"
DEST_DIR="/backups/$(date +%Y%m%d_%H%M%S)"

# Create destination directory if it doesn't exist
mkdir -p "${DEST_DIR}"

# Perform the backup using rsync
rsync -av --delete "${SRC_DIR}/" "${DEST_DIR}/"

# Check if rsync succeeded
if [ $? -eq 0 ]; then
    echo "Backup completed successfully."
else
    echo "Backup failed." >&2
    exit 1
fi
```

This script leverages rsync, a fast and versatile file copying tool commonly used for backups. The -a option ensures that rsync operates in "archive" mode, preserving symbolic links, file permissions, and other attributes. The –delete option synchronizes deletions from the source to the backup directory, maintaining an exact mirror.

The use of the date command in the destination path ensures that each backup is timestamped, preventing overwriting of previous backups. Error handling is accomplished by checking the exit status of the rsync command, providing feedback on the backup operation's success or failure.

For directory restoration, a corresponding script might look like the following:

```
#!/bin/bash

# Define the backup directory and the restore destination
BACKUP_DIR="/backups/20230101_123456"
RESTORE_DIR="/home/user/data"

# Ensure the backup directory exists
if [ ! -d "${BACKUP_DIR}" ]; then
    echo "Backup directory not found: ${BACKUP_DIR}" >&2
    exit 1
fi

# Perform the restore using rsync
rsync -av "${BACKUP_DIR}/" "${RESTORE_DIR}/"

# Check if rsync succeeded
if [ $? -eq 0 ]; then
```

```
    echo "Restoration completed successfully."
else
    echo "Restoration failed." >&2
    exit 1
fi
```

This script similarly uses rsync to copy files from the backup location to the restoration directory. It includes a check to ensure the backup directory exists before attempting the restore, reducing the risk of errors.

While rsync is suitable for many scenarios, there may be use cases requiring archive formats such as tar. The following example demonstrates a script that creates a compressed archive of a directory:

```
#!/bin/bash

# Define source directory and archive file
SRC_DIR="/home/user/data"
ARCHIVE_FILE="/backups/data_backup_$(date +%Y%m%d_%H%M%S).tar.gz"

# Create a compressed tar archive
tar -czf "${ARCHIVE_FILE}" -C "${SRC_DIR}" .

# Check if tar succeeded
if [ $? -eq 0 ]; then
    echo "Archive created successfully: ${ARCHIVE_FILE}"
else
    echo "Failed to create archive." >&2
    exit 1
fi
```

The tar command is utilized with the -c option to create an archive, -z to compress it using gzip, and -f to specify the output file. The -C option changes to the SRC_DIR directory, ensuring that the archive stores relative paths instead of absolute paths.

For restoring from the tar archive, a script might be:

```
#!/bin/bash

# Define archive file and restore destination
ARCHIVE_FILE="/backups/data_backup_20230101_123456.tar.gz"
RESTORE_DIR="/home/user/data"

# Ensure the archive file exists
if [ ! -f "${ARCHIVE_FILE}" ]; then
    echo "Archive file not found: ${ARCHIVE_FILE}" >&2
    exit 1
fi

# Extract the tar archive
tar -xzf "${ARCHIVE_FILE}" -C "${RESTORE_DIR}"

# Check if tar succeeded
if [ $? -eq 0 ]; then
    echo "Restoration from archive completed successfully."
else
```

```
    echo "Failed to restore from archive." >&2
    exit 1
fi
```

In this script, the tar command is used with the -x option to extract the archive, -z to filter the archive through gzip, and -f to specify the archive file. The extracted files are stored in the RESTORE_DIR.

These examples provide a foundation for developing robust file backup and restoration scripts. By incorporating thorough error checking and ensuring backups are consistently timestamped, one can achieve a reliable backup routine.

12.4 Log File Analysis and Management

Log files are essential for understanding and troubleshooting system behavior. Effective log file analysis helps administrators detect anomalies, plan capacity, and ensure security compliance. This section will delve into practical shell scripts for analyzing and managing log files.

To begin, we focus on extracting specific patterns from logs. Consider a scenario where you need to find all occurrences of the term "ERROR" in the system log located at /var/log/syslog.

```
#!/bin/bash
grep "ERROR" /var/log/syslog
```

This script uses the grep command to search for the string "ERROR" in the specified log file. The output is displayed directly on the terminal. For more complex searches, regular expressions can be employed. For instance, if we want to search for lines containing either "ERROR" or "WARNING" messages, the following script can be used:

```
#!/bin/bash
grep -E "ERROR|WARNING" /var/log/syslog
```

The -E flag enables extended regular expressions, allowing the use of the | operator to match multiple patterns.

Sorting and counting occurrences are common requirements in log analysis. Using the previous example, if you want to count the number of "ERROR" messages, you can combine grep with the wc command:

```
#!/bin/bash
grep "ERROR" /var/log/syslog | wc -l
```

The command wc -l counts the number of lines in the output provided by grep.

Analyzing logs can involve more advanced tasks, such as summarizing log entries by date. The following script extracts the date from each log entry and counts the occurrences of "ERROR" messages by date:

```
#!/bin/bash
grep "ERROR" /var/log/syslog | awk '{print $1}' | sort | uniq -c
```

In this script, we summarize the steps as follows:

- grep "ERROR" /var/log/syslog extracts lines containing "ERROR".
- awk 'print $1' extracts the date (assuming the date is the first field in each log entry).
- sort sorts the dates.
- uniq -c counts unique occurrences of each date.

For continuous monitoring, tail can be used to watch logs in real-time. The following script monitors the syslog for new "ERROR" messages as they are written:

```
#!/bin/bash
tail -F /var/log/syslog | grep --line-buffered "ERROR"
```

The -F option in tail follows the log file, and –line-buffered in grep ensures immediate output of matching lines.

Log rotation is a necessary management task to prevent logs from consuming excessive disk space. The logrotate utility is typically used for this purpose. A basic logrotate configuration for /var/log/syslog may look like this:

```
/var/log/syslog {
 daily
 rotate 7
 compress
 missingok
 notifempty
 postrotate
 /usr/lib/rsyslog/rsyslog-rotate
 endscript
}
```

- daily instructs logrotate to rotate the log file daily.

- rotate 7 keeps the last seven rotated logs.
- compress compresses the rotated logs to save space.
- missingok ignores missing log files.
- notifempty skips rotation if the log file is empty.
- postrotate and endscript define a script to run after rotation; in this case, it signals the rsyslog service.

For custom log rotation without logrotate, the following script rotates /var/log/custom.log manually:

```
#!/bin/bash
LOGFILE="/var/log/custom.log"
BACKUPDIR="/var/log/backup"

if [ -f $LOGFILE ]; then
    TIMESTAMP=$(date +%Y%m%d%H%M%S)
    mv $LOGFILE $BACKUPDIR/custom.log.$TIMESTAMP
    gzip $BACKUPDIR/custom.log.$TIMESTAMP
    touch $LOGFILE
fi
```

This script performs the following tasks:

- Checks if /var/log/custom.log exists.
- Moves the log file to a backup directory with a timestamp.
- Compresses the moved log file.
- Creates a new, empty log file.

These examples illustrate some of the essential techniques for log file analysis and management using shell scripts. By leveraging these scripts, system administrators can efficiently monitor, analyze, and manage log files to ensure smooth system operations and security.

12.5 Network Monitoring and Management

Effective network monitoring and management are paramount in maintaining the health and performance of IT infrastructures. Network monitoring involves collecting and analyzing information from network devices and inspecting network flows to ensure optimal performance, while network management involves controlling and coordinating network hardware, software, and protocols to ensure seamless operation. This section delves into practical shell script examples that can aid in these tasks.

One of the fundamental tools for network monitoring is ping. It allows verification of connectivity between the host and a target IP address or hostname. To create a simple network monitoring script using ping, consider the following example:

```
#!/bin/bash

# Define the target IP address or hostname
TARGET="8.8.8.8"

# Perform the ping test
ping -c 4 $TARGET

# Check the exit status of the ping command
if [ $? -eq 0 ]; then
    echo "Network is up"
else
    echo "Network is down"
fi
```

In this script, the TARGET variable holds the IP address we want to monitor. The ping -c 4 command sends four ICMP packets to the specified target. Based on the exit status of the ping command, the script prints whether the network is "up" or "down."

Moving beyond basic connectivity checks, more advanced monitoring requires tools like netstat, ifconfig, iptables, and tcpdump. These tools provide more comprehensive details about network interfaces, connections, and traffic.

For instance, to monitor the established TCP connections on a server, you can use a shell script with the netstat command:

```
#!/bin/bash

# Retrieve and display established TCP connections
netstat -an | grep 'ESTABLISHED'
```

This script filters the output of netstat -an to display only those lines which contain the string "ESTABLISHED," thus listing all active TCP connections.

Network management can involve analyzing interface statistics to determine utilization, errors, and other metrics. A practical script to obtain network interface statistics using ifconfig can be as follows:

```
#!/bin/bash
```

```
# Get network interface statistics
ifconfig -a | grep -E "^[a-zA-Z0-9]" | awk '{print $1}'

# Display the statistics for each interface
for IFACE in $( ifconfig -a | grep -E "^[a-zA-Z0-9]" | awk '{print $1}' ); do
    echo "Statistics for interface: $IFACE"
    ifconfig $IFACE
    echo "=================================="
done
```

This script first lists all network interfaces by parsing the output of ifconfig -a. For each interface, it displays detailed statistics, such as packet counts, errors, and network addresses.

Another critical aspect of network management is managing firewall rules. The iptables command allows administrators to set up, maintain, and inspect firewall rules in the Linux kernel. The following script can be used to list currently active iptables rules:

```
#!/bin/bash

# List all active iptables rules
iptables -L -n -v
```

This script uses iptables -L -n -v to output all current rules with detailed information, including packet counts and byte counts.

Network traffic analysis is another essential task. tcpdump is a powerful command-line packet analyzer. The following example script captures network traffic on a specified interface and writes it to a file:

```
#!/bin/bash

# Define the network interface and the output file
INTERFACE="eth0"
OUTPUT_FILE="/tmp/network_traffic.pcap"

# Capture network traffic
tcpdump -i $INTERFACE -w $OUTPUT_FILE
```

The tcpdump -i $INTERFACE -w $OUTPUT_FILE command captures all packets on the indicated interface and saves them to a file. This allows for later analysis using tools such as Wireshark.

Efficient network monitoring and management utilize a combination of these tools and scripts. They enable system administrators to maintain robust and performance-optimized networks. The detailed insights provided by these scripts facilitate proactive measures to mitigate potential issues.

```
#!/bin/bash
```

```
# Define the network interface to restart
INTERFACE="eth0"

# Restart the network interface
ifdown $INTERFACE && ifup $INTERFACE

# Verify the interface status
ifconfig $INTERFACE
```

In this script, the target network interface is defined in the INTERFACE variable. The interface is brought down using ifdown and then brought back up using ifup. Finally, ifconfig is used to verify the status of the interface.

12.6 Disk Usage and Cleanup Scripts

Monitoring and managing disk usage is a crucial aspect of maintaining the health and performance of a Linux system. Disk usage scripts help system administrators monitor file system usage, identify large files and directories, and automate cleanup tasks. This section illustrates how to create and utilize shell scripts for effective disk usage management and cleanup.

To begin with, we will discuss how to create a script that reports disk usage using the 'df' and 'du' commands. The 'df' command provides an overview of disk space usage on all mounted filesystems, while the 'du' command estimates file space usage for directories and files. Below is a simple script to display disk usage:

```
#!/bin/bash

# Disk usage report
df -h
```

The above script utilizes the '-h' option with 'df' to display the size in human-readable format (e.g., KB, MB, GB).

Next, for a more detailed analysis, we will write a script to report the usage of specific directories. This script will use the 'du' command:

```
#!/bin/bash

# Directory usage report
DIRECTORY=$1
if [ -z "$DIRECTORY" ]; then
    echo "Usage: $0 <directory>"
    exit 1
fi
```

```
du -sh $DIRECTORY/*
```

This script takes a directory path as an argument and displays the size of each sub-directory and file within it. The '-s' option summarizes the total usage of each argument, and the '-h' option provides human-readable output.

To automate cleanup tasks, we need scripts capable of identifying and deleting unnecessary files. The following script identifies and deletes log files older than a specified number of days:

```
#!/bin/bash

# Log file cleanup
LOG_DIR="/var/log"
DAYS_OLD=30

find $LOG_DIR -type f -name "*.log" -mtime +$DAYS_OLD -exec rm -f {} \;
```

In this script, the 'find' command is used to search for files in '/var/log' ending with '.log' and modified more than 30 days ago ('-mtime +30'). The '-exec' option executes the 'rm -f' command to delete the identified files.

Another useful script automates the removal of files from the '/tmp' directory that have not been accessed recently:

```
#!/bin/bash

# Temporary files cleanup
TMP_DIR="/tmp"
DAYS_NOT_ACCESSED=7

find $TMP_DIR -type f -atime +$DAYS_NOT_ACCESSED -exec rm -f {} \;
```

Here, the 'find' command searches for files in '/tmp' not accessed in the last 7 days ('-atime +7') and removes them.

For scenarios that require confirming deletions interactively, the following script incorporates a prompt for user confirmation before deleting each file:

```
#!/bin/bash

# Interactive cleanup with user confirmation
CLEANUP_DIR=$1
DAYS_OLD=$2

if [ -z "$CLEANUP_DIR" ] || [ -z "$DAYS_OLD" ]; then
    echo "Usage: $0 <directory> <days-old>"
    exit 1
fi
```

```
find $CLEANUP_DIR -type f -mtime +$DAYS_OLD -exec rm -i {} \;
```

The '-i' option with the 'rm' command prompts the user for confirmation before each deletion, enhancing control over the cleanup process.

Automating these scripts using 'cron' jobs ensures that disk usage is monitored and cleaned up regularly. The following 'cron' job example schedules the log file cleanup script to run daily at midnight:

```
0 0 * * * /path/to/log_cleanup.sh
```

Regular execution of such scripts helps maintain ample free disk space, ensuring optimal system performance and preventing unexpected storage-related issues.

12.7 Process Management Scripts

Process management is a crucial aspect of system administration, allowing administrators to monitor, control, and automate the execution of various processes on a Linux system. This section delves into practical shell scripts designed to address common process management tasks, including monitoring resource usage, terminating unresponsive processes, and automating process execution.

To begin with, let's consider a script that monitors resource usage for a specific process. This can be particularly useful for ensuring that no single process is monopolizing system resources. The script below uses the 'ps' and 'grep' commands to achieve this:

```
#!/bin/bash

# Check if process name is provided
if [ -z "$1" ]; then
  echo "Usage: $0 <process_name>"
  exit 1
fi

PROCESS_NAME=$1

# Get the PID of the process
PID=$(pgrep -f $PROCESS_NAME)

# Check if process is running
if [ -z "$PID" ]; then
  echo "Process $PROCESS_NAME not found."
  exit 1
fi

# Get CPU and memory usage of the process
```

```
CPU=$(ps -p $PID -o %cpu --no-headers)
MEM=$(ps -p $PID -o %mem --no-headers)

echo "Process $PROCESS_NAME (PID: $PID)"
echo "CPU Usage: $CPU%"
echo "Memory Usage: $MEM%"
```

This script takes a process name as an argument, retrieves the process ID (PID) using 'pgrep', and then uses 'ps' to display the CPU and memory usage. Note the use of the '–no-headers' option in 'ps' to exclude header lines from the output.

Next, let's explore a script that can terminate unresponsive processes. The following example uses the 'kill' command to send signals to a process:

```
#!/bin/bash

# Check if process name is provided
if [ -z "$1" ]; then
  echo "Usage: $0 <process_name>"
  exit 1
fi

PROCESS_NAME=$1

# Get the PID of the process
PID=$(pgrep -f $PROCESS_NAME)

# Check if process is running
if [ -z "$PID" ]; then
  echo "Process $PROCESS_NAME not found."
  exit 1
fi

# Send SIGTERM signal to the process
kill -15 $PID

# Wait for a grace period
sleep 5

# Check if the process terminated
if ps -p $PID > /dev/null; then
  echo "Process did not terminate, sending SIGKILL"
  kill -9 $PID
else
  echo "Process terminated successfully"
fi
```

This script attempts to gracefully terminate a process by sending the 'SIGTERM' signal ('kill -15'). If the process does not terminate within a specified grace period (5 seconds in this example), the script forcefully terminates it using the 'SIGKILL' signal ('kill -9').

Automating process execution is another common requirement in system administration. The following script demonstrates how to ensure that a particular process is always running, restarting it if it stops:

```
#!/bin/bash

# Check if script name is provided
if [ -z "$1" ]; then
  echo "Usage: $0 <script_name>"
  exit 1
fi

SCRIPT_NAME=$1

while true; do
  # Check if the script is running
  if ! pgrep -f $SCRIPT_NAME > /dev/null; then
    echo "Script $SCRIPT_NAME not running. Starting..."
    ./$SCRIPT_NAME &
  fi

  # Sleep for a defined interval
  sleep 10
done
```

This script takes another script name as an argument and enters an infinite loop where it checks if the specified script is running using ‘pgrep‘. If the script is not running, it starts the script in the background using ‘.$SCRIPT_NAME &‘. The script then sleeps for a defined interval (10 seconds in this example) before repeating the check.

Lastly, managing background jobs is an essential component of process management. The following example script demonstrates how to move a process to the background and disown it so it continues running even after the initiating shell session is closed:

```
#!/bin/bash

# Check if command is provided
if [ -z "$1" ]; then
  echo "Usage: $0 <command>"
  exit 1
fi

COMMAND=$@

# Run the command in the background
$COMMAND &

# Get the PID of the background process
PID=$!

echo "Process started with PID: $PID"

# Disown the background process
disown $PID
```

This script executes a given command in the background and immediately disowns it. The command to be run is captured in the variable

'COMMAND', and the PID of the background process is stored in 'PID' using '$¡. The 'disown' command is then used to disassociate the process from the current shell session, ensuring it continues to run independently.

By utilizing these scripts, system administrators can efficiently manage processes on a Linux system, ensuring optimal resource usage and system reliability.

12.8 User Account Management

User account management is a critical aspect of system administration that ensures secure and efficient utilization of system resources. In Linux systems, various commands and shell scripts are available to automate user account management tasks such as creating users, modifying user properties, deleting users, and managing group memberships. This section provides detailed examples to illustrate how these tasks can be accomplished using shell scripts.

Creating a New User

To create a new user, we can utilize the useradd command. The following script takes a username and password as arguments and creates a new user with the specified parameters:

```
#!/bin/bash

# Check if the script is run as root
if [ $(id -u) -ne 0 ]; then
  echo "You must run this script as root."
  exit 1
fi

# Check if a username and password are provided
if [ $# -ne 2 ]; then
  echo "Usage: $0 <username> <password>"
  exit 1
fi

USERNAME=$1
PASSWORD=$2

# Create new user
useradd -m $USERNAME

# Set user password
echo "$USERNAME:$PASSWORD" | chpasswd

echo "User $USERNAME has been created."
```

This script ensures that it is executed with root privileges and checks for the required arguments. It uses the useradd command to create a new user and the chpasswd command to set the user's password.

Modifying an Existing User

To modify an existing user, we can use the usermod command. For example, to change a user's shell, we can use the following script:

```
#!/bin/bash

# Check if the script is run as root
if [ $(id -u) -ne 0 ]; then
  echo "You must run this script as root."
  exit 1
fi

# Check if a username and new shell are provided
if [ $# -ne 2 ]; then
  echo "Usage: $0 <username> <new_shell>"
  exit 1
fi

USERNAME=$1
NEW_SHELL=$2

# Change user's shell
usermod -s $NEW_SHELL $USERNAME

echo "User $USERNAME's shell has been changed to $NEW_SHELL."
```

This script allows changing a user's shell by employing the usermod command with the -s option, followed by the new shell path and the username.

Deleting a User

To delete a user and their home directory, the userdel command is used along with the -r flag. The following script demonstrates how to delete a specified user:

```
#!/bin/bash

# Check if the script is run as root
if [ $(id -u) -ne 0 ]; then
  echo "You must run this script as root."
  exit 1
fi

# Check if a username is provided
if [ $# -ne 1 ]; then
  echo "Usage: $0 <username>"
  exit 1
fi

USERNAME=$1

# Delete user and their home directory
```

```
userdel -r $USERNAME

echo "User $USERNAME has been deleted."
```

This script verifies root privileges and the presence of a username argument before executing the userdel command to remove the user and their home directory.

Adding a User to a Group

Managing group memberships is another important aspect of user account management. The following script adds a specified user to a given group using the usermod command:

```
#!/bin/bash

# Check if the script is run as root
if [ $(id -u) -ne 0 ]; then
  echo "You must run this script as root."
  exit 1
fi

# Check if a username and group are provided
if [ $# -ne 2 ]; then
  echo "Usage: $0 <username> <group>"
  exit 1
fi

USERNAME=$1
GROUP=$2

# Add user to group
usermod -aG $GROUP $USERNAME

echo "User $USERNAME has been added to group $GROUP."
```

The script uses the -aG option of the usermod command to append the user to the specified group while retaining their existing group memberships.

Listing All Users

To list all users on the system, the /etc/passwd file can be parsed. The following script outputs all usernames present in the system:

```
#!/bin/bash

# Extract and display all usernames from /etc/passwd
cut -d: -f1 /etc/passwd
```

This script uses the cut command to extract the first field (username) from each line in the /etc/passwd file.

Checking User Existence

Before performing operations on a user account, it may be necessary to check if the user exists. The following script demonstrates how to check for the presence of a user:

```
#!/bin/bash

# Check if a username is provided
if [ $# -ne 1 ]; then
  echo "Usage: $0 <username>"
  exit 1
fi

USERNAME=$1

# Check if user exists
if id "$USERNAME" &>/dev/null; then
  echo "User $USERNAME exists."
else
  echo "User $USERNAME does not exist."
fi
```

The script uses the id command to check for the existence of the specified user and outputs an appropriate message.

Implementing User Account Management

Integrating these scripts into a single script can offer a comprehensive user account management tool. Below is an example that combines user creation, modification, and deletion into a single interactive script:

```
#!/bin/bash

# Check if the script is run as root
if [ $(id -u) -ne 0 ]; then
  echo "You must run this script as root."
  exit 1
fi

echo "User Account Management Script"
echo "1. Create a new user"
echo "2. Modify an existing user"
echo "3. Delete a user"
echo "4. Add user to a group"
echo "5. List all users"
echo "6. Check if a user exists"
read -p "Choose an option (1-6): " OPTION

case $OPTION in
  1)
    read -p "Enter username: " USERNAME
    read -s -p "Enter password: " PASSWORD
    echo
    useradd -m $USERNAME
    echo "$USERNAME:$PASSWORD" | chpasswd
    echo "User $USERNAME has been created."
    ;;
  2)
    read -p "Enter username: " USERNAME
    read -p "Enter new shell: " NEWSHELL
```

```
    usermod -s $NEWSHELL $USERNAME
    echo "User $USERNAME's shell has been changed to $NEWSHELL."
    ;;
  3)
    read -p "Enter username: " USERNAME
    userdel -r $USERNAME
    echo "User $USERNAME has been deleted."
    ;;
  4)
    read -p "Enter username: " USERNAME
    read -p "Enter group: " GROUP
    usermod -aG $GROUP $USERNAME
    echo "User $USERNAME has been added to group $GROUP."
    ;;
  5)
    cut -d: -f1 /etc/passwd
    ;;
  6)
    read -p "Enter username: " USERNAME
    if id "$USERNAME" &>/dev/null; then
      echo "User $USERNAME exists."
    else
      echo "User $USERNAME does not exist."
    fi
    ;;
  *)
    echo "Invalid option. Exiting."
    exit 1
    ;;
esac
```

This unified script verifies root privileges, presents a menu for different user account management tasks, and executes the corresponding operations based on user input.

By leveraging these scripts, system administrators can efficiently manage user accounts, thereby ensuring secure and consistent user access control in a Linux environment.

12.9 Automated Report Generation

Automated report generation is a vital aspect of system administration and data analysis, where recurring reports need to be created and disseminated without manual intervention. By leveraging shell scripting, we can produce reports that summarize system performance, user activities, network statistics, and much more. This section delves into crafting scripts for generating such reports, formatting them, and scheduling their creation.

- **Collecting System Information**

First, we consider a script that gathers information about the system, such as CPU usage, memory usage, disk space, and running processes. This information is essential for system administrators to monitor performance and to make informed decisions.

```
#!/bin/bash

OUTPUT_FILE=/var/reports/sysinfo_report.txt

echo "System Information Report" > $OUTPUT_FILE
echo "Generated on: $(date)" >> $OUTPUT_FILE
echo "=========================" >> $OUTPUT_FILE

echo "Uptime:" >> $OUTPUT_FILE
uptime >> $OUTPUT_FILE

echo "" >> $OUTPUT_FILE
echo "Memory Usage:" >> $OUTPUT_FILE
free -h >> $OUTPUT_FILE

echo "" >> $OUTPUT_FILE
echo "Disk Usage:" >> $OUTPUT_FILE
df -h >> $OUTPUT_FILE

echo "" >> $OUTPUT_FILE
echo "Top 10 Processes by Memory Usage:" >> $OUTPUT_FILE
ps aux --sort=-%mem | head -n 11 >> $OUTPUT_FILE

echo "" >> $OUTPUT_FILE
echo "Top 10 Processes by CPU Usage:" >> $OUTPUT_FILE
ps aux --sort=-%cpu | head -n 11 >> $OUTPUT_FILE
```

- **Formatting the Report**

To make the report readable and professional, we can format the output using markdown or HTML. Below is an example of wrapping the previous script's output in HTML tags:

```
#!/bin/bash

OUTPUT_FILE=/var/reports/sysinfo_report.html

echo "<html><body><h1>System Information Report</h1>" > $OUTPUT_FILE
echo "<p>Generated on: $(date)</p>" >> $OUTPUT_FILE
echo "<hr>" >> $OUTPUT_FILE

echo "<h2>Uptime:</h2>" >> $OUTPUT_FILE
echo "<pre>$(uptime)</pre>" >> $OUTPUT_FILE

echo "<h2>Memory Usage:</h2>" >> $OUTPUT_FILE
echo "<pre>$(free -h)</pre>" >> $OUTPUT_FILE

echo "<h2>Disk Usage:</h2>" >> $OUTPUT_FILE
echo "<pre>$(df -h)</pre>" >> $OUTPUT_FILE

echo "<h2>Top 10 Processes by Memory Usage:</h2>" >> $OUTPUT_FILE
echo "<pre>$(ps aux --sort=-%mem | head -n 11)</pre>" >> $OUTPUT_FILE
```

```
echo "<h2>Top 10 Processes by CPU Usage:</h2>" >> $OUTPUT_FILE
echo "<pre>$(ps aux --sort=-%cpu | head -n 11)</pre>" >> $OUTPUT_FILE

echo "</body></html>" >> $OUTPUT_FILE
```

- **Sending the Report via Email**

Once the report is generated, it may be essential to send it to stakeholders or system administrators through email. We utilize the mail utility to accomplish this.

```
#!/bin/bash

OUTPUT_FILE=/var/reports/sysinfo_report.html
EMAIL="admin@example.com"
SUBJECT="System Information Report"

echo "<html><body><h1>System Information Report</h1>" > $OUTPUT_FILE
echo "<p>Generated on: $(date)</p>" >> $OUTPUT_FILE
echo "<hr>" >> $OUTPUT_FILE
echo "<h2>Uptime:</h2><pre>$(uptime)</pre>" >> $OUTPUT_FILE
echo "<h2>Memory Usage:</h2><pre>$(free -h)</pre>" >> $OUTPUT_FILE
echo "<h2>Disk Usage:</h2><pre>$(df -h)</pre>" >> $OUTPUT_FILE
echo "<h2>Top 10 Processes by Memory Usage:</h2><pre>$(ps aux --sort=-%mem |
     head -n 11)</pre>" >> $OUTPUT_FILE
echo "<h2>Top 10 Processes by CPU Usage:</h2><pre>$(ps aux --sort=-%cpu |
     head -n 11)</pre>" >> $OUTPUT_FILE
echo "</body></html>" >> $OUTPUT_FILE

mail -a "Content-Type: text/html" -s "$SUBJECT" "$EMAIL" < $OUTPUT_FILE
```

- **Scheduling the Report Generation**

To ensure that reports are generated at regular intervals, use cron jobs. The cron daemon is a time-based job scheduler that enables scripts to be executed at specified times and dates.

```
0 6 * * * /path/to/report_generation_script.sh
```

This crontab entry schedules the report generation script to run daily at 6 AM.

Finally, proper permissions should be set for the script to ensure it executes without issues. Typically, the script needs permission to execute and write to the report directory.

```
chmod u+x /path/to/report_generation_script.sh
```

Through careful scripting and scheduling, automated report generation can be achieved with efficiency and reliability, freeing system administrators from repetitive tasks and ensuring up-to-date reporting.

12.10 Data Extraction and Transformation

Data extraction and transformation are critical tasks when dealing with large datasets, configuration files, log files, or any form of structured and unstructured data. The goal here is to extract relevant information, transform it into a desired format, and make it suitable for further analysis or processing. Shell scripting can be an effective tool to automate these processes.

To illustrate these concepts, we will discuss several examples, including text extraction using grep, data transformation with awk, and data manipulation using sed. We will also demonstrate how to chain these commands together using pipes for more complex tasks.

Example 1: Extracting Text with grep

The grep command is used to search for specific patterns within files. Consider a log file named server.log that contains various log entries. Suppose we want to extract all log entries related to the keyword "error".

```
grep 'error' server.log
```

The above command searches for the string "error" within server.log and prints each line that contains this keyword. For case-insensitive searches, use the -i option:

```
grep -i 'error' server.log
```

To extract lines containing either "error" or "warning", employ the -E option for extended regular expressions:

```
grep -E 'error|warning' server.log
```

Example 2: Transforming Data with awk

The awk command is a powerful tool for pattern scanning and processing. Assume we have a CSV file named data.csv with the following content:

Name	Age	Occupation
Alice	30	Engineer
Bob	24	Designer
Carol	40	Manager

We want to extract and print just the names and occupations:

```
awk -F', ' '{print $1, $3}' data.csv
```

The -F option specifies the field separator (in this case, a comma followed by a space). The $1 and $3 are used to reference the first and third columns, respectively.

To calculate the average age from the data.csv file:

```
awk -F', ' 'NR > 1 {sum+=$2; count++} END {print "Average Age: ", sum/count}'
    data.csv
```

Here, NR > 1 skips the header row, and sum+=$2; count++ aggregates the age values. The END block is executed after processing all records, calculating and printing the average age.

Example 3: Editing Data with sed

The sed command is a stream editor for filtering and transforming text. Suppose we need to replace all occurrences of "Manager" with "Director" in data.csv:

```
sed 's/Manager/Director/g' data.csv
```

The s/Manager/Director/g syntax denotes substitution, where g stands for global replacement within each line.

To delete lines containing "Designer":

```
sed '/Designer/d' data.csv
```

The /Designer/d syntax identifies lines containing "Designer" and deletes them.

Chaining Commands with Pipes

Chaining commands with pipes allows for the combination of multiple text processing steps. For example, to extract log entries containing "error" from server.log, and then count the number of such entries:

```
grep 'error' server.log | wc -l
```

This command uses grep to search for "error" and pipes the results to wc -l, which counts the number of lines.

To transform log entries to a specific format, we use a combination of grep, awk, and sed. Consider formatting log entries to display only the timestamp and the error message:

```
grep 'error' server.log | awk '{print $1, $3}' | sed 's/\[//g; s/\]//g'
```

In this case, grep filters the logs, awk extracts the first and third fields (assuming the first field is the timestamp and the third is the message), and sed removes square brackets from the output.

These examples illustrate the versatility of shell scripts in extracting and transforming data. By leveraging tools like grep, awk, and sed, users can efficiently process and manipulate text files to meet various requirements.

12.11 Integration with Other Tools

Shell scripting extends beyond performing standalone tasks; it is immensely powerful when combined with other tools to accomplish complex workflows. This section demonstrates how to integrate shell scripts with various tools to enhance functionality, improve efficiency, and leverage existing software capabilities.

Integrating with awk for Text Processing:

awk is a potent text processing tool that can be embedded within a shell script to parse and manipulate text or data files. Here is an example script illustrating integration with awk to process a CSV file containing user information and extract specific columns.

```
#!/bin/bash

# Define the input CSV file
input_file="user_data.csv"

# Extract and display the User ID and Name columns from the CSV
awk -F, '{ print $1, $2 }' $input_file
```

This script specifies the field separator as a comma (-F,) and prints the first two columns of each record. Such integration is beneficial for generating reports or transforming data based on specific criteria.

Interfacing with sed for Stream Editing:

sed (stream editor) is another essential tool for processing and transforming text streams. Consider a scenario where you need to replace all instances of a specific pattern in a configuration file. The following script integrates sed to replace a placeholder value within a configuration file.

```
#!/bin/bash
```

```
# Define the configuration file and the placeholder to replace
config_file="app_config.conf"
old_value="PLACEHOLDER"
new_value="actual_value"

# Use sed to perform the replacement
sed -i "s/$old_value/$new_value/g" $config_file
```

The -i option edits the file in-place, replacing PLACEHOLDER with actual_value throughout the configuration file. This integration automates configurations dynamically based on different environments or deployments.

Leveraging grep for Pattern Matching:

Incorporating grep into shell scripts allows for efficient searching and pattern matching within files. Suppose you need to find and list all error messages in a log file. The following script integrates grep to achieve this task:

```
#!/bin/bash

# Define the log file to search
log_file="application.log"

# Search for and display all lines containing "ERROR"
grep "ERROR" $log_file
```

grep scans the log file and outputs lines containing the specified pattern, in this case, ERROR. This integration is vital for log analysis and debugging purposes.

Combining with curl for HTTP Requests:

Integrating with curl facilitates sending HTTP requests and retrieving data from web servers. Consider a scenario where you need to monitor the status of a web service by making periodic HTTP GET requests. The following script exemplifies this integration:

```
#!/bin/bash

# Define the URL to check
url="http://example.com/status"

# Make an HTTP GET request and display the response
response=$(curl -s $url)

# Process the response
if [[ $response == *"OK"* ]]; then
  echo "Service is running"
else
  echo "Service is down"
fi
```

This script uses curl to send an HTTP GET request to the specified URL and then processes the response to determine the service status. Integrating with web services expands the capabilities of shell scripts for monitoring, automation, and notification tasks.

Interacting with jq for JSON Processing:

When dealing with JSON data, jq is an invaluable tool for parsing and manipulating JSON content within shell scripts. Suppose you need to extract specific information from a JSON API response. The following script integrates jq for this purpose:

```
#!/bin/bash

# Define the URL to get the JSON data
url="http://api.example.com/data"

# Fetch the JSON data
json_data=$(curl -s $url)

# Extract specific fields using jq
name=$(echo $json_data | jq -r '.name')
version=$(echo $json_data | jq -r '.version')

# Display the extracted fields
echo "Name: $name"
echo "Version: $version"
```

In this script, jq is employed to parse the JSON response and extract the name and version fields. This integration simplifies handling and processing JSON data within shell scripts.

Integrating with tar for Archive Management:

tar is commonly used for managing archives. Integrating tar into shell scripts enables automated archiving of files and directories. The following script demonstrates creating backups using tar:

```
#!/bin/bash

# Define the directory to backup and the backup file name
dir_to_backup="/path/to/directory"
backup_file="backup_$(date +%Y%m%d).tar.gz"

# Create a compressed tar archive of the directory
tar -czf $backup_file $dir_to_backup
```

This script creates a compressed archive of the specified directory, appending the current date to the backup file name. Such integration is vital for scheduling regular backups and maintaining data integrity.

Collaborating with Databases using mysql:

Automation often involves interacting with databases. Integrating mysql commands within shell scripts allows for executing SQL queries to manage and manipulate database records. Consider a script to back up a MySQL database:

```
#!/bin/bash

# Define database credentials and the backup file name
db_user="user"
db_password="password"
db_name="database"
backup_file="db_backup_$(date +%Y%m%d).sql"

# Perform the database backup
mysqldump -u $db_user -p$db_password $db_name > $backup_file
```

This script utilizes mysqldump to create a backup of the specified database, ensuring data preservation and facilitating recovery.

The power of shell scripting is amplified when integrated with these tools, offering extensive possibilities for text processing, stream editing, pattern matching, HTTP requests, JSON processing, archive management, and database interaction. This integration underpins the versatility and utility of shell scripts in automating and optimizing various tasks in a Linux environment.

12.12 Scheduling Scripts with Cron

Cron is a time-based job scheduling daemon found in Unix-like operating systems, including Linux. It allows users to schedule scripts or commands to run at specific times or intervals. Understanding how to use cron is essential for automating repetitive tasks, ensuring regular maintenance, and enhancing overall system efficiency.

A crontab file defines the schedules and commands that the cron daemon executes. Each line in a crontab file follows a specific structure:

MINUTE HOUR DAY_OF_MONTH MONTH DAY_OF_WEEK COMMAND

- **MINUTE** — Minute field (0 - 59)
- **HOUR** — Hour field (0 - 23)
- **DAY_OF_MONTH** — Day of the month field (1 - 31)
- **MONTH** — Month field (1 - 12)

- **DAY_OF_WEEK** — Day of the week field (0 - 7) where both 0 and 7 represent Sunday
- **COMMAND** — The command or script to be executed

An asterisk (*) in any field represents every possible value for that time unit. Multiple values can be separated by commas, and ranges can be specified with a hyphen.

To create or edit a crontab file, use the following command:

```
crontab -e
```

This command opens the crontab file in the default text editor. After adding or modifying entries, save and exit the editor. The cron daemon will automatically detect the changes and apply the new schedule.

Consider the following examples of crontab entries:

- Schedule a script to run every day at midnight:

  ```
  0 0 * * * /path/to/script.sh
  ```

- Schedule a script to run at 3:00 PM every Monday:

  ```
  0 15 * * 1 /path/to/script.sh
  ```

- Schedule a script to run every five minutes:

  ```
  */5 * * * * /path/to/script.sh
  ```

Cron also supports several predefined special strings to simplify common scheduling expressions. These include:

- @reboot — Run once, at startup.
- @yearly or @annually — Run once a year, equivalent to 0 0 1 1 *.
- @monthly — Run once a month, equivalent to 0 0 1 * *.
- @weekly — Run once a week, equivalent to 0 0 * * 0.
- @daily or @midnight — Run once a day, equivalent to 0 0 * * *.
- @hourly — Run once an hour, equivalent to 0 * * * *.

For example, to schedule a script to run daily using a special string:

```
@daily /path/to/script.sh
```

To facilitate monitoring and debugging, cron jobs can be configured to generate output logs. By default, cron sends job output via email to the user who scheduled the job. To redirect output to a log file instead, modify the crontab entry:

```
0 0 * * * /path/to/script.sh >> /path/to/logfile.log 2>&1
```

In this example, standard output (stdout) and standard error (stderr) are redirected to /path/to/logfile.log. This approach helps trace issues by reviewing the log files for error messages and verifying successful execution of the commands.

To view all scheduled cron jobs of the current user, execute:

```
crontab -l
```

To remove all the user's cron jobs, use:

```
crontab -r
```

To edit the cron jobs of another user (administrative privileges required), use:

```
sudo crontab -u username -e
```

These commands provide essential control over cron job management, enabling users to add, remove, and modify scheduled tasks efficiently.

Understanding and utilizing cron effectively allows users to automate a wide array of tasks, enhancing system maintenance and productivity. By leveraging these scheduling capabilities, administrators and users can ensure that routine activities are performed consistently and without manual intervention.

12.13 Case Studies and Real-World Examples

In this section, we will delve into comprehensive case studies illustrating the application of shell scripting in diverse real-world contexts. These examples are designed to consolidate your understanding and demonstrate the practical utility of the concepts covered in this chapter, including system maintenance, file management, network monitoring, report generation, and integration with other tools.

Consider the following scenarios:

Case Study 1: Automated System Health Check and Reporting

This script performs regular system health checks and compiles a comprehensive report. The report includes CPU and memory utilization, disk space usage, and the status of critical services. The script is scheduled to run daily, with the output emailed to the system administrator.

```
#!/bin/bash

# Define the report file
report="/var/log/system_health_report.txt"

# Get CPU and memory usage
cpu_usage=$(top -b -n1 | grep "Cpu(s)" | awk '{print $2 + $4}')
mem_usage=$(free -m | awk 'NR==2{printf "%.2f", $3*100/$2 }')

# Get disk usage information
disk_usage=$(df -h | grep "^/dev/" | awk '{print $5 " " $6}')

# Check services
services=("nginx" "mysql" "ssh")
service_status=""

for service in "${services[@]}"; do
    if systemctl is-active --quiet "$service"; then
        status="active"
    else
        status="inactive"
    fi
    service_status+="$service: $status\n"
done

# Compile report
echo -e "System Health Report \n" > $report
echo -e "CPU Usage: $cpu_usage%\n" >> $report
echo -e "Memory Usage: $mem_usage%\n" >> $report
echo -e "Disk Usage:\n$disk_usage\n" >> $report
echo -e "Service Status:\n$service_status" >> $report

# Send report via email
mail -s "Daily System Health Report" admin@example.com < $report

exit 0
```

Case Study 2: Backup and Restoration of Important Files

This script creates a backup of specified directories and restores them upon request. It's designed to retain daily backups for a week, after which the oldest backups are discarded.

```
#!/bin/bash

# Set backup source and destination
```

```
src="/home/user/important_data"
dest="/backup/important_data"

# Create the backup folder if it doesn't exist
mkdir -p $dest

# Function to create a backup
create_backup() {
    timestamp=$(date +"%Y%m%d%H%M")
    tar -czf $dest/backup_$timestamp.tar.gz $src
}

# Function to restore a backup
restore_backup() {
    latest_backup=$(ls -t $dest/backup_*.tar.gz | head -n 1)
    tar -xzf $latest_backup -C /
}

# Check command line argument
case "$1" in
    backup)
        create_backup
        ;;
    restore)
        restore_backup
        ;;
    *)
        echo "Usage: $0 {backup|restore}"
        exit 1
        ;;
esac

# Remove backups older than 7 days
find $dest -type f -name "backup_*.tar.gz" -mtime +7 -exec rm {} \;

exit 0
```

Case Study 3: Log File Analysis and Cleanup

This script analyzes log files to extract and archive error messages while rotating logs to prevent them from growing indefinitely. It retains log archives for a month.

```
#!/bin/bash

# Define log files and archive directory
log_file="/var/log/application.log"
archive_dir="/var/log/archive"

# Create the archive directory if it doesn't exist
mkdir -p $archive_dir

# Extract error messages and create an archive
grep "ERROR" $log_file > $archive_dir/error_$(date +"%Y%m%d%H%M").log

# Rotate logs
cat /dev/null > $log_file

# Remove archives older than 30 days
find $archive_dir -type f -name "error_*.log" -mtime +30 -exec rm {} \;
```

```
exit 0
```

Case Study 4: Network Bandwidth Monitoring

This script monitors network bandwidth usage on an interface and logs the data. It checks the bandwidth usage every minute and logs the average usage every hour.

```
#!/bin/bash

# Define network interface
iface="eth0"
log_file="/var/log/network_bandwidth.log"

# Function to measure bandwidth
measure_bandwidth() {
    RX=$(cat /sys/class/net/$iface/statistics/rx_bytes)
    TX=$(cat /sys/class/net/$iface/statistics/tx_bytes)
    sleep 60
    RX_NEXT=$(cat /sys/class/net/$iface/statistics/rx_bytes)
    TX_NEXT=$(cat /sys/class/net/$iface/statistics/tx_bytes)

    RX_RATE=$((($RX_NEXT - $RX) / 60))
    TX_RATE=$((($TX_NEXT - $TX) / 60))

    echo "$(date +"%Y-%m-%d %H:%M:%S"): RX $RX_RATE bytes/s, TX
          $TX_RATE bytes/s" >> $log_file
}

# Monitor network bandwidth every minute
while true; do
    measure_bandwidth
done

exit 0
```

Case Study 5: Automated Disk Cleanup

This script regularly cleans up temporary files and caches to free up disk space. It also provides a summary of the space reclaimed.

```
#!/bin/bash

# Define directories and files to be cleaned
dirs=("/tmp" "/var/tmp")
files=("/var/log/*.log" "/home/user/.cache/*")

# Cleanup directories
cleanup() {
    for dir in "${dirs[@]}"; do
        rm -rf $dir/*
    done

    for file in "${files[@]}"; do
        rm -rf $file
    done
}
```

```
# Log initial disk usage
initial_usage=$(df / | tail -1 | awk '{print $4}')

# Run cleanup
cleanup

# Log final disk usage
final_usage=$(df / | tail -1 | awk '{print $4}')
reclaimed=$((initial_usage - final_usage))

# Summary report
echo "Disk Cleanup Summary"
echo "Space reclaimed: $reclaimed KB"

exit 0
```

Each of these scripts exemplifies the pivotal role of shell scripting in administrative tasks, ensuring smooth, efficient, and reliable system operations. The presented scripts are highly customizable to meet varying organizational requirements, fostering a deeper comprehension of their application in real-world scenarios.

Made in the USA
Monee, IL
05 November 2026

67814345R00213